Praise for *Open*

"This book is an invitation to open oneself up for a journey of transformation. With unapologetic clarity, Braxton invokes the power of the Spirit, breath of God, and Nommo, the spoken word, to usher in a radical hermeneutic on Christian theopraxis. Leveling the playing field by intent and example, Braxton speaks to the diversity of our circumstances, callings, and commitments to a communion with God that charts a new course for ecumenical, interfaith, and human engagement. Praise for *Open*—'gonna trouble the water.'"

—Rev. Dr. Iva E. Carruthers, general secretary,
Samuel DeWitt Proctor Conference

"*Open* is a compelling blend of memoir, penetrating biblical analysis, and pragmatic advice for scholars, seminarians, grassroots leaders, and ministers interested in social justice work within a transgressive theological model. Braxton dives into historical abuses and misuses of Scripture and uncovers the historical and cultural resources needed to build progressive interfaith organizations and theologically inclusive congregations."

—Dr. Terrence Johnson, professor of African American
religious studies, Harvard Divinity School

"In this intriguing collection of essays, Rev. Dr. Brad Braxton, biblical scholar, gospel preacher, and social justice advocate, explores the unorthodox orthodoxy of progressivism as an expansive vision of the Jesus story. Chapters explore classic Christian themes including justification, sanctification, sacraments, and community as entry points for a grace-filled openness inside and outside the church. It is a powerful study of and for our times."

—Dr. Bill J. Leonard, professor of divinity emeritus,
Wake Forest University

"This thrilling read is a compelling application of Christian thought rooted in theology, biblical analysis, and real-world experiences that serves as a firmly rooted and unapologetic foundation for progressive reflection and action. It's a call for critical engagement of religious, cultural, and academic institutions to boldly speak amid the deafening din of hurtful and stagnant doctrine."

—Rev. Dr. Derrick McQueen, pastor, St. James
Presbyterian Church, Harlem, New York, and
assistant director, CARSS at Columbia University

"Like an open tomb that extends into an open future, Brad Braxton reveals the liberating and life-giving present and future of God as a capacious and gracious broad meadow. Rooted in the tradition of the unknown black bards, Braxton presses the church to be open like the enslaved singing seers and preach, 'There's room for many-a more.' If you are finished with the old fences of theology and yearn for a new promised land of humanity, this book is for you!"

—Rev. Dr. Luke A. Powery, dean of Duke University
Chapel and associate professor of homiletics at
Duke Divinity School; author of *Becoming Human:
The Holy Spirit and the Rhetoric of Race*

"Dr. Brad Braxton invites us to imagine and co-create a world in which religion nurtures the belonging of everyone, especially those who have traditionally found the doors of the church/mosque/synagogue barred and the windows latched. His invitation is audacious and unapologetic, but it is not undemanding. Dr. Braxton challenges us to look at our structures, our assumptions, and our narrow places with intellectual rigor and courage. Generously and lovingly, he offers his own life stories to accompany us as we do so."

—Rabbi Elissa Sachs-Kohen,
Baltimore Hebrew Congregation

"Only Dr. Brad Braxton would have the audaciousness and capacity to offer Christendom and the world a book that discusses pluralism, reparations, sex talk, and the environment with heft and without hesitation. This is the book that seminary professors, seminary students, clergy, and laity must read if they want to better understand hermeneutics, homiletics, biblical studies, and the church of the twenty-first century."

—Rev. Dr. Martha Simmons, coauthor of
Preaching with Sacred Fire: An Anthology of African American Sermons, 1750 to the Present

OPEN

OPEN

UNORTHODOX
THOUGHTS
ON GOD AND
COMMUNITY

BRAD R. BRAXTON

Fortress Press
Minneapolis

OPEN
Unorthodox Thoughts on God and Community

Cover design: Laurie Ingram Art + Design.com
Cover image: Abstract colorful oil painting on canvas texture,
Nongkran Pornmingmas / Alamy Stock Photo

Print ISBN: 978-1-5064-8881-3
eBook ISBN: 978-1-5064-8882-0

Contents

Introduction

*The openness of our hearts and minds can be measured
by how wide we draw the circle of what we call family.*

—Mother Teresa

Open about Being Open: A Prelude on Progressivism

Since you took the time and energy to open this book—whether
by turning a page or scrolling on your digital device—the least I
can do is be open with you from the beginning. I am an unapologetic and unorthodox progressive. Progressives are frequently
referred to as being on "the left." Thus, the reflections in this book
come from, and move toward, the left.

In these difficult days—when right-wing politics and conservative religion are curtailing opportunities for diverse manifestations of community, democracy, and the sacred—we need more
progressives to be audaciously open about being open. When
writing with a pen or eating with a fork, I am right-handed.
However, everything else about me and the open approach to
theology in this book are left-wing!

Interestingly, the Latin word for "left" is *sinister*. This word
gives us our English word "sinister," which carries connotations
of "negativity" or "evil." In many places, and especially religious
spaces, certain people have characterized my progressive perspectives as evil.

For example, I lectured once in a Baptist church and challenged the Bible's supposed "inerrancy" (i.e., the traditional
belief that the Bible has no errors). During the question-and-
answer session after the lecture, a minister in the audience, who

was troubled by my open thinking, forcefully accused me of espousing demonic views.

I did not intend in that lecture to be the "devil's advocate." Nor is that my intention in this book. When people use the phrase "devil's advocate," I often politely interrupt and encourage them to be an "angel's advocate" because the "devil" is doing fine. According to the womanist ethicist Emilie Townes, evil refers to a society's ability to "produce misery and suffering in relentlessly systematic and . . . structural ways." According to this definition, the "devil" needs no more advocates, since our world is clearly full of evil.[1]

On the contrary, my aim in this book is to be an "angel's advocate." The Greek word that gives us the English word "angel" (*aggelos*) literally means "messenger." I am not trying to stir up devilment, negativity, or needless trouble. My goal is to share positive, progressive messages designed to move us forward to bigger truths and better forms of community.

When that minister accused me of aiding the devil, I was not offended. He correctly assessed that I was offering perspectives from the "left field." In other words, I was articulating ideas not normally conveyed by the orthodox teachers of Christianity. If that minister had seriously examined, let alone adopted, my perspectives, he might have had to significantly change his opinions about God and the boundaries of his community. Rather than open himself up to a potential reassessment of his core beliefs, he summoned "demonic" language to shut me out and to shut down his engagement with my unorthodox approach to Christianity.

I interpreted his visceral response to my lecture as a palpable sign that my itinerary was clear. I was inviting the listeners of that lecture to travel with me out in the open—beyond safe, sheltered thinking about God. I am inviting readers of this book to do the same—to roam with me into progressive thinking that empowers us to ponder unorthodox thoughts about God and our communities without fear or shame. In the spirit of openness, permit me to expand upon my understanding of progressivism.

I am a black scholar of religion and a Christian pastor who has spent my entire adult life studying ancient religions and cultures and especially Judaism, Christianity, and African Traditional Religions. Thus, I respect the wisdom and ways of the past and realize that recklessly ignoring the past is an act of moral arrogance.

I am also a *progressive* black scholar of religion and a Christian pastor. Accordingly, I believe that the uncritical submission to the values and voices of the past is also an act of moral laziness as well as an abdication of moral responsibility. With the inevitable benefit of hindsight and the progress of time, we possess certain insights—not just scientific/technical expertise but also moral wisdom—that the ancients did not have or have as well as we now do. For example, the denigration and oppression of women and LGBTQ people are categorically wrong no matter what certain verses in the Bible or other ancient religious texts and traditions say.

Therefore, progressivism is a commitment to fearlessly discern what beliefs and practices—past and present—might assist us in advancing efforts to foster more justice, peace, and inclusive love in our families, communities, and the broader society. Progressives are not afraid to scrutinize orthodox traditions, philosophies, and practices and even discard them if they discriminate or promote hate. There is nothing holy about hate, even if hate is endorsed by so-called holy people who ironically hold "Holy Bibles" in their hands. Could it be that some Christians' tight grip on the Bible prevents more love from flowing to and from their hearts?

This book seeks to open our thinking about God and community in ways that allow more love—*radically inclusive love*—to flow among us. When our mental and moral pipes get clogged, the wellsprings of wisdom, generosity, and restorative justice will be severely restricted and eventually blocked. In short, bad things usually happen when the pipes get clogged. I learned this lesson the hard way once during a holiday.

Unclogging the Pipes in a Baltimore Suburb

After months of waiting, the long-anticipated holiday arrived on Sunday, February 1, 2015. Since I am a devoted fan of the National Football League, Super Bowl Sunday is a holiday and virtually a religious observance in our home. My wife, Lazetta; our daughter, Karis; and I had attended the Sunday morning worship service at The Open Church of Maryland, where I led worship and preached. Now, as the evening darkness drew near, I was ready to dine on the sumptuous spread of food on the kitchen table in our suburban Baltimore home. It was time to kick back, relax, and watch Super Bowl XLIX between the Seattle Seahawks and the New England Patriots.

The extensive Super Bowl pregame show had ended. The referee had already tossed the coin to determine that the Patriots would receive the opening kickoff. As the football sailed through the air, I started hearing a strange, gurgling noise coming from the basement bathroom. Although I tried to ignore the noise, it persisted and grew louder. I eventually went to investigate the noise, and to my utter dismay, water was coming up through the drain in the basement bathtub. We had an emergency on our hands, and it was all hands on deck!

Lazetta, Karis, and I used towels and buckets to prevent the water from flooding the entire basement. In response to an emergency phone call, a plumber came to our house and helped us prevent further damage. Amid the chaos, I missed the entire Super Bowl (which the New England Patriots won dramatically in the final seconds of the game) because I was keeping an anxious eye on the basement bathtub and toilet bowl.

The plumber we hired was compassionate and knowledgeable. After helping us with the immediate dilemma of the water backup, he dutifully attempted to locate the ultimate source of the problem. With a flashlight in hand, he went to the front yard and peered underneath the drain cover leading to the sewer pipes for our house. Within moments, he discovered the source of the backup.

Large rocks were blocking the sewer pipes, thus causing the backup. The town house in which we lived was newly constructed, and we had just moved in. The construction company, in its haste, had left considerable debris in the sewer pipes leading into the house. The plumber assisted us in contacting an industrial plumbing company to resolve the problem. The industrial plumbing company arrived the next day with large machinery to extract the debris and unclog the pipes.

When seeking to convey the stability of our cultural and religious traditions, we often use metaphors associated with rocks because rocks provide sturdy foundations upon which to build. Yet as I discovered years ago, rocks can sometimes get in the way, particularly if they clog the pipes and restrict the flow. Open approaches to theology realize that on various occasions, our "rocks"—those orthodox, traditional ways of thinking about God and community—have clogged the pipes. Backups and other bad things tend to happen when the pipes get clogged.

Unclogging the Pipes in a Biblical Story

My personal story about clogged pipes reminds me of an ancient biblical story where the process of "unclogging the pipes" resulted in a newfound embrace of openness. In addition to recounting the creation of the universe, the book of Genesis chronicles stories about certain mythic ancestors of the human family. More specifically, Genesis traces branches of a family tree that would eventually become the ancient Israelites. Beginning in Genesis 12, the stories focus especially on how God fulfills promises to a quintessential Israelite ancestor—Abraham—and the successive generations of his family.

In Genesis 26, shortly after Abraham's death, Isaac (Abraham's son), Rebekah (Isaacs's wife), and their family find themselves in a dire situation. When a famine arises and threatens their well-being, God instructs Isaac and Rebekah to remain in the land of Gerar (i.e., the southwest section of contemporary Israel-Palestine). The Philistines, a group often in contention with the Israelites, controlled Gerar. Interestingly, Genesis 20 recounts an episode when Abraham and Sarah (Isaac's parents) had sojourned previously in Gerar. This narrative detail accentuates the theme of generational repetition. The new generation covers ground previously traversed by their ancestors, facing the opportunities and dilemmas their ancestors also encountered.[2]

Following God's instructions, Isaac and Rebekah remain in Gerar, and they accumulate wealth and gain social prominence. The success of this Israelite family creates tension among the Philistines. Consequently, the Philistines demonstrate their displeasure by clogging the wells that Abraham had established a generation ago when Abraham and Sarah resided in Gerar. When Abraham and Sarah were in Gerar, they had wells built to ensure a regular supply of life-sustaining water. A generation later, when Isaac, Rebekah, and their family are in the same location, these wells are still providing water. However, due to conflict and ill will, the wells get clogged.

Clogged wells in this ancient story, like the clogged pipes in my personal story, pose a serious dilemma. In ancient agricultural settings, such as those depicted in biblical texts, people, flocks of animals, and crops needed regular access to water. Clogged wells prevented that access. In this biblical story, these are not just any wells; they are historic, ancestral wells established by an earlier generation to nourish succeeding generations.

However, due to rising tensions between Isaac's family and Philistine leaders, Isaac, Rebekah, and their family depart Gerar, leaving the first set of ancestral wells clogged. This family then travels to the nearby valley of Gerar where they find additional ancestral wells that Abraham had established. The Philistines had clogged up these wells after Abraham's death. Thus, a second time, Isaac is confronted by the dilemma of clogged wells.

However, on this occasion, Isaac instructs servants to unclog these wells. I imagine his instructions were direct and clear: "Dig out the dirt! Remove the rubbish! Open the system so that precious water might replenish our bodies and spirits!" Ancestral wells are a central feature of Genesis 26. Ancestral wells are resources given to us by others, but we cannot benefit from them fully until we unclog them.

It is not far-fetched to symbolically interpret the wells established by Abraham as representations of our cultural and religious heritages—cherished principles, places, and practices that orient us morally and sustain us spiritually. Occasionally, these wells become clogged. Stuff in the system must be removed so these wells might continue to provide spiritual irrigation and promote social transformation. I renew my earlier assertion: problems arise when "the pipes" (or "ancestral wells") get clogged.

As an unashamed progressive, I feel compelled to unclog the wells. Christianity is a marvelous ancestral well. However, across the millennia, "rocks, dirt, and debris" have clogged the pipes and limited the ability of this well to satisfy the thirst of people parched from injustice and exclusion. For instance, sexism, the culturally sanctioned superiority of males, is clogging the well. Racism, the culturally sanctioned privileging of white people's norms and practices, is clogging the well. Heterosexism, the culturally sanctioned privileging of heterosexual identity, is clogging the well. Christocentrism, the culturally sanctioned privileging of Christianity as the ultimate path to "righteousness and salvation," is clogging the well.

Returning to the unfolding plot in Genesis 26, we encounter a fascinating story of discovery. In accordance with Isaac's instructions, the servants unclog Abraham's ancestral wells. We might characterize the servants' earnest efforts as renovation. The servants fix or enhance irrigation systems that others had previously established.

Isaac's servants are not satisfied with mere renovation. Isaac's servants also dig in the valley of Gerar and discover a well of fresh water. Instead of resting after renovating old wells, Isaac's servants also purposefully dig and search for new wells.

Why do these servants dare to push beyond the boundaries of Abraham's reopened wells in search of new wells? They realize that additional resources would be necessary to sustain life. I admire the tenacity and audacity of these servants as they dig and search. At this point, we might characterize their earnest efforts as the quest for innovation—the persistent push to move beyond the status quo in search of fresh life-sustaining resources.

Despite the resolute search that results in the discovery of a fresh well, Isaac's servants meet resistance as they explore new territory. According to Genesis 26:20–21, shepherds from Gerar arrive and argue with Isaac's servants, claiming that the new well belongs to them. In response to the contestation and energized by a spirit of innovation, Isaac's servants continue digging and find another well.

Shepherds from Gerar once again dispute ownership of the newly discovered well. Amid the controversy and arguments surrounding these new wells, Isaac appropriately names these wells *Esek* (which means "contention" in Hebrew) and *Sitnah* (which means "hostility" in Hebrew). These names offer us a cautionary note about the importance of vigilance when pursuing innovation. We should expect arguments, hostilities, and insecurities to attend the progressive search for fresh resources.

Isaac's servants remain undaunted amid the challenges of renovation and innovation. When seeking to unclog the pipes and find new wells, it is imperative to keep moving. Rather than remaining in tight, contested spaces among quarrelsome people, Isaac, Rebekah, and their crew journey onward.

After two contentious attempts at digging new wells, they eventually move to a new, wide-open space where there are no disputes, no bitter arguments, and no petty jealousies. In this wide-open space, they dig yet another new well and name that well *Rehoboth*. In Hebrew, this word means "broad spaces" and carries other connotations such as "breathing room" and my favorite nuance, "broad meadows."

Throughout the winding narrative of Genesis 26, the combination of diverse people (the Israelites and the Philistines) and seemingly limited resources (water and wells) creates contentious social contexts. Yet this story reveals that more expansive and peaceful possibilities exist. Opening the clogged pipes of Abraham's ancestral wells sets the stage for a bigger and more significant openness. Isaac's crew eventually discovers a wide-open space. A commitment to openness leads to more openness. The discovery of this wide-open space is so momentous that it requires memorialization with a special name: Rehoboth or "broad meadows."

Open thinking involves the innovative, progressive pursuit of understandings of God and configurations of community that honor and create beautiful "broad meadows." In my estimation, Rehoboth is not just a name of a place; it is also a characteristic of God and all that is sacred.

God is capacious. In honor of a capacious God, we should strive to create capacious, noncontentious spaces that make ample room for the differences and similarities existing among the human family and the nonhuman environmental partners that share the planet with us. Insisting that there is room for all of us, an open approach to theology is a theoretical and pragmatic outworking of the impulse for innovation and inclusion: innovation in how we explore the sacred, build communities, and create meaning and values; and inclusion of diverse groups of people and unorthodox approaches to our principles and practices, irrespective of our cultural identities and the religious, spiritual, or ethical worldviews we espouse.

Fewer Fences and More Broad Meadows

This book is an assemblage of my selected essays and sermons—composed across more than two decades of my service as a pastor, professor, philanthropic program officer, museum professional, and diversity, equity, and inclusion practitioner. While written at different moments and for distinct audiences, each writing represents an attempt to articulate aspects of my open thinking. Some writings seek to bring a scholarly perspective to concepts and practices integral to Christianity, such as the identity of Jesus or the practices of baptism and holy communion. Other writings reflect upon my pragmatic pastoral experiences of preaching and establishing a progressive religious community—The Open Church of Maryland.

In addition to theorizing about an open approach to theology, I have collaborated with others to create an open community. For eleven years, I have served as the founding senior pastor of The Open Church in Baltimore, Maryland, a congregation committed to radically inclusive love, courageous social justice activism, and compassionate interfaith collaboration.[3] The Open Church affirms LGBTQ equality and regularly participates in intercultural and social justice initiatives with partners from African diasporic, Baha'i, Buddhist, Christian, Humanist, Jewish, Muslim, and religiously unaffiliated communities.

When I teach open approaches to theology in divinity schools and seminaries, the initial response of some students is "Doc, you can't really preach and teach this progressive stuff in local churches." My straightforward response to any would-be doubters is "Yes, you really can, and yes, I really have!" The Open Church offers tangible evidence of what is possible when a community embraces open thinking with courage and curiosity.

My career has attempted to connect the precision of the academy and the passion of local congregations so that leaders and communities can respond positively to the opportunities and obligations of an increasingly pluralistic world. The offerings in this book move seamlessly between the ivory tower and the grassroots. Consequently, I hope the book will find a wide readership among scholars of religion and culture, leaders in diverse religious communities, educators, social activists, and broad audiences interested in progressive approaches to culture and the creation of radically inclusive communities.

My different professional positions and the diverse geographic and institutional spaces I have inhabited have influenced the open thinking in this book. For example, my trip to Israel and my multiple pilgrimages to the African continent (and especially the visits to African sites associated with transatlantic slavery) have significantly impacted my thinking about God and community. My preaching in historic pulpits such as Westminster Abbey in London, England, and The Riverside Church in New York City has also influenced this book. Furthermore, the brilliant people I have encountered—in my pastorates and social activism, in my professorships and lectureships, and in my service in venerable institutions such as the Ford Foundation and the Smithsonian Institution—have enhanced my reflection on and practice of an open approach to theology.

Amid the different contexts in which I have worked and from which I have written, there is a clear, discernible theme or "through-line" connecting these writings—an unwavering commitment to openness and an abiding desire to move our thinking about God and community into broader, more open places.

Attempts to fence in or place gates around a great big God diminish us spiritually and make us more prone to small-mindedness and mean-spiritedness. Many religious people specialize in installing fences and gates around God and our communities. These people function as if God is so frail that God cannot withstand robust contact with the real world, which is full of marvelously diverse people, practices, and principles. God does not need our protection, our fences, or our gates.

The tendency to establish barriers around the sacred might appear as a form of religious devotion that maintains proper boundaries between the holy and the profane. Upon closer inspection, religious fence building and gatekeeping are often efforts to avoid authentic engagement with God, especially a God who transgresses the tidy barriers of pious dogma to connect diverse people. Some religious people insist that their faith-based fences ensure righteousness, lest the vices and distorted values of a wicked world creep into their religious communities. Yet these attempts to seal off the world often create closed hot houses of bigotry, narrow-mindedness, and injustice.

During my more than twenty years in Christian ministry and theological education, my biggest challenges and deepest emotional wounds have occurred as "church folk" erected fences and gates in their liturgical practices and governance policies. Instead of fostering more fellowship in Sunday church services and Saturday church business meetings, some church folk have used fences and gates to create "cage matches" between competing groups and interests. The hostility I have witnessed in some church gatherings resembled a wrestling match on pay-per-view television instead of a godly gathering for personal edification and social transformation.

As I often tell students in divinity schools and seminaries, "Ain't no love like church love, and ain't no mean like church

mean." When church folk are at their best, they can demonstrate a compassion and vulnerability that can soften the hardest
hearts. Alternatively, when church folk are at their worst, they
can wield a vindictiveness that can wound people for a long time,
if not a lifetime.

Some church folk are especially mean when they erect fences
and gates around God and our communities. Fences and gates
come in many forms:

- "Women cannot serve as pastors and lay leaders in this
  church."
- "LGBTQ relationships are sinful. Marriage can only occur
  between a man and a woman."
- "Divorced people and members of other denominations
  and religious traditions cannot come to our communion
  table."
- "The Bible says it, that settles it, and I believe it."
- "Only Christians will be saved."

Many churches are so theologically fenced in that their steeples are
not symbolic signs pointing to a loving God. Their steeples instead
are symbolic barbwire to dissuade people from trespassing on the
premises with probing questions about problematic dogmas.

Religious practices and principles do not have to be restrictive
and exclusionary. On the contrary, religious practices and principles can be broad meadows characterized by openness, diversity, and radically inclusive love. While the writings in this book
reflect my attempts as an adult to express an open approach to
theology, the seeds of my passion for broad meadows were sown
in my childhood. I have been thinking about open approaches to
theology and broad meadows for a long time.

Living into My Name: "Broad Meadow"

I was raised in a black family and religious community where
the idea of divine calling was taken with utmost seriousness. "Calling" means the responsible use of our gifts that move beyond

self-fulfillment to the glorification of God and the enhancement of the world. My parents and community encouraged me to care about the ultimate meaning of my life and the lives of others. My father, James Braxton Sr., was a Baptist pastor, and my mother, Louise Braxton, is a retired educator. My parents modeled integrity, kindness, and steadfast community service before my three siblings and me.

The theological orientation of First Baptist Church in Salem, Virginia, the black congregation of my youth, was moderate and oriented toward civic engagement. There was significant emphasis on piety and the importance of a personal relationship with Jesus. There was also significant teaching about our responsibility as Jesus's disciples to be "the salt of the earth" (Matt 5:13). In other words, I was taught to follow Jesus not only as a means for me to "go to heaven" but also as a means for me to enrich other people while on earth. My parents and the surrogate spiritual mothers and fathers in that church constantly encouraged me to walk uprightly, thereby honoring God's name and my family's name.

In my mature years, I am developing a deeper appreciation for the spiritual significance of names and, in this case, my given name: Brad. I now understand my ministry and purpose in life—which are conveyed in my efforts to facilitate open thinking—as the evolving process of "living into my name." In many cultures, naming is important. For instance, the Bible recounts various stories, as discussed above, where the naming of people or places reveals their meaning and predicts their destiny (e.g., Rehoboth in Gen 26:17–22). To name is to chart a course for the future.

By naming me "Brad," my parents, who have been my wisest and best teachers, shaped my calling to be a progressive scholar, pastor, and social activist with profound commitments to diversity and social justice. In Old English, "Brad" means "broad meadow." In my personal and professional endeavors, I strive to create broad spaces where people from diverse backgrounds with divergent beliefs can peacefully probe their differences and celebrate their similarities for the sake of a better world. How did I move from "Brad" simply being my name to the realization that the creation of "broad meadows" is my mission in life?

My parents used the sage words of two great thinkers to enlarge my mind, thereby fostering in me a passion for intellectual breadth and depth. My parents placed two inspirational posters on the walls of my adolescent bedroom. These posters set me on a lifelong course of being an intellectually courageous nonconformist eager to challenge traditional boundaries.

On the first poster were words from Oliver Wendell Holmes Sr.: "A mind, once stretched by a new idea, never regains its original dimensions."[4] On the second poster were words from Martin Luther King Jr.: "Rarely do we find people who willingly engage in hard, solid thinking. There is an almost universal quest for easy answers and half-baked solutions. Nothing pains some people more than having to think."[5] Through these quotations, my parents insisted that my mind be nimble enough to expand to new situations and tough enough to avoid naïveté.

Consequently, when my exposure to the academic study of religion led me to question the traditional doctrines of my religious heritage, my parents did not recoil. When my first pilgrimages to Europe and Africa unleashed my curiosity about cultural pluralism, my parents encouraged my cultural exploration. Additionally, when friendships with LGBTQ colleagues galvanized my commitment to be a heterosexual advocate for LGBTQ equality, my parents supported me. On these and other issues, my parents simply invited me to count the cost of whatever courageous stance I was willing to take.

In a fascinating study on innovation, the theorist Steven Johnson insists that some environments punish innovation and "squelch new ideas," while other environments "seem to breed them effortlessly."[6] My parents created for me a permissive intellectual environment that untethered me from slavish adherence to stifling traditions. In that environment, audacious new ideas about diversity and progressive social transformation began germinating in my soul.

In my family of origin, my parents encouraged me to become a broad meadow. Long before I encountered Mother Teresa's inspirational quotation that opens this introduction, my family inspired me to widen "the circle of what we call family."

If you are interested in unclogging the pipes, creating broad meadows, and widening the circle of what we call family, please keep this book—and your hearts and minds—*open*!

Part 1

Essays

1

"Every Time I Feel the Spirit"

Black Christology for a Pluralistic World

*In so many ways ... our lives have been deeply touched
and influenced by the life and character, teaching and
spirit, of Jesus of Nazareth. He moves in and out on the
horizon of our days like some fleeting ghost. At times ...
some startling clear thrust of his mind moves in upon
us ... reminding us of what we are, and what life is ...
kindling anew dead hopes, giving to leaden spirits wings
that sweep. We owe so much to the spirit which he let loose
in the world.*

—HOWARD THURMAN, *THE CENTERING MOMENT*

The Hopes of a Concerned Father

This chapter focuses on Jesus, the Jewish, itinerant preacher who
proclaimed the imminent arrival of God's reign.* His message
and methods antagonized certain leaders within his religious
tradition. His crucifixion revealed Rome's intolerance for the
messianic pretension surrounding his message and methods.[1]

---

* This chapter was originally published as "'Every Time I Feel the Spirit':
African American Christology for a Pluralistic World," in *Radical Christian Voices and Practice: Essays in Honor of Christopher Rowland*, edited
by Zoë Bennett and David Gowler (New York: Oxford University Press,
2012), 181–99. Reprinted with permission of Oxford University Press.

Multiple quests to discover the "historical Jesus" have occupied countless generations, and the history of those histories needs no rehearsal here.[2] Such a rehearsal would obscure the personal passion motivating this christological exploration (i.e., theories about the identity and significance of Jesus). Historical study has a rightful place in any christological conversation, since "bad history cannot lead to good theology."[3] I, however, confess that my interests are thoroughly theological, unapologetically contextual, and even autobiographical.

Fourth- and fifth-century CE debates among church fathers concerning Jesus's divinity and humanity are not my ultimate concern. Nevertheless, fatherhood is central to this chapter. As the father of Karis—our beautiful, brilliant, seventeen-year-old, black daughter—I am motivated to think carefully about Christology. Several years ago, my wife, Lazetta, and I hung a picture of an African Jesus on Karis's bedroom wall as an antidote against the white privilege that inaccurately portrays the historical Jesus as European. At the time, Karis was attending a church-sponsored elementary school where her teachers shared with her wonderful stories about Jesus. Even as a young child, Karis began connecting the stories from the schoolhouse with the picture in our house. Stories, songs, and questions about Jesus were, and are, constant features of our family interactions.

We eagerly want our daughter to know and follow Jesus. Religious communities across the millennia have depicted Jesus in myriad ways. Many of these depictions might stunt the emerging faith of an intellectually sharp, strong-willed, young black woman growing up in an increasingly pluralistic world.

In her dealings with Christianity, and especially black churches, I am hopeful that Karis will continue to encounter a liberating, not lethal, Jesus. Otherwise, as she matures, she might abandon Jesus and churches as outdated instruments of oppression. If Karis abandons churches that convey oppressive, and even lethal, understandings of Jesus, I will understand and applaud her decision.

I believe that black churches can be beacons of hope and healing in the twenty-first century, as they often have been during previous centuries. To maintain their identity as prophetic institutions providing social liberation and spiritual refuge, black churches will have to recalculate some of their christological conceptions. The positive implications of such a reassessment might enable me with a clear conscience to continue encouraging our daughter to engage with black churches.

The Power and Perils of Black Churches

I write not only as a father but also as a "son." The roots of the latter identity burrow deeper than my biological family tree. My parents, James Braxton Sr. and Louise Braxton, provided sterling examples of moral integrity to my three siblings and me. My parents also recognized the need for additional "parental" support. Thus, they wisely invited black churches—those venerable religious communities that have been a "mother" and a "father" to countless children—to guide us spiritually even as they nurtured us physically. Black churches reared me, and I am a proud and grateful "son."

Black churches represent a creative, cogent response to the racism facilitated by large segments of white culture and consecrated by many white churches. A distorted version of Christianity provided the religious justification for nations such as Portugal, France, the Netherlands, England, and the United States to exploit, brutalize, and murder millions of Africans in the transatlantic slave trade during the fifteenth through nineteenth centuries. Amid this ineffable violence, new moral communities arose in the United States—black churches.

Enslaved and free Africans in the United States transformed the religion they received from white Christians. These Africans removed the racist elements of white Christianity and replaced them with African practices and cultural wisdom, thereby moving Christianity in the United States closer to Jesus's message of justice. In the creative mixture of Christianity and African Traditional Religions, of biblical stories and African folklore, of Christian message and African music, black churches were forged.[4] Black churches sustained the liberation longings of

Sojourner Truth and Harriet Tubman, of Henry McNeal Turner
and Frederick Douglass. Later, some black churches became
incubators for civil rights protests that persuaded the United
States to embody its noble creeds through just deeds.

Furthermore, had it not been for the rhetorical and moral
imagination of black churches, a *black person* might never
have occupied the *White House*. The lyricism of former president Barack Obama's language is the mother tongue of black
churches. If President Obama's oratory is soaring, it is because
Trinity United Church of Christ, the black Christian congregation where he and his family worshipped for many years, placed
wings on his back.

Additionally, "the audacity of hope"—the title of Obama's
best-selling book and an implicit theme of his legendary 2008
presidential campaign—was derived from a sermon preached
by his then pastor, Jeremiah Wright, a fearless black prophet.
Despite the politically motivated vilification of Obama's former
congregation and pastor, fair-minded people cannot ignore
that a black Christian congregation and pastor mentored the
United States' first black president into his position and power
on the global stage. I am proud to be a part of the progeny of
black churches.

Irrespective of my pride, I am critically aware of the perils
facing black churches. Simply stated, black churches are in danger of forfeiting their prophetic witness. Many black Christian
congregations remain numerically solid and culturally vibrant.
Nevertheless, four stubborn factors, amid others, continue to
whittle away the moral heft historically associated with black
churches: (1) the promotion of sexism; (2) the lack of social justice engagement; (3) the reticence to embrace interfaith dialogue
and collaboration; and (4) the inhospitality, and even hostility,
toward LGBTQ people. A subsequent chapter in this book will
focus on black churches and LGBTQ people. Thus, this chapter focuses on these first three issues.

As Karis's father and a concerned "son" eager to aid an ailing
"parent" (black churches), I raise these questions: (1) What contemporary christological understandings are needed to ensure

that black churches do not suffocate the leadership potential of girls and women under the shroud of a Jesus-sanctioned sexism? (2) How might black churches enable their members to follow Jesus while still appreciating and learning from the beautifully diverse religious, spiritual, and ethical traditions around the globe? To resist the principalities and powers of sexism and religious chauvinism, contemporary black Christology should heed time-honored African wisdom—namely, to go forward, we must first go backward.

Sankofa: Womanist Christological Reflections

Sankofa, an African term from the Akan language meaning to "return and take," refers to the "wisdom in learning from the past, to help improve the future."[5] When I traveled to Ghana, Kofi Amos, a Ghanaian friend, provided me with a vivid explanation of *sankofa*. He spoke about a mother who, on a journey with her child, notices that the child has left garments behind. The mother says to the child, "Go back and get what is yours." Accordingly, *sankofa* teaches us that to go forward on our journeys, we must reclaim our valued possessions. In this picturesque example, the parent urges the child to reclaim valuable possessions. In this chapter, I, the "child," urge the "parent" (black churches) to reclaim valuable possessions.

The resources for a liberating Christology are already present in the rich intellectual and cultural resources of black religious communities. Many black religious leaders neglect these resources because of their preoccupation with Eurocentric theological conceptions.[6] Womanist theologian Delores Williams underscores this preoccupation with an incisive question: "What are the appropriate tools for exploring the meaning of Jesus in an Afrocentric American context rather than an 'Afro-Saxon,' Eurocentric American context?"[7] Twenty-first-century black churches would do well to reclaim (*sankofa*) womanist wisdom from the late twentieth century. To illustrate, I will highlight christological proposals from three womanist theologians: Jacquelyn Grant, Kelly Brown Douglas, and JoAnne Terrell.

Jacquelyn Grant: *White Women's Christ and Black Women's Jesus*

Jacquelyn Grant sent shock waves across the feminist landscape by highlighting the significant limitations and omissions of white, feminist Christologies. She argues that those Christologies were inattentive to black women's experiences and that they failed to examine the multiple dimensions of racism, sexism, and classism.[8] While affirming that white women and black women were sisters in the struggle against gender oppression, Grant insists that many white women knew little about class oppression and practically nothing about racial oppression. Consequently, black women's qualitatively different oppression required a new term and approach—"womanist"—which Alice Walker coined in her now famous definition: "Womanist, from *womanish*. (Opp. of 'girlish,' i.e., frivolous, irresponsible, not serious). A black feminist or feminist of color. From the black folk expression of mothers to female children, 'You acting womanish,' i.e., like a woman. Usually referring to outrageous, audacious, courageous or *willful* behavior."[9]

Walker's culturally resonant definition sparked a potent movement of theological inquiry—womanist theology: "the systematic, faith-based exploration of the many facets of African American women's religiosity" that emphasizes "the imagination and initiative that African American women have utilized in developing sophisticated religious responses to their lives."[10]

Employing indigenous black resources, Grant's Christology accentuates egalitarian understandings of Jesus among nineteenth-century black activists, such as Sojourner Truth and Jarena Lee. These ancestors insisted that "the significance of Christ is not his maleness, but his humanity."[11] Grant also calls for christological proposals that focus on the life of Jesus and enable resistance to class-based injustice.

Kelly Brown Douglas: *The Black Christ*

Kelly Brown Douglas provides a sweeping history of the black Christ—the connection of Jesus's biological ancestry with African origins and the identification of Christ's redemptive activity with the survival and empowerment of black people. Of particular interest is her highlighting of the Christologies from three twentieth-century black male theologians: Albert Cleage, James Cone, and J. Deotis Roberts.

Cleage based his belief in Jesus's ethnic blackness on biblical genealogy. Cone asserted that Christ was symbolically black, which means that Christ identified with the oppressed people of the first century and thus is revealed in contemporary black people's experiences of racial oppression. Roberts's Christology promoted a reconciling, universal Christ who relates to all groups of people, which means that Christ can relate specifically to black people.

A word concerning Cleage is appropriate. Cleage's use of genealogy to determine Jesus's ancestry is not without problems. Nevertheless, his insistence on Jesus's ethnic blackness has proven to be more factual than fanciful. Some scholars are questioning the designation of first-century Jews as people from the "Near East" or "Middle East." These Eurocentric terms obscure the geographic fact that "the land of Palestine actually sits on the two continental plates that comprise the African continent."[12] Consequently, it is accurate to refer to Jesus, a first-century Palestinian Jew, as "African."

Furthermore, forensic anthropologist Richard Neave constructed a portrait of a typical, first-century Jewish male such as Jesus of Nazareth.[13] Neave's portrait possesses features associated with people of African ancestry.[14] Jesus was an African Jew who likely was dark complexioned. We should not underestimate this first-century probability in twenty-first-century cultural contexts where racism is resurgent and white privilege remains stubbornly entrenched and even theologically endorsed.

Douglas argues that womanist Christology should hold accountable black institutions (e.g., churches) that are guilty of oppressing people as well as foster an enhanced global focus among black people.[15] Additionally, womanist Christology will avoid entanglement in early Christian creeds (e.g., the Nicene and Chalcedonian creeds) that focus on the metaphysics of Christ's coequality with God and Christ's simultaneously divine and human natures.[16]

JoAnne Terrell: *Power in the Blood?* *The Cross in the African American Experience*

JoAnne Terrell focuses womanist wisdom on the cross, "the central cultic symbol of Christianity."[17] She questions the ethical and liturgical appropriateness of theories of sacrificial atonement, especially in the light of the unmitigated and unredemptive suffering characterizing large segments of black history. Terrell's sensitivity to the liturgical implications of atonement theology is especially noteworthy.

According to a long-standing black Christian axiom, a sermon is incomplete unless it "goes to Calvary" and recounts in considerable detail Jesus's suffering on the cross. When divorced from theological reflection and cultural history, the excessive emphasis on Jesus's suffering unwittingly perpetuates the "hermeneutics of sacrifice," a problematic social ethic that emphasizes love without an equally adamant emphasis on justice.[18] The glorification of sacrifice eventually became an ideological pillar buttressing the European and American slave empires. Ultimately, for Terrell, the power of Jesus's story is not in the blood he shed but rather in the life he lived. Jesus's sacrifice was the "result of his confrontation with evil" and stands as a sacrament to the power of a life unwilling to surrender to injustice.[19]

Taken as a whole, these womanist scholars call for christological proposals that (1) focus on the life of Jesus, (2) provide indigenous resources for resistance to social oppression external and internal to black communities, (3) challenge traditional theories of atonement, and (4) enable greater global awareness among black people. This *sankofa* pilgrimage to the past can facilitate the christological pilgrimage into the future.

A Spirit-Centered Christology

A liberating black Christology should be grounded in a central feature of many African-influenced religions—*the activity of the Spirit*. Furthermore, it should embrace a fully human Jesus whose hospitality to God's Spirit during his ministry led God to incorporate or adopt Christ into God's divinity. In short, I argue for a fully human Jesus who *became* a divine Christ.

Judged by orthodoxy, my assertions are heretical. It has been said that heresy is the revenge of a suppressed truth.[20] Too often we live by truths that are "greatly reduced."[21] Thus, the promotion of heresy might lead to *holiness*, or at least move us toward *wholeness*, if it brings to light suppressed truths that expand our appreciation for the robust revelation of a capacious God.

My christological proposals seek to address social injustices and religious chauvinism, especially in black communities. Although Jesus remains central to the liturgical life of black congregations, many of these congregations fail to adopt a serious social justice agenda. Since Jesus, an ancient prophet for justice, is so important to the black *religious* imagination, why is there so much unmitigated *social* pathology in black communities?

Undoubtedly, centuries-long structural injustices foisted upon black communities are the source of many of these pathologies. Yet problematic christological conceptions might contribute, at least indirectly, to the incapacity to deal with these debilitating dysfunctions. At their prophetic best, black churches have creatively wed Jesus and justice. The current separation of Jesus and justice is not irreparable, but reconciliation may require different christological approaches.

We must deemphasize christological concepts not native to black communities. We cannot continue writing a theological story that ignores our cultural grammar.[22] The creeds from Nicaea and Chalcedon present at least two significant cultural challenges for black communities committed to the liberation struggle.

First, the presence and patronage of Roman emperors at those councils have left ruling-class fingerprints all over those creeds. In the case of the Council of Nicaea, the Roman emperor "Constantine not only called the council but also funded the travel and expenses of the bishops, determined the agenda, and chaired the meetings."[23] The imperial agenda involved the use of Christian creeds to solidify and celebrate the "unity" of the Roman Empire. In fairness, many of those ancient bishops might have had a holier agenda. Nevertheless, it would be naïve to believe that the imperial presence and largesse did not influence and co-opt those theological proceedings.

In short, the Christology of those early creeds comes from imperial contexts designed to suppress plurality. Should black churches take their christological cues from ruling-class contexts? It would be a leap in logic to implicate those ancient councils in the atrocities of transatlantic slavery and racism, but might the ruling-class drive to suppress pluralism be an indirect link connecting those councils and later episodes of genocidal violence endorsed by many Christians?

Many centuries after those councils, a European slave trader would haul Africans into captivity in a slave ship named "Jesus." In the name of Jesus, some Europeans *suppressed* the cultural plurality of Africans and *compressed* African flesh into the hull of a Jesus ship, ignoring the Africans' humanity in the name of unifying an economic empire. The brutal connections across the centuries between imperial theology and genocidal sociology should motivate black Christians to locate our Christology elsewhere.

The ancient Roman Empire impaled its undesirables on wooden crosses. The colonial European empire inventoried its undesirables in wooden ships. The contemporary United States empire incarcerates its undesirables in steel cages—prisons that are disproportionately populated by black people. The presence and practices of empire are alive and well. Therefore, we should think twice about siding with theologies possessing an imperial pedigree.

Second, elite, powerful men historically have used the theological ambiguity of those ancient creeds to preserve patriarchal practices. The creeds' insistence on the mysterious comingling of the divine and the human in Christ has resulted in the deification of Jesus's maleness. The maleness of Jesus is assumed to be divine, while often the mission of Jesus becomes an afterthought: "It is hardly an accident that the life of Christ is not mentioned in the creeds. . . . The challenge to empire posed by the life of Christ would have just been too great."[24]

Perhaps we should understand Christ—and by extension Christology—more as a process than a person. Rather than simply being Christ, the human Jesus faithfully yielded his life to a Christ process that resulted in deification. Thus, men are not inherently better bearers of the Christ process, since faithfulness to this process is not gender specific. Consequently, women can preside over churches as pastors and popes as well as lead countries as prime ministers and presidents. The likelihood that a woman will become president of the United States before a woman presides at the Vatican speaks volumes about the orthodox confusion of maleness with divinity. Before examining the process to which the human Jesus yielded his life, a brief discussion of the Spirit in African cosmologies is appropriate.

African Cosmology: "Every Time I Feel the Spirit"

A fuller appropriation of African cosmology is the key to a liberating black Christology. A prominent thread running through African cosmologies is the centrality of the Spirit—the eternal life force animating the universe with divine purpose.[25] As the Supreme Deity, the Spirit links visible and invisible dimensions of existence into a tightly connected ecosystem. The material world is significant. Furthermore, beyond the parameters of sensory perception, there are vibrant dimensions of existence as significant, if not more so, as the material world. The *Spirit* connects multiple dimensions through the *spirits*—divine emissaries of the Supreme Deity. These spirits possess considerable power but ultimately are accountable to the Spirit.[26]

Spirits are benevolent forces who guard and guide life in various realms of existence. African cosmologies also are keenly aware of evil cosmic powers who visit misery and mischief upon the world. In distinction to benevolent spirits, these evil forces are often referred to by names such as "mysterious powers" or "sorcery."[27] These wicked forces do not impugn the goodness of the Spirit. The Spirit is ultimately the creator of everything, but spirits and evil forces can exercise their will somewhat in their realm of influence.

Beholden to enlightenment rationality, European and American colonizers inaccurately interpreted African cosmologies as "pagan fetishes," which further justified their exploitation of those "dark-hued heathens." Contemporary science, however, reveals the plausibility of ancient cosmologies that privilege the invisible "transformative energies" of Spirit/spirits, such as the cosmologies emanating from some African and Indigenous American cultures.[28]

Quantum physics asserts that the universe teems with "quanta," invisible, pulsating packets of energy. Certain quantum particles vibrate in ways that transcend the limitations of four-dimensional reality.[29] Quantum particles move erratically from one energy state to another—hence the expression "a quantum leap." In some African cosmologies, spirits could be equated with quantum energy obedient to the holy purposes of the Spirit. Evil forces are erratic quantum energy that have jumped into a state of rebellion against the Spirit's purposes. Employing different terminologies, some African cosmologies and quantum physics bear witness to the same truth—the universe abounds with visible *and invisible* power.

Accordingly, some African cosmologies declare that harmonious living involves balancing four interrelated dimensions of invisible and visible existence: (1) "the realm of the spirit (inclusive of the Supreme deity, the sub-divinities, the ancestral spirits)"; (2) "the realm of tribal or ethnic community"; (3) "the realm of family"; and (4) "the individual person."[30] Communal, familial, and individual equilibrium is contingent on harmony with the Spirit/spirits. Cosmology is the framework for appropriating ethical power in many African-centered cultures.

Slavery's Middle Passage did not eradicate the African belief in the ethical power of the Spirit/spirits. Recalling African cosmologies focused on the life-giving Spirit, enslaved black people insisted that the Spirit provided tools for survival and emancipation in this life, not simply some utopian life to come.[31]

As some of the earliest practical theologians in the United States, enslaved black people deposited their sophisticated cosmological and ethical understandings of the Spirit in the beautiful, subversive art form called the spirituals—faith-based folk songs sung in the key of freedom. While some white scholars wrote textual commentaries on the Bible to justify slavery and colonialism, enslaved black people sang spirituals as "a living, vocal commentary" designed to foster restorative justice and reconciliation.[32]

The much-loved spiritual "Every Time I Feel the Spirit" might serve as a fascinating christological connector, uniting African cosmology, the story of Jesus, and black people's ongoing quest for cultural empowerment and social emancipation. In the everyday language of the people, the refrain of this spiritual recalls the moving Spirit, whom Africans knew long before they encountered missionary imperialism disguised as Christian evangelism:

> Ev'ry time I feel the Spirit moving in my heart, I will pray,
> Ev'ry time I feel the Spirit moving in my heart, I will pray.

A verse in this spiritual plunges us directly into the story of Jesus and the struggle for justice:

> Ol' Jordan River, chilly and cold, It chills the body, but not the soul.
> There ain't but one train that's on this track, It runs to heaven and runs right back.

The Jordan River alludes to the story of Jesus's ancient baptism and justifies believers' contemporary baptism in their "Jordan River." Simultaneously, the "river" and "train" serve as covert codes for enslaved people seeking freedom on the "underground railroad," whose tracks traversed rivers into states where black people enjoyed freedom. In this spiritual, a Spirit-centered cosmology, the story of Jesus, and the search for justice converge to sponsor new ethical and social possibilities.

In accordance with *sankofa*, this spiritual symbolizes a valuable Christology that black Christians should carry into the future. This Christology can propel us beyond passive adoration

of Christ into active imitation of Jesus's hospitality toward the
Spirit—the process that led to the elevation of Jesus as Christ. I
now examine key moments in Mark's Gospel where Jesus "feels
the Spirit," thereby providing a pattern for what it means *to do*
Christology.

Holy Hospitality: The Process of Hosting the Spirit

Since Mark "tells the history of Jesus as the history of the Spirit
with Jesus," this Gospel seems an appropriate touchstone for my
christological reflections.[33] Mark affirms the centrality, and even
divinity, of Christ. However, unlike Matthew, Luke, and John,
Mark possesses greater ambiguity about the point at which Jesus
became the divine Son of God.[34]

This ambiguity invites *improvisation*, another hallmark of
black culture. Four key moments, among others, encapsulate
Jesus's hospitality to the Spirit: (1) Jesus's baptism, (2) Jesus's
conversion *by* the Syrophoenician woman, (3) the crucifixion's
unmasking of ungodly power, and (4) the grassroots gospel of
the risen Christ. As the first instance of hospitality, the baptism
will receive fuller exposition. Hopefully, the cursory statements
about the remaining three moments will provide sufficient
clues about the possibilities of this christological proposal.

Jesus's Baptism and the Beginning of His Ministry: Mark 1:1-15

Mark's first sentence forecasts the political implications of the
forthcoming drama: "The beginning of the good news of Jesus
Christ, the Son of God" (Mark 1:1). In the context of first-century
Roman imperialism, "good news" (*euangelion*) often referred
to the emperor's benevolent deeds.[35] Contrary to Rome's pro-
paganda, Mark declares that the real "good news" comes from
God's messiah.

The repetition of "way" (*hodos*) in verses 2–3 substantiates the
political nature of the "good news." The "way" is the road upon
which God will travel to rescue the oppressed from imperial

captivity.[36] As with Israel's first exodus, the way of the Lord involves the wilderness (Mark 1:4). In Isaiah's prophetic imagination, to which Mark alludes, this wilderness way also connotes a divine transformation of cosmic dimensions, which creates an entirely new world (e.g., Isa 40–42).

With eschatological passion, John the Baptizer, an Elijah-like prophet, initiates a revolutionary people's movement at the Jordan River in the Judean wilderness. This wilderness is a cosmic threshold between two competing powers: the oppressive power of Roman imperialism in league with Jewish aristocratic leaders and the liberating power of God's new order.[37] In light of the cosmic setting of Mark 1:1–8, the emergence of another key character in verse 8 is appropriate—the Holy Spirit. John prophesies that a person coming after him would baptize with the Holy Spirit. But to baptize with the Spirit, this anticipated figure must have the Spirit.

Jesus's baptism marks the inception of his hospitality to God's Spirit. God's ability to trust Jesus with the Spirit is confirmed by Jesus's intentional boundary crossing and willingness to endure political risk. Jesus is from the northern province of Galilee, but John's movement occurs in the southern province of Judea. Certain people in various parts of ancient Israel held prejudices and stereotypes about people from other parts of the country, even to the point of harboring hostility.[38] Irrespective of his humble origins in the insignificant northern town of Nazareth, Jesus journeys across intracountry boundaries to join John's movement.

Additionally, submission to John's baptism reveals Jesus's courage. His baptism is a dangerous decision to join a dangerous group. Any group that would dare question the power of the ruling class for the sake of the emancipation of the "underclass" should expect retaliation. Indeed, the retaliation against John is swift and eventually lethal (Mark 1:14; 6:27).

Despite the potential of ridicule and risk, Jesus willingly joins John's revolutionary movement. Since God's Spirit is a boundary-transcending power, the Spirit considers Jesus, a boundary-transcending person, a kindred spirit. Thus, the Spirit descends upon Jesus (Mark 1:10). God's pleasure in

Jesus is not an affirmation of preexistence but an endorsement of Jesus's politics (Mark 1:11).

Evil forces are unable to deter Jesus from God's way (Mark 1:12–13). As a result of Jesus's hospitality to the Spirit, the Spirit sends the assistance of other cosmic emissaries to minister to Jesus. While some commentators identify the animals in the wilderness as instruments of evil, is it not plausible that Jesus finds solace in fellowship *with* the animals in the wilderness (Mark 1:13)? In line with an African cosmology, harmony with life in the visible world enables resistance to demonic onslaughts from the invisible world. Fidelity to God's way is revealed in Jesus's continuance of John's mission of repentance (Mark 1:14–15). Participation in God's revolutionary community requires a radically new mindset.

Jesus's Conversion *by* the Syrophoenician Woman: Mark 7:24–30

Jesus's resistance to evil in the wilderness reveals an earnest commitment to host the Spirit. As the Spirit works with and through him, he accumulates other notable victories against evil (e.g., Mark 1:21–45; 4:35–41; 5:1–43). Jesus, however, would soon confront the pointed truth conveyed in the spiritual "Elijah Rock": "Satan is a liar and a conjurer too, if you don't watch out, He'll conjure you." Satisfied with external success against evil, Jesus momentarily ignores evil's covert operation within his own heart. The *process* of Christology is delicate and fraught with ever-present temptations to misuse or withhold the Spirit's power.

Jesus travels into Tyre, which is "foreign," gentile territory (Mark 7:24). Like imperial armies and greed-driven transnational corporations, evil spirits have no regard for cultural or national boundaries. Thus, the presence of an unclean spirit that oppresses a "foreign" child from another culture, unfortunately, is no surprise (Mark 7:25–26). What surprises us is Jesus's derogatory dismissal of this woman, this child, and this crisis in need of the Spirit's compassionate touch. No amount of exegetical maneuvering can lessen the sting of Jesus referring to these females as "dogs" (Mark 7:27). Jesus had just "lectured" others about how the evil that comes from inside a person defiles a person (Mark 7:1–23), and now words from inside of him defile others. Physician, heal thyself!

In this instance, Jesus *receives* healing before he offers it. Like so many audacious black women seeking healing for their tormented children, the Syrophoenician woman preaches a one-sentence sermon that converts Jesus from his racism and sexism.[39] Consequently, the girl is released from the grip of evil, and Jesus realizes anew that those who preach repentance must also practice it. The beloved community requires everyone—even Jesus—to vigilantly dismantle the barriers in the most guarded, secluded neighborhood of all—the human heart.[40]

The Crucifixion's Unmasking of Ungodly Power: Mark 15:33–39

I approach the cross cautiously, bearing in mind the womanist critique of "glorified suffering." At the beginning of Mark, the Spirit descends upon Jesus prior to his first temptation. In the end, the Spirit departs from Jesus after his last temptation. The cry of dereliction—"My God, my God, why have you forsaken me?"—is about abandonment. Not God's ultimate abandonment of Jesus but Jesus's final abandonment of any conceptions that hospitality to God's Spirit will lead necessarily to earthly success.

Grappling with this final temptation is a profoundly *spiritual* task with cosmic consequences, signaled by midnight darkness at midday (Mark 15:33). After Jesus's final cry, the verb translated "he breathed his last" is repeated (*ekpneō*; Mark 15:37, 39). Does this verb simply indicate Jesus's physical death? Or does it also connote the Spirit's departure from him, not as a sign of desecration but rather as a sign of divine affirmation?

God's affirmation of Jesus's faithfulness is visible and verbal. The torn temple veil symbolizes God's desire to rip apart religion's tendency to create "insiders" and "outsiders." The centurion's words—"Truly this man was a son of God"—are not a confession of Jesus's divinity but an unveiling of the depths to which people will plunge to destroy good and the common good. If a centurion, a ruthless Roman henchman, can recognize the injustice of ungodly power, maybe the empire is not as invincible as it appears. If we can resist the idolatrous desire to control God's Spirit—like the attempts to control exemplified by chauvinistic theology, patriotic civil religion, or prosperity preaching—we can dismantle cross-making systems before more people are strung up. We take up our crosses only because we trust that empires must eventually tear their crosses down.

The Grassroots Gospel of the Risen Christ: Mark 16:1–8

Mary Magdalene, Mary the mother of James, and Salome travel to the tomb with spices, fragrant mementos of their love for an ally martyred for the beloved community. Having ministered with Jesus in life, how could they not minister to him in death? For understandable reasons, the women consider the stone a hindrance to their death ritual. Had the stone remained, they would have missed the fullness of the empty tomb. So the obstacle is removed, perhaps through the agency of the cosmic figure in a white robe, a startling contrast to Jesus's blood-stained burial cloth.

Upon entering the tomb, the women receive an announcement of cosmic significance: "He has risen!" The verb "to raise" (*egeirō*) is passive, indicating God's activity (Mark 16:6). Jesus *is raised* by God's Spirit. "The Spirit liberates; that's her vocation. . . . *Pneuma*, spirit, is the source of Jesus's power to restore life; indeed, *pneuma* resurrected him."[41]

The Spirit miraculously transcends death and Jesus's limitations of mortality (i.e., his social identity and human attributes). Furthermore, God ushers Jesus into a new form of life, which is no longer constrained by time and space. The Spirit Jesus breathed out on the cross is breathed anew into Christ. Christ becomes a cosmic spirit, universally available to assist the Supreme Spirit in building the beloved community.

Yet the universality of the risen Christ manifests itself in Christ's continual engagement in local, grassroots struggles—a crucial theme for those committed to justice and peace. Christ's resurrection is only part of the message. The messenger exhorts the women and other disciples to meet the risen Christ in Galilee. Galilee was the site of Jesus's resistance to evil, and "Galilee" is a symbol of the ongoing resistance to evil waged in the memory of Jesus and through the power of Christ. "Galilee" exists

wherever grassroots folks are tapping into the redemptive energy of the beloved community;
wherever the demons of religious chauvinism, racism, sexism, heterosexism, and economic exploitation are being exorcised;
wherever people are being healed of the "leprosy" of drug addiction and incarceration.

The risen Christ does not liberate us from service but rather for service. Accordingly, the biblical scholar Ched Myers poignantly observes, "The resurrection is not an answer, but the final question."[42] The question is will we follow the risen Christ and take the good news to the grassroots?

My commitment to the grassroots gospel was solidified as a graduate student at the University of Oxford. My Oxford teacher and mentor, Christopher Rowland, held a professorship in the "ivory tower," but his *discipleship* is firmly planted in the grassroots. His pioneering work in liberation theology has motivated me and many others to ground pastoral practices and theological reflection in "the struggles of millions for recognition and justice."[43]

Whether I am preaching a sermon, publishing a book, or protesting injustice, Professor Rowland's voice reminds me that "the experience of poverty and oppression . . . is as important a text as the text of Scripture itself."[44] Genuine disciples are not content merely to read Scripture in the comfortable confines of a church sanctuary. Rather, they are compelled by the risen Christ to embody the grassroots gospel in "Galilee" as people fend off evil's encroachments and create communities abounding in indomitable hope and invincible love.

Embracing a Pluralistic Christ

Liberating possibilities emerge if we read Mark's Gospel as an unfolding process of a fully human Jesus who provides hospitality to the Spirit. Jesus of Nazareth was not divine. He submitted faithfully to a divine process involving God's providential selection of his life as a demonstration of the holy power that dethrones the dehumanizing power of empires.

If we forge partnerships with God's Spirit and with one another, our inhumanity to humanity can be broken, and the beloved community, where social differences no longer divide, can emerge. Jesus's purpose was not to inspire faith in him but rather to inspire fidelity to the inbreaking "*kin*-dom"—our mutual enjoyment of God's fullness that unites us as siblings who possess equally the image of our Divine Parent.[45]

Christologies that support the "superiority" of Christianity foster the imperial spirit against which Jesus struggled. The Roman Empire suppressed plurality in service of its lord, Caesar. Often, the "Christian Empire" follows suit in service of its lord, an exclusive Christ. By insisting on the exclusive lordship of Christ, are we making religion a "zero-sum game" where there can be only one "winner"?[46]

In light of the complex problems around the globe, religious communities should work collaboratively. Empires persist by causing the opponents of empires to squabble among themselves. R. S. Sugirtharajah, a postcolonial scholar, encourages an approach to pluralism that enables us to follow more faithfully the paths of justice and peace: "In a multireligious context like ours, the real contest is not between Jesus and other savior figures like Buddha or Krishna, or religious leaders like Mohammed . . . it is between mammon and Satan on the one side, and Jesus, Buddha, Krishna, and Mohammed on the other. Mammon stands for personal greed, avariciousness, accumulation, and selfishness, and Satan stands for structural and institutional violence."[47]

This is not the time for religious communities to perpetuate intolerance and hatred. We should direct our energies toward providing hospitality for the Spirit—the holy energy flowing through the cosmos that desires abundant life for all. When Jesus hosted the Spirit at his baptism, the Spirit called him "beloved." Womanist ethicist Emilie Townes declares, "To be called beloved is the marvelous yes to God's what if . . . to ask the question . . . what would it look like if we actually believed that we are washed in God's grace?"[48] Let us pray that the Spirit also might call us "beloved."

"Ev'ry time I feel the Spirit moving in my heart, I will *pray*." Prayer is revolutionary openness to God's what if. "What if we actually believed that we are washed in God's grace?" As people in black churches often say enthusiastically, "Amen and Amen." Yes, our spirits say, "Yes!"

2

Religion, Reparations, and Racial Reconciliation

A Postcolonial Approach to 2 Corinthians 3:12–18

> *If God is the Spirit of freedom for the least in society, then this spirit has to be active as an event and process of struggle even where the name of Jesus is not known. . . . Among the cries of all the marginalized peoples, God reveals God's self in all faiths around the globe. To deny this is to possibly participate in a new form of imperialism—a Christocentric imperialism against the majority of the other faiths on earth.*
>
> —Dwight Hopkins, "A Black American Perspective on Interfaith Dialogue"

Postcolonial Studies: Moving from the "Ancient" and the "Academic"

I am passionately concerned about the contemporary theological and ideological implications of biblical texts in general and Pauline texts in particular.[1*] These concerns were formed by the inspiring worship and pastoral preaching at First Baptist

---

* This chapter was originally published as "Paul and Racial Reconciliation: A Postcolonial Approach to 2 Corinthians 3:12–18," in *Scripture and Traditions: Essays on Early Judaism and Christianity in Honor of*

Church in Salem, Virginia, the black Christian congregation
of my youth, where my father served as pastor and my mother
as a strong lay leader. There, I witnessed how biblical texts
shaped people's understanding of God and transformed their
daily lives.

Later, as I pursued university training and began my professorial career, I began to understand more clearly the theological
and ideological implications of biblical interpretation. In my first
published book (which was originally my Emory University PhD
dissertation), I investigated how the apostle Paul confronted
the perplexing problem of Greco-Roman slavery in the Corinthian congregation.[2] Furthermore, this book examined how
nineteenth- and twentieth-century interpretive debates about
1 Corinthians 7:17–24 continued and expanded the theological
and ideological struggles evident in that biblical text.

This chapter is a natural continuation of my earlier exegetical work on Paul. Previously, I examined how a text from the
Corinthian correspondence shaped nineteenth- and twentieth-
century conversations about slavery. In this chapter, I pursue
a related question: How might a reading of another text in the
Corinthian correspondence shape twenty-first-century conversations about racial reconciliation among people still affected
by the transatlantic slavery of the fifteenth through nineteenth
centuries?

Given my theological and ideological concerns, postcolonial
approaches to biblical interpretation provide an excellent way
forward. Postcolonial studies are a diverse and expanding set
of interpretive practices and theories that place the colonialism and neocolonialism of Europe and the United States at the
center of interpretive conversations. Postcolonial practitioners
debate the definitions of terms such as "colonialism," "imperialism," and "postcolonialism." While these debates reflect the
intellectual vibrancy, cultural relevance, and methodological

Carl R. Holladay, edited by Gail O'Day and Patrick Gray (Boston: Brill,
2008), 411–28. Reprinted with permission of Brill.

maturity of postcolonial studies, the specifics of the debates will not detain us now.

Broadly defined, postcolonial studies engage "the overlapping issues of race, empire, diaspora, and ethnicity."[3] More specifically, postcolonial studies are concerned with colonialism—"the organized deployment of racialized and gendered constructs for practices of acquiring and maintaining political control over other social groups, settling their lands with new residents, and/or exploiting that land and its peoples through military and administrative occupiers."[4] Closely associated with colonialism is "imperialism," which consists of a "more coherent organizational form" by which colonizers present themselves as missionaries to the world.[5] Postcolonial studies also examine the attempt of the literal and figurative descendants of former colonizers to reassert their colonial influence ("neocolonialism" or "neoimperialism"). Additionally, postcolonial studies consider the political and cultural possibilities that emerge when formerly colonized people resist and transcend colonialism's oppressive effects ("decolonization").[6]

In recent decades, Pauline scholars have explored ancient imperialism as an inescapable aspect of early Christianity.[7] These studies have charted a promising course that has yielded specific exegetical refinements. For example, attention to ancient Roman imperialism has prompted interpreters to rethink key Pauline terms such as "righteousness/justice" (*dikaiosunē*), "gospel" (*euangelion*), and "faith" (*pistis*). These studies also have reminded us of the blurry boundaries between religion and politics in the first-century CE Mediterranean world. In general, the emphasis in many recent political readings of Paul's letters has been on the ancient world. Yet as noted above, postcolonial studies invite interpreters to acknowledge more readily the current manifestations of imperialism that abound in many cultures.

While I appreciate innovative readings of Paul's letters that demonstrate awareness of the political realities of his time, I am more interested in the political realities of my time. To read Paul against the backdrop of ancient Rome is intellectually profitable, but the Roman Empire crumbled centuries ago. A more intriguing question is the following: What happens if postcolonial critics begin to engage Pauline texts more fully with respect to the neoimperialism of the twenty-first century?

Biblical scholarship must engage more thoroughly the impulse of empire that runs through so much political, economic, academic, and religious life in the United States and other so-called first world countries in the Northern Hemisphere. If biblical scholarship avoids such engagement, it will fall prey again to that sharp critique the biblical scholar Walter Wink presented half a century ago: "The outcome of biblical studies in the academy is a trained incapacity to deal with the real problems of actual living persons in their daily lives."[8]

As a politically engaged black scholar, I cannot ignore the contemporary empire. It is the legislative decisions made by the Potomac River and the financial decisions made by the Hudson River—not the ancient machinations of the Caesars by the Tiber River—that currently threaten the well-being of so many people in the United States and abroad. Thus, this chapter unapologetically moves the interpretive conversation concerning Pauline texts from an emphasis on ancient imperialism to an emphasis on contemporary imperialism.

A Contemporary Social Struggle: Racial Reconciliation and Transatlantic Slavery

In light of my interest in postcolonial approaches, I began pondering how a postcolonial reading of a Pauline text might facilitate the demanding, but necessary, work of contemporary racial reconciliation,[9] a social cause to which I am deeply committed.[10] Two events galvanized my efforts to create a dialogue among a Pauline text, a postcolonial methodology, and the issue of racial reconciliation. First, 2007 marked the bicentennial commemoration of the abolition of the transatlantic slave trade in the British Empire.[11] Second, in conjunction with this international commemoration, I was selected to give the 2006–7 Bray Lectures. A word concerning both events is now in order.

Bicentennial Commemoration of the Abolition of the Transatlantic Slave Trade

In 1807, courageous social agitation and revolt and coordinated abolitionist efforts finally brought an end, at least in legal principle, to the international trading of Africans as slaves in the British colonies.[12] For centuries, this "triangular trafficking" had shipped whiskey and guns from England to West Africa, enslaved people from West Africa to the Caribbean and the Americas, and sugar and cotton from the Caribbean and the Americas to England. On March 25, 1807, an act of the British Parliament abolished this international trade.[13]

This event in 1807 forecasted the possibility of a more humane era in interpersonal and international relations, especially between people of African and European descent. Abolitionist activities—before and after 1807—released palpable positive energy into the moral universe. However, for two centuries, many well-intentioned people have ignored, resisted, or failed to operate fully under that moral energy. Therefore, more than two hundred years later, genuine reconciliation between groups estranged by slavery is still, in many regards, an unrealized hope. Thus, the bicentennial commemoration seemed to me an opportune occasion to address the role of the Bible, and especially the role of Paul's letters, in contemporary efforts to heal past injustices concerning slavery.

The use of Paul's letters in the ideological justification of slavery is well documented.[14] In light of the bicentennial commemoration, I raised a different question: How might Paul's letters provide theological and ideological energy for contemporary conversations about racial reconciliation? Instead of ignoring Paul or maligning him for the role of his letters in promoting the "iniquitous institution" of slavery, I wanted to engage his letters for the healing balm they might possess.[15] While contemplating these issues, a fortuitous invitation provided me with further incentive to pursue this line of inquiry.

Bray Lectures in Ghana and England

The United Society for the Propagation of the Gospel (USPG) and the Society for Promoting Christian Knowledge (SPCK), two London-based missionary organizations, selected me as the 2006–7 Bray Lecturer. Named in honor of Thomas Bray, a seventeenth-century British missionary, this lectureship provided an opportunity for an academic theologian with church connections to learn and give lectures in two international contexts.[16]

I traveled to Ghana in December 2006 for the first part of the lectureship. Ghana seemed an appropriate choice since it was preparing to celebrate another auspicious anniversary in addition to the bicentennial commemoration of the abolition of the slave trade. In March 2007, Ghana would mark its fiftieth year of independence from British colonial rule. While in Ghana, I learned about the history of the country before and after European slavery and colonialism. I met with religious leaders and presented seminars on the role of religion in the oppression and liberation of people of African descent. My itinerary also included visits to historical sites, such as the home of W. E. B. Du Bois in Accra;[17] the memorial to Kwame Nkrumah, Ghana's first president; and the slave castles in Cape Coast and Elmina, where thousands of Africans were enslaved prior to being shipped to the Caribbean and the Americas.

The second part of the lectureship occurred in England in March 2007. I gave numerous presentations throughout England, including formal lectures exploring how communities still impacted by transatlantic slavery can strive for reconciliation and a more just and peaceful world. I also received the honor of preaching at the 11:15 a.m. Sung Eucharist service at Westminster Abbey in London on Sunday, March 11, 2007.[18]

My selection as the Bray Lecturer provided an ideal opportunity to pursue a postcolonial reading of a Pauline text in two cultural contexts dramatically impacted by colonial and postcolonial realities—Ghana and England. The itinerary of the lectureship permitted me to retrace geographically and theologically parts of the triangular route of slavery. Furthermore, the slave castles in Ghana—those dark, suffocating dungeons designed to brutalize the bodies and spirits of their inhabitants—have indelibly influenced my exegetical and theological agenda.

Paul and Reparations for Slavery

In the summer and fall of 2006, as I began my initial research for the Bray Lectures, I had planned to offer a postcolonial reading of a Pauline text to support the granting of reparations for persons impacted by transatlantic slavery. By "reparations," I mean "payment for the repair of an injury or wrong done."[19] Social activists and scholars in many disciplines are intensely debating reparations for slavery.[20] While some religious leaders and theologians have added their voices to this debate, I am unaware of many overtly exegetical approaches to this important conversation.[21] In the Bray Lectures, I wanted to address the lack of exegetical resources concerning reparations for slavery.

My initial thinking about reparations followed this logic. Transatlantic slavery inflicted cultural, economic, and psychic wounds upon the African continent and the African diaspora. The African continent and diaspora have been hemorrhaging ever since. Despite this massive bleeding, African people the world over, to their credit, have transformed every aspect of global culture, from commerce to cuisine. As a Ghanaian clergy said to me in Ghana during the Bray Lectures, "The whole world has been made rich by Africa."

Yet to ignore conversations about reparations is akin to enjoying the riches from people of African descent while simultaneously allowing those people to bleed profusely from the wounds of slavery. To continue with the metaphor, reconciliation is often depicted as an embrace or hug that overcomes hostility. But hugging a person bleeding profusely, without attending to the gaping wound, is more a kiss of death than a hug to end hostility.

Just as reconciliation is a complex process that must involve reparations, so too is reparations a complex term with many nuances. Opinions about the meanings and possible administrations of reparations are wide ranging. For instance, Molefi Asante, a progenitor of contemporary African-centered scholarship, maintains that there should be four dimensions of reparations: the moral, the legal, the economic, and the political.[22] While a discussion of the multiple dimensions of reparations will not detain us now, there is a growing consensus among some scholars and activists that reparations should involve financial compensation for people of African descent and their institutions. Since chattel slavery reaped untold *economic* profits for many white Europeans and Americans, it seems only just that the currency of reparations should also be at least partly economic.

Nevertheless, slavery exacted from African people not only an economic toll but also a psychic toll. In that regard, British pounds and American dollars alone will be insufficient to redress the wrong. In my research and reflection about reparations, I left open the question of the form of reparations. Yet I have grown increasingly convinced that without reparations, there will be no genuine, abiding reconciliation among those estranged by the violence of transatlantic slavery.

Thus, I initially set out to offer a postcolonial reading of a Pauline text that would support the cause of international reparations for persons affected by slavery. I soon discovered, however, that my desire was premature. It began to occur to me how uncomfortable some people were with even the mention of reparations.

As I pondered the cultural discomfort that even the term "reparations" creates among some people, another question occurred to me: If we can barely mention the term "reparations" in polite, cultural conversations, let alone seriously entertain it as a socioeconomic reality, how will reparations ever happen?

At this point, I altered my exegetical agenda for the Bray Lectures. No longer would I read a Pauline text to directly address the issue of reparations. Instead, I would read a Pauline text to discern why it is so difficult even to have the conversation about reparations in the first place, especially in intercultural settings. How might Pauline exegesis create the conditions for a much-needed conversation about the dimensions of racial reconciliation in the twenty-first century?

A Postcolonial Approach to 2 Corinthians 3:12-18

To proceed with my theological and exegetical investigation, I posed this question to myself: Why do certain people—religious, well-meaning, justice-seeking people—frequently renounce even the mention of reparations? As I pondered this question, it seemed to me that there are ideological obstacles that prevent meaningful intercultural, international dialogues about reparations and hence prevent reconciliation. Reparations and reconciliation cannot be seriously examined, let alone embraced, until some ideological obstacles are identified and addressed. In this effort, 2 Corinthians appeared a suitable place to seek assistance.

In many Christian conversations about reconciliation, 2 Corinthians 5:17-21 is a touchstone text, and especially verse 19: "In Christ God was reconciling the world to [God's] self." Christian proponents of reconciliation are right to centralize 2 Corinthians 5:17-21. Yet it occurred to me that conversations about 2 Corinthians 5 are premature without sustained attention to 2 Corinthians 3, especially verses 12-18.

In 2 Corinthians 3, Paul plumbs the depths of the challenges facing the Corinthian congregation and the world. The deeper issue in 2 Corinthians is epistemology—how we know and think.[23] To investigate epistemology is to ask this question: What characteristics allow us to know truth from falsehood?

As I grappled afresh with 2 Corinthians, Paul seemed to be saying that the world will never arrive at truth or reconciliation without a transformation in our way of knowing and thinking. Before there can be a new world, there must be new ways of thinking about the world. Second Corinthians 3 was, and is, a call for repentance—an apocalyptic action that transforms our thinking.

In 2 Corinthians 3:12-18, Paul identifies the epistemological obstacle that must be removed: "the veil"! The veil distorts how we know and obscures right perceptions of the world. Paul's interpretation of the veil is filled with exegetical intricacies. I summarize below my interpretation of 2 Corinthians 3.

God has ushered in a new moment in salvation history.[24] This new era, whose chief architect is Jesus Christ, is both similar and dissimilar to the old era, whose chief architect was Moses. Both the old and new eras reflect God's glory. Yet there is a crucial distinction between the old and new eras. The old era actually places a veil over people's thinking. A relationship with Jesus Christ removes the obscuring veil and bestows upon persons a radically new orientation. With the veil removed, people are able to detect God's surprising plans.

What does the veil in 2 Corinthians 3 have to do with contemporary racial reconciliation among people still impacted by transatlantic slavery? An answer emerges if we read 2 Corinthians 3 from the contextual framework of my trip to Ghana in the fall of 2006 for the first part of the Bray Lectures. I led a seminar for scholars and clergy at St. Nicholas Seminary, an Anglican theological school in Cape Coast, Ghana. On the Thursday night before that Friday seminar, I read again 2 Corinthians 3:12–18, the principal text for the seminar, and I also read again the text upon which that 2 Corinthians passage is predicated, Exodus 34.

Exodus 34 concludes a pivotal three-chapter section of Exodus, which begins in Exodus 32. In Exodus 32, Israel commits idolatry, thus provoking God's fierce judgment. In Exodus 33, Moses pleads with God to restore God's presence to Israel, for without God's presence, Israel would cease to be. God promises to allow God's face to go with Israel, but God refuses to allow Moses to see God's face. In Exodus 34, God renews the covenant with Israel on Mount Sinai.

At the end of the covenant renewal, there is a mysterious reference to a veil that Moses places on his face in Exodus 34:29–35. Moses's direct encounter with God's transcendence left Moses's face shining. Thus, when speaking with the people after this divine encounter, Moses put the veil on. Moses then took the veil off when he spoke to God.

Scholars debate the meaning of the veil. For instance, the biblical scholar Walter Brueggemann suggests that the veil might be protection for Israel or an instrument to prevent God's glory from being profaned by contact with masses of people.[25] Thus, the veil appears to fulfill some positive or at least protective purpose.

However, as Paul interprets Exodus 34 in 2 Corinthians 3:12–18, this veil is not positive. Instead, the veil prohibits the proper perception of reality. It is an instrument of concealment. Moses uses the veil to hide from people his fading glory, which for Paul signals the inability of the old era to provide ultimate life. Therefore, when Paul interpreted Exodus 34 in his context, the veil assumed new, negative significance.

On a warm Ghanaian Thursday night, prior to the seminar at St. Nicholas Seminary, I, too, began to realize that the veil was problematic and was hiding something. The veil was hiding the horrific colonial violence that Exodus places in the mouth of God. In Exodus 34, the covenant is renewed but at the expense of Indigenous people.

There had been a veil on my mind in previous engagements with Exodus 34. When I read Exodus 34 in a Ghanaian context, this text was no longer an innocent affirmation of covenant renewal. In Ghana, a country only then fifty years removed from the bondage of British colonialism, Exodus 34:11–16 arrested my attention.

In the seminar with my Ghanaian colleagues, I played "jazz" with the scriptures, inserting different ethnic or tribal names in Exodus 34:11–16. My "improvisation" revealed how dangerous this text could be:

> Observe what I the God of colonial violence and greed command you—my colonial British missionaries to the Gold Coast of Africa. As you invade the Gold Coast to enslave the people and pillage their resources, I will drive out before you the Akan, and the Fante, and the Ga, and the Ewe, and the Mossi, and the Yoruba. . . .
>
> Tear down their altars of African Traditional Religions where they have met the Great God for centuries; cut down their sacred poles where they have named and dedicated their children to the Great God and raised their families in righteousness.
>
> And in the name of colonial religion, refer to their sacred traditions as "fetishes," and call those dark people "pagans."

Even though those Indigenous Africans were the architects of religion and knew the Great God millennia before the Christian religion was formulated, convince them that their sacred traditions are demonic rituals.

My improvisational reading revealed that Exodus 34 for Indigenous West Africans could be a "text of terror,"[26] which employs "a theological justification in order to serve the vested [and violent] interest of a particular ethnic/racial group."[27] Indeed, religious faithfulness in Exodus 34 required the destruction of Indigenous peoples. My point was not to impugn Moses or by extension to foster contemporary anti-Judaism. My aim was to unmask the colonial violence at the center of Exodus 34. Paul in the first century and the twenty-first-century African participants in my seminar had a strong premonition that the veil posed a serious problem.

The veil prevents us from perceiving reality properly. This lack of proper perception has created the conditions for cultural chauvinism and violence. The veil is not a cloth fabric for the face. It is a philosophy that cloaks the mind.

Until we lift the veil in our contemporary cultural conversations, we cannot have probing conversations about reparations and genuine racial reconciliation. If religious communities and social activists want to be ambassadors of justice, they must lift the veil from their own attitudes and actions. Then with sharpened moral perception, these religious communities and social activists will be empowered to guide global conversations about justice and reconciliation.

Spiritual Inspiration from W. E. B. Du Bois

My emphasis on the veil as an instrument of oppression seemed especially appropriate in a Ghanaian context. W. E. B. Du Bois— the distinguished nineteenth- and twentieth-century scholar who emigrated to Ghana and died there in 1963—had likened the psychic and social oppression of black people to a "veil" in his classic work *The Souls of Black Folk*. This veil prevented black people from accurately perceiving who they are, leaving them instead with the distorted self-images propagated by white racism.

Scholars suggest that Du Bois constructed the image of the veil partly from Paul's words about seeing through a glass dimly in 1 Corinthians 13:12 and partly from the veil of the Tabernacle in Exodus 26:33.[28] Du Bois believed that the veil would have to be destroyed or transcended in order for black people to achieve the psychic and social wholeness that allowed them to integrate their "Negro" identity with their "American" identity.[29]

Interestingly, during my stay in Ghana for the Bray Lectures, the first historical site my tour guide arranged for me to visit was Du Bois's home in Accra. This visit occurred two days before the seminar at St. Nicholas Seminary discussed above. As I walked through Du Bois's home, sat in his study, and knelt at his grave outside his home, I began a "postcolonial conversation" with his spirit. My thoughts went like this: "Dr. Du Bois, you turned, at least in part, to the apostle Paul for a powerful image describing the oppression of black people—the veil. In spite of the courageous, pioneering work of you and other freedom fighters, the veil still exists. With your blessing, I want to explore another Pauline text dealing with the veil, with the hopes that these lectures in Ghana and England will move us closer to the final removal of the veil."

As I shared these thoughts at Du Bois's grave, with tears falling from my eyes, I felt a numinous presence surrounding me. I believe it was Du Bois's spirit blessing my efforts to wrestle, once again, with the apostle Paul and with the veil for the sake of liberty and justice for all, and especially for all black people. Inspired by this "visitation" with Du Bois, I set out in my lectures and seminars to understand afresh the nature or "texture" of the veil.

The "Fabric" of Colonialism

There are at least two interlocking "fabrics" that compose the veil. As I intimated above, the first fabric of the veil is colonialism and neocolonialism. Indeed, "colonial" Christianity was a primary ideological pillar of transatlantic slavery.

The collusion of colonial Christianity and slavery became viscerally real to me as I visited the Ghanaian slave dungeons in Cape Coast and Elmina during the Bray Lectures. In Cape Coast, the male slave dungeon was literally beneath the chapel in which Europeans were holding their so-called Christian worship services. In Elmina, the slave auction block was literally beneath the chapel for worship. Colonial Christianity, along with its hegemonic biblical hermeneutics, was propped up by the backs and bones of enslaved Africans.

Religious organizations such as United Society Partners in the Gospel (USPG) should be commended for inviting various contemporary communities to ponder the diverse roles of Christianity in the support and abolition of chattel slavery. Furthermore, the Bray Lectures were a noteworthy effort by USPG to address its role in promoting colonial Christianity in its early years. In this regard, USPG placed its mark on contemporary conversations for justice and reconciliation.

Yet reconciliation will never come unless we, in the words of the ethicist Barbara Holmes, move beyond "polite and reserved academic discourses."[30] According to Holmes, such "discourses are inappropriate responses to genocide."[31] Thus, as we address the lasting legacies of the colonial genocide of transatlantic slavery, we cannot only speak politely about USPG's mark on contemporary conversations.

We must also risk being impolite and remember that USPG's historical antecedent, the Society for the Propagation of the Gospel, marked people in the eighteenth century in a much more infamous way. According to the historian Adam Hochschild, slaveholders associated with SPG branded the mark "Society" into the skin of the enslaved persons they owned in the Caribbean.[32] An eighteenth-century enslaved African on that *Christian-sponsored* Caribbean plantation could have uttered words from another Pauline text: "I carry the marks of Jesus branded on my body" (Gal 6:17). Indeed, some colonial slaveholders transformed the symbolic "branding" of Jesus into an excruciatingly literal practice. In the name of Jesus, Christian missionaries "marked," maimed, and murdered countless Africans.[33]

Furthermore, the historian Christopher Brown has examined the role of Anglo-American religious groups, such as the Quakers and Evangelical Anglicans, in the antislavery movement.[34] Yet Brown also reminds us that many Anglo-American Christians condemned slavery while rarely, if ever, questioning the colonialism and empire building that inflicted another kind of violence on the African continent and diaspora.

Additionally, it must be noted that neocolonialism is alive and well and being fostered by policies implemented by nations such as the United States. One example substantiates the claim. In Ghana, in order to pay their loans from international banks, local farmers must charge higher prices for their rice than the cheaper rice imported from the United States. Consequently, Ghanaians tend to buy rice from the United States rather than from their own farmers.

When I addressed a group of clergy in Ghana during one of the Bray seminars, they spoke passionately about how these trade policies were bringing slow but certain economic and physical death to their communities. For these clergy eager to resist neo-colonial policies and practices, *abstract* musings about Pauline themes such as "death" and "resurrection" were meaningless. So many Ghanaians continue to die prematurely. No longer are they dying in violent forced slave marches to the Ghanaian coast or in the hulls of slave ships. Now Ghanaians die from a lack of economic development. The slower economic development in Ghana—and in many other places around the globe formerly colonized by Europeans and North Americans—is related, in large measure, to the economic despondency and scarcity of social infrastructures (e.g., potable water, health care, sufficient roads, and schools) left in the wake of transatlantic slavery and colonialism. Thus, in Ghana, a postcolonial approach to "resurrection" that overcomes "death" must account for practical, tangible realities like the price of rice.

The "Fabric" of Fundamentalism

In addition to colonialism, there is another interlocking "fabric" from which the ideological veil has been woven: fundamentalism.

Fundamentalism also obscures proper perceptions and poses a serious threat to racial reconciliation.[35] When I speak of fundamentalism, I am not identifying a particular segment within a religious community, per se. Rather, I mean an overall approach to reality that transforms *culturally conditioned* criteria for truth and relevance into *universal criteria*. Furthermore, fundamentalism vigorously and, sometimes, violently compels acceptance of those criteria.

Fundamentalism "replaces the awesome depth of Mystery with a flat surface of barren forms,"[36] and it tends to demonize diversity and ambiguity. While some scholars locate the formal emergence of fundamentalism in the late nineteenth century, the veil of fundamentalism had fallen over the minds of many a long time before that. Indeed, one could argue that fundamentalism provided ideological support for colonialism, and colonialism was the political embodiment of fundamentalism.

Fundamentalism does not restrict itself to *religious* doctrines. It can subsume *cultural philosophies* such as "white privilege" and invest them with a divine mandate. Thus, even after the abolition of the slave trade and emancipation from slavery, white Christian missionaries felt "called by God" to enlighten and evangelize the "dark natives" in Africa, Asia, and the Americas. This historical collusion between fundamentalism and colonialism reveals the fine line between mutually edifying intercultural interaction and a patronizing "white man's burden" to civilize and "Christianize" the world.

Given my apprehension about fundamentalism, my emphasis on 2 Corinthians 3:12–18 could seem strange. This passage appears to support a kind of fundamentalism, where Paul seeks to flatten the mystery of his ancestral religion, Judaism, in the name of making everyone a "Christian." In some sense, Paul does to Judaism what later Christian missionaries did to African Traditional Religions: deny their enduring validity. Thus, at the very point where Paul assists us in lifting the veil of colonialism, he seemingly lowers the veil of fundamentalism further upon our minds.

However, 2 Corinthians 3:16–17 might provide a way forward. Verse 16 makes Jesus Christ central to the removal of the veil. But if the veil is raised only through Jesus Christ, then this passage becomes an instrument of fundamentalism, where only followers of Jesus have proper perception. To avoid the dangers of fundamentalism, did Paul unwittingly appeal to the language of the Spirit in verse 17? "Now the Lord is the Spirit, and where the Spirit of the Lord is, there is freedom." Just when it appears that this text has clearly marked the boundaries of religious insiders and outsiders, this text moves into the boundary-transcending territory of the Spirit.

Jesus said that the Spirit blows where it wills (John 3:8). By invoking God's Spirit in 2 Corinthians 3:17, Paul suggests that the Spirit's ultimate concern is not partisanship on the basis of religious group identity. Rather, the Spirit's ultimate concern is the last word in the Greek text and English translation of 2 Corinthians 3:17: *eleutheria*, or "freedom." Where the Spirit is there is *freedom*, and where *freedom* is, there is the Spirit.

Thus, attempts to restrict sacred truth to any one religious worldview create inhospitable conditions for the Sacred Spirit who wants to inspire freedom and flourishing for the creation and all its inhabitants. Undoubtedly, for Paul, the phrase "Spirit of the Lord" possessed overt christological meaning. For him, the Lord is Christ. Yet the Greek translation of the Hebrew Scriptures (i.e., the Septuagint) reveals that the term "Lord" (*kyrios*) is sufficiently flexible to include both a broader reference to God and a more specific reference to Jesus Christ.

As a Christian, I am deeply invested in the story and significance of Jesus. Nevertheless, I do not want to be limited by that christological story. Said differently, as a Christian, I believe that in the messages and methods of Jesus, I have all the sacred truth I often can handle, but I do not have all the sacred truth there is. Others also have sacred truth, for example, those who practice African Traditional Religions or seek right relationships with God through the Torah or the Qur'an. By linking with and learning from them, we all are enriched.

In one of my seminars in Ghana, an African Anglican clergy welcomed my attempt to loosen the Spirit in 2 Corinthians 3:17 from a dogmatic Christocentrism. He rightly sensed that my interpretation represented an embrace of religious pluralism. During our dialogue, he insisted that my interpretation was the kind of theological resource he had long desired.

He is a Christian. His wife is a Muslim. In addition to their devotion to their respective religious traditions of Christianity and Islam, they are also seeking God through various approaches in African Traditional Religions. He has grown weary of neocolonial, dogmatic Christianity that disparages the religious validity of other approaches to the sacred. Instead, he and his family are seeking approaches to religion that honor the particularities of various religious traditions while acknowledging the complexity and ambiguity of the desire to grasp, or to be grasped by, the sacred.

Continuing the Conversation

The time has come to lift the veil—the veil of colonialism and fundamentalism. In my preparation for and presentation of the Bray Lectures, and in the reflection on those events in this chapter, I have marshaled cultural and biblical resources that hopefully will facilitate honest conversations about reparations for transatlantic slavery. Such conversations can further foster the conditions for genuine racial reconciliation.

In retrospect, the lectures in Ghana and England appear to have been well received. My postcolonial approach in these lectures and subsequent reflections remained intensely aware of the hermeneutical implications of transatlantic slavery, and the lectures sparked lively international conversations about the complex dimensions of racial reconciliation in the twenty-first century.[37] Admittedly, my reading of 2 Corinthians 3:12–18 can be refined, but I am energized about the possibility of engaging Pauline texts for their assistance in the demanding work of contemporary racial reconciliation.

My current exploration has revealed several areas for further investigation, which I present as questions:

1. Given the interest in reconciliation in Paul's letters (e.g., Rom 5:10–11; 2 Cor 5:18–19; Eph 2:16; and Col 1:20–22),

how should transatlantic slavery influence contemporary exegetical and theological reflection about restorative justice (e.g., reparations), healing, forgiveness, and
reconciliation?

2. How can postcolonial readings of the interethnic dialogue in Paul's letters foster more probing conversations
about the construction of ethnic identity in diverse
twenty-first-century contexts?

3. To what degree are the similarities and differences in the
understanding of ethnic and racial identity among African, European, and North American audiences related
to the experiences of slavery and colonialism, and how
do these similarities and differences impact exegesis?

4. Given Paul's interest in epistemology and divine revelation, how can postcolonial readings of such themes
address and correct the false perceptions perpetuated by
white racism and other forms of xenophobia?

I hope that my exegetical efforts in the Bray Lectures and in
this chapter have served the "truth." According to the biblical
scholar Elisabeth Schüssler Fiorenza, "Truth is not . . . a process
of discovering the hidden or forcing into the open a divine that
is buried. Rather, truth is a historical process of public deliberation for the creation of radical democratic equality for every
wo/man in the global village. . . . A conception of 'truth' in this
sense comes close to the biblical notion of 'doing the truth,' a
truth that 'will set you free.'"[38]

Many colonial readings of Paul's letters facilitated the enslavement of millions of Africans. I believe that emerging postcolonial
readings of those same letters can assist the heirs of the enslaved
and of the enslavers in their quest for reconciliation. Let it be so
in the name of the Spirit that brings *eleutheria*—freedom!

3

An Experiment in Radical Religious Openness

How do we achieve progressive change? By celebrating our divine discontent with the way things are. . . . To be divinely discontent is to want our democratic ideals and egalitarian hopes to be realized in the world around us. It is to challenge conformity, to push the boundaries of "the ways things are" to the "way things should be."

—MANNING MARABLE, "BLACK LEADERSHIP, FAITH, AND THE STRUGGLE FOR FREEDOM"

Opening The Open Church

On October 8, 2011, fifty-five people gathered in a Baltimore library to initiate an experiment in radical religious openness.* A library, a repository of ancient wisdom and emerging knowledge, seemed a perfect place to ask a poignant question: Is it possible for a community to love and serve God apart from the cultural discord and theological dogma that can make religion so dangerous? For three hours on that auspicious morning, we sang and prayed. We laughed and embraced. We discussed Scripture and dreamed a big dream about a bold, new congregation whose chief characteristic would be *openness*—openness to radically inclusive love, courageous social justice activism, and

---

* This chapter was originally published in *Intercultural Ministry: Hope for a Changing World*, edited by Grace Ji-Sun Kim and Jann Aldredge-Clanton (Valley Forge, PA: Judson, 2017), 81–96. Copyright © 2017 by Judson. Reprinted with permission of Judson.

compassionate interfaith collaboration. At the meeting's conclusion, The Open Church of Maryland had begun.[1]

Eleven years later, The Open Church is a viable faith community of approximately one hundred active members who have raised nearly two million dollars to support the congregation's ministries. With purpose and passion, The Open Church is pushing cultural boundaries and challenging theological assumptions. For example, The Open Church (1) considers the weekly worship service as a "political assembly" for creating citizens who are preparing to live in God's inbreaking kin-dom[2]; (2) supports the moral and civic equality of LGBTQ persons; (3) sensitizes congregants about social injustices such as classism; and (4) embraces interfaith collaboration as an antidote to Christian arrogance and imperialism.

At a typical gathering of The Open Church, a millennial, white lesbian agnostic with a master's degree might sit next to a blue-collar heterosexual black nationalist in his sixties as they collaborate to bring healing and hope to Baltimore's blighted communities. The Open Church is increasingly becoming a resource in local and national initiatives concerning diversity, equity, and inclusion. For example, The Open Church's advocacy for marriage equality received national attention through a PBS television interview.[3] Additionally, a feature article on The Open Church appeared in a popular magazine highlighting innovative agents of social change.[4]

On the one hand, our progress in building an intercultural church has been remarkable. On the other hand, as the founding senior pastor, I realize how precarious the experiment still is. Some congregants remain reticent about the joyful embrace of radical inclusion and the discarding of problematic religious perspectives. For example, although there is a healthy balance between heterosexual and LGBTQ persons in the congregation, some heterosexual and LGBTQ congregants worried that The Open Church was (or would become) the "gay church." Additionally, the emphasis on Jesus's humanity and questioning Jesus's divinity, dismissal of narrow definitions of biblical authority, and use of gender-inclusive language (especially when referencing

God) initially sparked discomfort and respectful resistance in some persons.

Furthermore, attracting newcomers is a constant challenge. Many persons for whom The Open Church has been designed are understandably skeptical of religion or were badly hurt in previous encounters with congregations. When religion behaves, it is beautiful and empowering. When religion misbehaves, it is vile and vicious.[5] Unfortunately, certain Christian communities have misrepresented God's inclusive intentions, thereby making it difficult to attract people who are willing to take another chance on "organized religion."

Additionally, some persons who say they desire an intercultural experience renege when they understand how many dimensions of culture and diversity The Open Church is audaciously exploring. At The Open Church (and for the purposes of this chapter), culture is understood in an expansive way that includes and extends considerably beyond race/ethnicity.

The theologian Sheila Davaney defines culture as "the process by which meaning is produced, contended for, and continually renegotiated and the context in which individual and communal identities are mediated and brought into being."[6] The Open Church is predominantly black, with a growing presence of people from other racial/ethnic groups. Nevertheless, The Open Church is intercultural because of the conscious embrace of diverse cultural factors that mediate meaning and delineate identities such as religious beliefs, gender and sexual identities, and class status.

The aforementioned challenges must be addressed in order for the experiment to succeed and reach scale. Scalability is crucial. There needs to be a critical mass of vibrant, healthy congregations practicing "good religion" that liberates people in order to counteract the profusion of unhealthy congregations promulgating "bad religion" that asphyxiates people.

This chapter will explore the historical background, theological commitments, and religious practices that have bolstered The Open Church's development, guided by our vision statement recited regularly in worship.

The Open Church Vision Statement

All: The Open Church is a sacred place where those who are hurting, confused, and in need can find healing and hope, regardless of color, culture, or creed.

Leader: It is a wide place where "Abraham's family"—Christians, Jews, and Muslims—can dialogue with Buddhists and Bahá'is and where Hindus can dialogue with Humanists.

All: The Open Church is a joyful place where children, seniors, migrant workers, people experiencing homelessness, and scholars eagerly learn from and teach one another.

Leader: It is a safe place where varied ethnicities and capabilities, genders and sexual identities, social and economic groups gather in peace to break bread at Christ's communion table as we break down stereotypes.

All: As sacred siblings born to our Heavenly Father who is Divine Mother of us all, we practice radically inclusive love that proclaims and builds up the "_kin_-dom of God."

(Auto)Biography Is Theology

During the last fifty years, contextual theologies (e.g., black theology, women's theologies [feminist/womanist/_mujerista_], postmodern theology, postcolonial theology, and queer theology) have insisted that responsible theological discourse must be grounded in our personal stories and cultural histories.

Our personal stories and cultural histories are not obstacles to be overcome in the pursuit of "universal objectivity." On the contrary, these experiences are doorways to a critically informed and culturally nuanced subjectivity. My context is not a perfunctory "pretext" to be heedlessly discarded. My context is a priceless "text" to be thoroughly excavated for its insights and impact. The stories of who we are influence the stories of who we understand God to be. (Auto)Biography is theology.

As the founding senior pastor, my story, which includes my implicit and explicit theologies, has greatly influenced the congregation's development. An organizational development consultant reminded me of the crucial role that beginnings play in a congregation's genetic evolution. When analyzing organizations that are decades or even centuries old, this consultant continually returns to the founding narratives of organizations for key insights, because much of the organizational DNA is determined in the beginning.

In order to understand The Open Church, we must pay attention to important elements of its beginnings. Furthermore, in order to understand its beginnings, we must pay attention to important elements of my personal and professional pilgrimage. Thus, I highlight certain autobiographical details that galvanized my decision to establish The Open Church and that continue to impact my leadership as its founding senior pastor.

The Two Churches That Led to the Third

The Open Church is the third congregation that I have shepherded. The Open Church would not exist were it not for important experiences in my previous two churches: Douglas Memorial Community Church and The Riverside Church.

Douglas Memorial Community Church (1995–2000)

My first pastorate was from 1995 to 2000 at the Douglas Memorial Community Church, a medium-sized, nondenominational church in downtown Baltimore founded in the early twentieth century. Douglas Church called me at the age of twenty-six to succeed its legendary retiring pastor and civil rights veteran Marion Bascom, who was seventy and had served Douglas Church for forty-six years. Bascom had a razor-sharp mind, and the pulpit that he bequeathed to me was free from any bondage to theological provincialism.

In my first pastorate, I inherited an ecclesial "broad meadow" of tough-minded, tender-hearted believers who were ready to embrace change and embrace me as their new spiritual leader. In that "broad meadow," many beautiful things blossomed across five years. For example, two hundred people joined the congregation. An intellectually robust Wednesday Bible study was created with regular attendance in excess of one hundred persons. Exciting interfaith initiatives with Baltimore's Jewish community occurred.

Having completed my PhD at Emory University in 1999, I was called in 2000 to the "broad meadow" of university teaching. Wake Forest University in Winston-Salem, North Carolina, had established a new divinity school with a progressive theological orientation. The school's founding dean, Bill Leonard, invited me to serve as the first preaching professor.

Through a sacred partnership between people and pastor, Douglas Church had been revitalized.[7] I came to Douglas Church as a scholar. I left as a scholar and a pastor. It was now time for me to mentor other scholars and pastors, and that is what I attempted to do from 2000 to 2008.

I was privileged to serve on two distinguished divinity school faculties—four years as an assistant professor at Wake Forest University and four years as an associate professor at Vanderbilt University. In those eight years, I served with outstanding deans, faculty, and staff; taught preaching and biblical studies to brilliant students; published three books; made three pilgrimages to Africa; and clarified the intellectual and spiritual dimensions of my progressive, intercultural agenda.

I thoroughly enjoyed my professorial ministry. Yet I knew that at some point, the professor had to return to the pastorate. The call to what I thought would be my second and final pastorate came in the fall of 2008. I was leaving the university to return to the church, without realizing that in this next church, I would matriculate in the advanced curriculum in the school of hard knocks.

The Riverside Church (2008–9)

I was called in 2008 to be the sixth senior minister of The Riverside Church in New York City. The Riverside Church, founded in 1930 by a sizable bequest from John D. Rockefeller Jr., is a large, historic, intercultural institution. At the age of thirty-nine, I was the youngest senior minister ever called by the congregation and the second African American. In spite of the challenges that besieged my brief tenure at Riverside, I count it a privilege to have served that remarkable congregation.

After several months of serving as senior minister, long-standing tensions within the congregation severely hindered forward progress in executing the church's stated intercultural mission and vision. Undoubtedly, I made tactical leadership errors. For example, I could have introduced modest programmatic changes more deftly. Nevertheless, the acrimonious assaults on my professional pedigree and leadership, orchestrated by a small and organized cadre of congregants, revealed that I was a lightning rod for internal congregational storms that had raged for decades. The attacks began a month before my formal confirmation as senior minister and lasted the duration of my nine-month tenure.

Thus, rather than force the issue and create additional strife, I voluntarily resigned from the pastorate of The Riverside Church in the hope that all parties would benefit from new beginnings. The shock and sadness among many congregants resulting from my rapid resignation revealed a growing affection between many congregants and me. Many congregants quietly hoped that we could have outlasted this bitter squall.

Thirteen years have passed since my departure from Riverside. For eight of those thirteen years, Riverside has been without a permanent senior minister, an intriguing detail perhaps indicating unresolved congregational issues. Amy Butler, my pastoral successor, was the first woman to serve as Riverside's senior minister. She made generous gestures to foster healing and reconciliation between the congregation and me, including my participation in her pastoral installation in 2014 and Riverside's eighty-fifth anniversary in 2015.[8] In the intervening years since my departure, hindsight has taken on its twenty-twenty character. I have increasing clarity concerning how the experience at Riverside prepared me for The Open Church.

During my Riverside pastorate, the key source of contention was "power." I came to Riverside as a tenured professor with a PhD in biblical studies. However, I quickly realized that for a vocal and influential faction in that church, the most sacred text was not the Bible but instead the congregation's bylaws.

During my yearlong candidacy for Riverside's pastorate, I read accounts of Riverside's history and interviewed many people familiar with the congregation.[9] As part of my due diligence, I searched for clues to Riverside's institutional DNA. In addition to Riverside's splendid external reputation, my investigation into Riverside's DNA also revealed a more disturbing internal narrative of congregational divisiveness, unclear boundaries between clergy and lay leaders, and an ineffectual governance structure that hamstrung the senior minister.

These issues of power became acutely pronounced during the tenure of the third senior minister, Ernest Campbell. Governance matters more than thirty years prior to my being called to Riverside prompted Campbell to resign from Riverside in 1976.[10] The change in pastoral leadership necessitated by Campbell's resignation did not change these divisive internal dynamics. Governance issues also beset the pastorate of the fourth senior minister, William Sloane Coffin.[11]

If Ernest Campbell and William Sloane Coffin—who were white pastors—struggled with these governance issues when the church remained predominantly white, one can imagine how these governance issues intensified during James Forbes's tenure and my tenure—a time when Riverside was led by its first two black pastors. During Forbes's pastorate, the racial dynamics shifted significantly, and Riverside became a predominantly black congregation. The shock waves of that seismic demographic shift reverberated throughout Forbes's pastorate and my brief Riverside tenure. These demographic issues during Forbes's pastorate and mine complicated already complex and contested governance matters by unearthing the "white anxiety" that often occurs when intercultural ministry decenters white people and white cultural priorities.

Intercultural Lessons Learned at The Riverside Church

The Power in Understanding Power: This abbreviated retelling of portions of my Riverside experience is germane to the founding of The Open Church in crucial ways. First, my Riverside pastorate compelled me to think more explicitly and theologically about issues of power when building an intercultural community.

Congregational leaders often deem issues of power as unsavory at best or evil at worst. "Spiritual people" supposedly should not be preoccupied with a seemingly manipulative topic like "power." Defining power by its worst manifestations, many congregations operate with problematic understandings of power and avoid theological analyses of power. This avoidance can result in power imbalances, where unhealthy amounts of power are concentrated in the hands of an individual or a small group.

Furthermore, until issues of power are addressed, congregations interested in intercultural ministry often confuse "representation" for "diversity." The influx of a minority community into a majority community does not necessarily equate to diversity. That influx might simply mean that there is greater intercultural representation in that community. Diversity genuinely surfaces when minority groups are represented in sufficient numbers to organize and thus challenge and change power structures in a community.

Even though Riverside's racial demographics had shifted, its overall cultural ethos and approach to religious practices remained firmly anchored in white cultural narratives and priorities. Racial justice educators and activists have long noted that covert, institutional racism—not overt, individual racism—is the more difficult form of racial injustice to overcome. Joseph Barndt insists, "The distinctive mark of racism is power—collective, systemic, societal power. Not simply the power of one individual over another, but shared power expressed through political, economic, educational, cultural, religious, and other societal systems and institutions. . . . Buried within the systems and institutions of our society are the mechanisms for racism's power."[12]

Barndt's framework explains why even my small attempts at Riverside to question or decenter the assumed "superiority" of white perspectives and approaches aroused serious opposition, and the leaders of the opposition on some occasions were black people. Internalized oppression is often subtle and runs very deep. Frequently, members of a minority group will extensively adopt the cultural perspectives and practices of the dominant majority group in an effort to "fit" within the cultural climate and legitimize themselves before the majority group. This explains why some women, ironically, are fierce opponents of feminist liberation efforts and why some people of color vigorously oppose efforts to dethrone white privilege.[13]

For an intercultural agenda to thrive in a congregation, leaders and congregants must consider power an appropriate topic for theologically nuanced discussion. Leaders must attend to issues of power with the same care that they attend to liturgical practices such as preaching and praying. I now tell persons aspiring to be pastors, especially in intercultural contexts, to "spend as much time with the bylaws as you do with the Bible. Both the 'devil' who can harm you and the 'angel' who can heal you are in the details about how power is understood and applied in a community."

A Nimble Governance Structure: My experience at Riverside also influenced my desire to create an intercultural congregation with a nimble governance structure. In the years between leaving Riverside and founding The Open Church, I mused frequently on this question: How can a congregation have governance structures that are responsible for fiduciary matters yet open to the sometimes-transgressive leadership of the Holy Spirit?

As Jesus says to Nicodemus in John 3:8, the wind of the Spirit blows wherever it wills. The unruly Spirit often disrespects the decorum and deliberations of the parliamentary procedures prescribed by *Robert's Rules of Order*. Governance structures can become so burdensome that they prevent a congregation from discerning the unexpected thing that God wants to do. Envisioning The Open Church and its governance structures, I repeatedly called to mind poignant observations from the theologian Justo González: "The function of the Spirit is not so much to create the structures and procedures by which the church must live forever, but rather to break *open* structures so that the church may be obedient as it faces each new challenge."[14]

When faced with the opportunity of embracing genuine intercultural ministry, many faith communities across the millennia have said a defiant "No!" to these opportunities. Their negations often have been inscribed institutionally in restrictive governance structures that frustrate the boundary-breaking movement of the Spirit.

My experience at Riverside was both humbling and hurtful. It was for my family and me (and for many people at Riverside) a tragedy. Yet from tragedy, one can extract truths that lead to future triumphs. I departed that painful episode eager to envision a new intercultural faith community characterized by permissive power structures that enabled the default answer of a congregation to be "Yes!"

The Open Church: Pursuing *Openness on Purpose*

After my departure from Riverside, I relocated with my family to Chicago, where I took a yearlong professional sabbatical. After the sabbatical, I served for two years as a distinguished visiting scholar at McCormick Theological Seminary, a vibrant and hospitable theological institution on Chicago's South Side. McCormick's administrators, faculty, staff, and students were invaluable dialogue partners as The Open Church's vision was conceived and born.

I wanted to form an intercultural community held together by three core theological commitments: (1) progressive ministry, (2) prophetic ministry, and (3) pluralistic ministry.

1. **Progressive Ministry:** Progressive ministry believes that sacred texts and authoritative traditions must be

critically engaged and continually reinterpreted in light of contemporary circumstances, or religion becomes a relic.

2. **Prophetic Ministry:** Prophetic ministry insists that God desires to save us not only from our personal sins but also from the systemic sins that oppress neighborhoods and nations.

3. **Pluralistic Ministry:** Pluralistic ministry is a liberating call to "uncertainty, to a sense of human and religious limitedness. It is an affirmation that what we think we know certainly and absolutely is, in fact, neither certain nor absolute."[15] Truth held in a *vise grip* often leads to the *vice* of arrogance. On the contrary, by *opening* our hands and hearts, we make it possible to grasp, and be grasped by, larger truths.

Like sturdy beams supporting a floor, these three core commitments undergirded every aspect of The Open Church's founding meeting in October 2011. Thus, in the very foundation of the congregation is an explicit commitment to radical openness.

In the founding meeting, and subsequent meetings across these eleven years, we envisioned, and have endeavored to be, *The Open Church*, not just *The Open Door* Church. Many churches have referred to themselves as "open door" churches. I do not disparage congregations with open doors. However, The Open Church has loftier ambitions in its pursuit of openness. In some churches, the doors may be open, but the windows are nailed shut through denominational dogma, burdensome bureaucracy, and an obsession with outdated orthodoxies (to name a few nails). Consequently, the free-flowing "Wind (of the Spirit)" cannot circulate properly, and the air becomes stagnant.

We purposed to create a church whose entire existence—and not just its "doors"—was open. We envisioned the following: A church open to any persons and perspectives that are truthful, just, and compassionate. A church open to theistic and nontheistic religions and to Humanist and atheistic moral philosophies. A church open to sexual diversity so that LGBTQ persons could emerge from the closets they often inhabit in religious spaces for fear of "assault and battery" by the Bible. A church open to the courageous reimagining and embracing of the feminine dimensions of God as an act of resistance to sexism. A church open to class diversity that would enable white-collar salary workers and blue-collar shift workers to learn with and from one another.

Although openness is an obvious commitment at The Open Church, an equally central commitment buttressing our intercultural work is *purpose*. Purpose must be the partner to openness. In a world where so many people are closed off from opportunities, from sources of abundance, and even from one other, intercultural communities will not occur by accident. Benjamin Mays, the sage who mentored Martin Luther King Jr., understood well the irreverent insistence needed to ignite personal and social transformation across cultural boundaries. Mays remarked, "I would rather go to hell by choice than to stumble into heaven following the crowd."[16]

Too many faith communities are stumbling in their efforts to promote diversity and social justice because they are comfortably following the crowd. They are afraid to engage in audacious, purposeful actions to create the conditions for diversity and social justice to thrive. Apparently, in many churches, 2 Timothy 1:7 has been removed from their Bibles: "For God did not give us a *spirit of cowardice*, but rather a spirit of power and of love, and of self-discipline." I frequently offer in my sermons and pastoral exhortations at The Open Church my contemporary remix of Mays's insight on purpose: "If radical inclusion sends me to hell, then I am going to hell *on purpose*, and I will take the express train there! God, if your heaven is exclusive, then it is a place I would rather not be because *all* my sacred siblings are not welcome there."

This brazen statement encapsulates the ultimate sacredness of openness for me. In my theology, an inclusive hell is more sacred than an exclusive heaven. Shortly after I composed the congregational vision statement, the Spirit also placed a simple purpose pledge in my spirit. We conclude every worship service at The

Open Church and many other congregational gatherings by reciting this simple, heartfelt pledge:

> *We live on purpose!*
> *We love on purpose!*
> *We lift on purpose!*

I briefly chronicle below examples of how The Open Church is pursuing radical religious openness *on purpose*.

Wrestling with Biblical Authority *on Purpose*

At The Open Church, we question the Bible and acknowledge its moral ambiguities. We often say, "Not everything in the 'Good Book' is good news." We intentionally renounce the regrettable role that the Bible has played in legitimizing vilification and violence, especially as it relates to historically marginalized groups such as women and LGBTQ people.

We are constructing notions of biblical authority that invite people to engage the Bible with intellectual honesty as well as reverence. In an early sermon at The Open Church, I placed biblical authority front and center in the congregation's ministry of inclusion:

> In my estimation, biblical authority is about engagement with the Book, not necessarily agreement with the Book. . . . Because I know what I believe and in whom I believe, I can listen to you talk about what you believe and in whom you believe. Biblical authority simply means, "Let's engage!"
>
> So as we ponder the meanings of biblical authority, I will not coerce you to agree with me. Rather I offer my perspectives as a catalyst for you to voice your perspectives, with the hope that from multiple perspectives, we might assemble some fragments of truth.[17]

This sermonic reframing of biblical authority assisted some congregants in their emancipation from a stifling submission to biblical dogma.

Creating a Culture of Inquiry *on Purpose*

The Open Church also fosters an atmosphere where we lovingly question one another. Creating a culture of healthy, respectful inquiry is a critical component of the intercultural experience. We conceive of The Open Church as a "republic"—a sacred "political assembly" where we are learning to share power for the sake of a better world. A key congregational mantra is "At The Open Church, *everyone* is a minister." Accordingly, everyone's voice is crucial as we discern collaboratively what the good news is and how the good news compels us to act.

We amplify the voices of everyone by frequently holding dialogue-driven services dealing with major theological and social issues, such as the humanity/divinity of Jesus, the interplay of sexuality and spirituality, immigration, homelessness, and violence. We regularly place in the bulletin discussion questions based on the worship service and sermon for that day, and the question-and-answer period occurs immediately after the sermon. On some occasions, discussion questions and the dialogue around them constitute the entire worship service.

At The Open Church, the invitation to dialogue is as important as the invitation to discipleship. Kathleen Neal Cleaver, the freedom fighter and legal scholar, said, "No one can speak truth to power until they know what is true."[18] In order to know what is true, we must listen to, reason with, and question one another.

When we shifted our Sunday worship and fellowship gathering to an online format in 2020 due to the Covid-19 pandemic, we enhanced our culture of inquiry by formally implementing a "Sundays with Sacred Siblings" series. Now, on the fourth Sundays of most months, we invite to our pulpit via videoconference persons from diverse religious, spiritual, and ethical traditions as the major Sunday speaker. Our invitation to them is simple: inspire, instruct, and challenge us about the meaning of values-centered living from the depths of your respective traditions.

In recent months, we have had religious and civic leaders, scholars, activists, and artists from diverse traditions, including but not limited to African diasporic, Buddhist, Humanist,

Jewish, Muslim, and religiously unaffiliated communities. After our "Sacred Sibling" partners offer their message/presentation on these Sundays, we engage them in a time of facilitated dialogue, questions, and answers. Members of The Open Church and our "Sacred Sibling" partners have commented on how valuable it is to have a safe and open forum where we can engage our differences and similarities in a spirit of curiosity and courage.

Dethroning Sexist Language *on Purpose*

Language possesses both life-giving and death-dealing power. Thus, what we say and how we say it are matters of great moral consequence. At The Open Church, we embrace gender-inclusive language as a moral act that creates an inclusive environment. Early in the development of our congregation, I wrote the following statement and placed it in the bulletin:

> As Christians, we are a people of the word. According to Genesis 1, God created in the beginning with the spoken word. We gather in worship to listen to and wrestle with the words of scripture in the hope that those words will lead us to the living word of God's truth for us here and now.
>
> The lyrics of many of our sacred songs were composed at a time when God was thought to be "male." Unfortunately, the exclusive imaging of God as male has contributed to the horrific injustice of sexism, the assumed superiority of males. This injustice affects us all, but it especially injures women and girls.
>
> Yet we know that God is neither male nor female. God is a living Spirit. So at The Open Church, we value inclusive language as a reminder that none of our terms for God can accurately capture God's majestic presence and infinite essence. There is nothing wrong with calling God "Father," but in fairness we should not mind calling God "Mother" either. God is a good God. Yes, *She* is! Furthermore, when we have the opportunity to avoid pronouns, we should not mind simply referring to God as God.

Eboo Patel, a friend and noted interfaith educator, intimates that our language practices and stories can either build bombs to destroy or bridges to unite.[19]

Opening the Communion Table *on Purpose*

At The Open Church, the table where we share holy communion is radically open. In some Christian traditions, there are strict preconditions for who can serve and partake of this simple meal of bread and wine (or juice) that symbolizes the price that Jesus paid to justly resist injustice. For example, in some Christian denominations, only ordained clergy and lay leaders are authorized to consecrate and serve the meal. Additionally, only baptized believers can partake of the communion elements in some denominations, and children who have not yet "officially" become members of the church are prevented from sharing the meal.

At The Open Church, anyone can serve holy communion, and everyone who desires the meal is welcome at the table. In a world full of hungry and thirsty people, it is unconscionable to me to serve a meal, even a symbolic one, and not attempt to invite as many willing people to the table as possible.

Furthermore, in light of Jesus's deep affection for children as witnessed in the New Testament (e.g., Matt 19:13–15), placing children's hands on holy communion makes the meal even holier. Thus, at The Open Church, we especially delight in inviting children to serve the meal. I typically use some variation of the statement below to invite the community to the table: "At this table, no reservations are needed, and no priority seating is allowed. At The Open Church, God's welcome table is *open*, *radically open*, to whosoever will. You don't even have to believe in God to come to this table, because even if you don't believe in God, God still believes in you. Come!" The response to our radically open table has been overwhelmingly positive, even if some congregants come to the table questioning why they previously belonged to faith communities that placed "fences" around a table designed to foster *communion*.

The fourth stanza of The Open Church's congregational vision statement invites people "to break bread at Christ's communion table, as we break down stereotypes." Through dialogue, the congregation is considering an adaptation of that line. We may change the language from "Christ's communion table" to "God's welcome table." This change would cohere with the congregation's commitment to interfaith collaboration and our attempts to decenter problematic versions of atonement theology that focus on Jesus's death as a "cleansing of our sins."

Womanist theology emphasizes that our "salvation" is not found in Jesus's death but rather in the liberating message and methods of his life. Fostering a sense of radical welcome was an integral aspect of Jesus's message and methods. Thus, referring to the congregation's fellowship table as "God's welcome table" represents the good news that God sent Jesus to proclaim—namely, that at God's table, everyone is welcome!

Next Steps: Playing a Love Supreme *on Purpose*

I am thankful for how far The Open Church has come and mindful of the long journey ahead. As the congregation's chief visionary leader, my primary responsibility is "romantic" in nature. Pushing the boundaries toward radical religious openness will involve wooing people to open their hearts even more to a love supreme. The Open Church's vision is bold, global, and even cosmic. We believe that radically inclusive love is the heartbeat of God and the ultimate impulse in an infinite and expanding universe. Through the ages, apostles and prophets have tried to seduce us with this love.

In 1965, the acoustical apostle John Coltrane released his monumental album titled *A Love Supreme*. With his saxophone, Coltrane preached a sermon. A love supreme—a soaring, unconditional love not detained by dogma nor constrained by color or creed—is the missing note in the jam session for restorative justice and intercultural inclusion. The Open Church is a tool through which God can push boundaries. The Open Church is an instrument on which God can play *A Love Supreme . . . on purpose!*

4

Aiding and Abetting New Life

"Sex Talk" in the Pulpit, Pew, and Public Square

Christianity is about forming a people who take seriously resurrection in their everyday lives and move their bodies and lives into places where their embodied power can make a difference. . . . Whenever the power of death cannot silence the power of life, I believe we are standing in the presence of resurrection.

—CHRISTINE MARIE SMITH, "A LESBIAN PERSPECTIVE:
MOVING TOWARD A PROMISED PLACE"

A Practical Approach to "Sex Talk"

Black churches have been incubators of life in deadly circumstances.* However, concerning sexuality, many black churches create hostile environments, especially for lesbian, gay, bisexual, transgender, and queer (LGBTQ) persons. Congregational leaders, scholars, and activists must encourage these congregations to stop unholy "character assassinations" and to aid and abet new life among sexually diverse people.

---

* This chapter was originally published in *The Sexual Politics of Black Churches*, edited by Josef Sorett (New York: Columbia University Press, 2022), 173–89. Copyright © 2022 Columbia University Press. Reprinted with permission of Columbia University Press.

While increased theoretical sophistication in discussions of sexuality is beneficial, *practical* implementation is necessary to achieve two objectives in black congregations and the larger society: (1) healthier conversations about sexuality and (2) greater affirmation for LGBTQ persons. Thus, *practical theology* provides the methodological framework for this chapter. The word "practical" is often misconstrued to mean "simplistic" or "uncritical." Practical theology seeks to correct this misunderstanding.

Practical theology is concerned with the profound cultural knowledge and moral wisdom contained in and conveyed by practices. The theologian Dorothy Bass remarks, "Focusing on practices invites theological reflection on the ordinary, concrete activities of actual people. . . . Focusing on practices demands attentiveness to specific people, doing specific things together within a specific frame of shared meaning."[1]

Grounding its theories in everyday life, practical theology considers our experiences of love and lovemaking as vital locales for learning about ourselves and God. As a *fleshly* approach attentive to the activities of our bodies, practical theology is well suited to foster progressive and welcoming environments for constructive "sex talk." To return to Bass's statement, this chapter will consider specific people (black Christians) doing specific things (religious practices such as pastoral care, preaching, and worship) within a specific frame of shared meaning (the beliefs that people are created in God's image and that God desires peace and abundant life for individuals and communities).

Practical theology also investigates the relationship between religious practices inside faith communities and other practices in the public square. The theologians Kathleen Cahalan and James Nieman insist, "Practical theology, though oriented toward discipleship and ministry in faithful communities, always looks outward to explore its mission in the world. . . . The field therefore seeks to connect with wider publics especially in order to focus on practices where there may be shared interest."[2] Thus, the chapter concludes by examining how faith communities can embody important values that foster healthy dialogue and moral discernment in the public square about significant contemporary issues.

An Inclusive Gospel

The kin-dom of God—God's beloved community where social differences no longer divide, and access to God's abundance is equal—was the primary theme of Jesus's ministry.[3] Jesus desired loving communities that would serve as a foretaste of the coming commonwealth of God. When Christians exclude people based on social identity, we defame the character of Jesus whose primary impulse was inclusion. The theologian and preacher Peter Gomes observes, "If Jesus Christ is the center of the biblical witness . . . how do we reconcile his expansive and inclusive behavior as recorded in scripture with what has so often been the constricted and exclusive practice of the church? . . . Jesus' generosity and hospitality got him into terrible trouble. . . . Nowhere in scripture do we find the mantra 'Love the sinner and hate the sin;' history has shown that it is the 'sinner' rather than the sin that is usually ostracized, criticized, and even crucified."[4]

Christians should model reconciling, inclusive love. Jesus describes the gospel this way: "The thief comes only to steal and kill and destroy. I came that they may have life, and have it abundantly" (John 10:10). Abundant life is the heart of the gospel. However, by promoting patriarchal perspectives on gender and puritanical perspectives on sexuality, some black congregations steal the peace, kill the joy, and destroy the hope of many women, LGBTQ persons, and people advocating for their empowerment. Congregations should aid and abet God's bestowal of life upon all who seek better ways to become better people for the sake of a better world.

Jesus encouraged his followers to go into the "streets and lanes of the town" with an inclusive invitation to God's party so that God's house would be filled (Luke 14:15–24). In the spirit of Jesus's teaching, congregations should be "holy house parties" where hospitality is abundant, and the sacredness of diverse forms of covenant love and sanctified sexuality are celebrated. As a heterosexual ally with LGBTQ persons, I raise this question: How do we take an inclusive gospel to the streets?

Pastoral Theology: Taking It to the Streets

My pastoral experiences reveal the importance of harmony between means and ends. If the goal is to sponsor *real* change in congregations, we must "keep it real" as it relates to our means. We must avoid the confusing language and irrelevant theorizing that frustrate genuine transformation in the grassroots and on concrete streets. The pastor and ethicist Samuel Proctor remarks, "Theology never comes alive in abstract debate. It is best understood when it is lived. A good pastor will take the time to show the people how life should be lived. . . . The pastor recognizes that life must be lived in very pedestrian ways and that people who are lacking in sophistication need teaching at the street level. Not everyone needs such help, but the pastor must always be ready to give it."[5] Reaching black congregations at the "street level" with progressive understandings of sexuality will require (1) relevant styles of communication (i.e., keeping it real) and (2) an emphasis on the importance of relationships (i.e., keeping it relational). A discussion of each point follows.

Keeping It Real

Many forms of black communication involve "body talk." The homiletician Teresa Fry Brown highlights the prevalence of black "sisterspeak," which is "informal, no-pretense, at-home, dangling-participles, double-negative, tell-it-like-it-is, intense-body-language speech."[6] Many black "brothers" also use these forms of communication. The stereotype of embodied black communication—head swerving, hand moving, body swaying—is anchored in some truth. The anthropologist and writer Zora Neale Hurston referred to these dramatic, fleshly (even sexualized) forms of communication as the "characteristics of Negro expression": "Every phase of Negro life is highly dramatized. . . . Everything is acted out. . . . Frequently the Negro, even with detached words in his vocabulary . . . must add action to it to make it do. . . . A Negro girl strolls past the corner lounger. Her whole body . . . posing. A slight shoulder movement that calls attention to her bust. . . . She is acting out 'I'm a darned sweet woman and you know it.' These little plays by strolling players are acted out daily in a dozen streets in a thousand cities, and no one ever mistakes the meaning."[7]

"Body talk" is a major strand of black cultural DNA. The contemporary theological task is to demonstrate how sexuality and the inclusion of LGBTQ persons in black congregations are also forms of "body talk." Bodies are on the line here: lesbian, gay, bisexual, transgender, queer, and heterosexual bodies—all constituting the body of Christ. If scholars retreat, in the name of academic respectability, into disembodied, abstract language typical of much elite, intellectual discourse, we might fail to connect with the very bodies in the pews and on the streets we want to heal and convert through a gospel of radical inclusion.

The homiletician Martha Simmons insists that if religious leaders are going to take an inclusive gospel to the streets, they must mix "James Brown" with "James Cone."[8] James Cone was the revered father of black liberation theology, whose writings sparked many liberation movements. Yet to fully activate an inclusive gospel of liberation, we also need the communication of James Brown, the godfather of soul, whose unshackled bodily movements conveyed freedom and truth at a level deeper than pure rationality. The transformation of sexual attitudes and values will require more than scholarly argumentation. Practical teaching methods that illustrate deep truths will also be necessary.

An example of "keeping it real" is instructive. I served for five years as the senior pastor of Douglas Memorial Community Church, a socially engaged black congregation in Baltimore, Maryland. Once during a sermon series on relationships, I preached a sermon titled "Sanctified Sexuality." The pastoral aims were to depict sexuality as our sacred desire for emotional and physical intimacy and promote approaches to sexual expression that glorified God and edified the community.

The sermon could have begun with a dry rehearsal of theories about sexuality, but a sermon about sexuality needed "sex appeal." So my wife, Lazetta, had a small cordless microphone attached to her dress as she sat in the congregation. The sermon began with the two of us reading passionately to each other erotic love poetry from the biblical book the Songs of Songs. While we were spatially distant from one another, our voices caressed and revealed to congregants that on other occasions, more than just our voices had caressed.

Eavesdropping on this erotic dialogue, one female parishioner started fanning herself with the worship bulletin. Perhaps she was having a "hot flash" recalling a "hot time" from yesteryear or maybe yesterday. Preaching openly about sex and sexuality will bring a range of emotions to the fore, and it will no doubt make some churchgoers (and readers) uncomfortable. Yet like good foreplay, this dramatic sermon introduction opened minds and lubricated hearts so that people could interact more intimately with their sexual existence in the context of church.

Keeping It Relational

"Street-level" teaching will also emphasize the development of godly relationships amid social diversity. To enlist an analogy, streets are sites of "intersections," and "intersections" imply plurality—the convergence of diverse people, experiences, and ideas. "Street-level" theology should facilitate people's ability to safely navigate cultural and theological intersections without committing vehicular homicide. When people recklessly converge at intersections, destruction and death result. However, when intersections are negotiated with care and work constructively, they facilitate travel and allow people going the wrong way to find new directions.

Enabling constructive encounters with diversity is a primary pastoral task of congregations. Pastoral care ultimately is the responsibility of an entire congregation and not a duty to be fulfilled exclusively by clergy.[9] Clergy facilitate the ministry of care through example and instruction. However, presenting God's multidimensional truth and multifaceted love requires a multiplicity of voices. Apart from diversity, the pursuit of truth becomes an idolatrous affair of a community worshipping its limited perspectives, and the practice of love becomes egotistical self-adoration. By welcoming diversity in the embodied presence of others—in this case, LGBTQ persons—congregations enhance their capacity to offer and exemplify truth and love.

The door leading to godly truth often swings on the hinges of social diversity. Even the Bible was the result of complex debates spanning thousands of years and involving many languages, diverse cultures, and a host of political decisions about which books to admit and omit. The plurality of voices in Scripture reveals a clear biblical message: sacred truth demands diverse perspectives. The pastoral theologian Emmanuel Lartey celebrates diversity's role in truth-making: "Truth, knowledge, and justice are not attained in solitary thought. . . . Truth involves . . . a basic act such as engaging in dialogue with the Other. . . . To practice truth is to welcome the Other."[10]

Similarly, the pastoral task of "making love" requires an affirmation of diversity. The phrase "making love" should not be reduced exclusively to erotic activity. Making love is the mission of the church. The apostle Paul's beautiful love hymn reminds the church of its lovemaking mandate: "If I speak in the tongues of mortals and of angels, but do not have love, I am a noisy gong or a clanging cymbal. . . . Love is patient; love is kind. . . . Love never ends" (1 Cor 13:1, 4, 8). This hymn entices believers to embrace the practice of genuine love—the compassionate concern for others that transcends sheer self-interest and removes the fear of people who differ from us.

Imagine how much more *care-full* Christian congregations would be if they caressed people with Paul's gracious words about love in 1 Corinthians 13 instead of battering them with his ungenerous words about gay and lesbian people in Romans 1. Furthermore, our neglect of another biblical "love note" has diminished our love life: "There is no fear in love, but perfect love casts out fear" (1 John 4:18). The cultural critic bell hooks observes, "Fear is the primary force upholding structures of domination. . . . When we are taught that safety lies always with sameness, then difference, of any kind, will appear as a threat. When we choose to love we choose to move against fear—against alienation and separation. The choice to love is a choice to connect—to find ourselves in the other."[11] Diversity is crucial for pursuing truth and making love. Consequently, there is no more pressing pastoral task than teaching people how to encounter diversity without the fear and fanaticism that terminate dialogue and destroy difference.

Studies indicate that personal experiences with loved ones or LGBTQ persons who are open about their sexual identity (i.e., "out" LGBTQ persons) significantly contribute to the development of "more inclusive perspectives regarding sexual differences."[12] This was true in my experience. While academic study facilitated my journey toward inclusive theology, the decisive moments involved friendships with "out" LGBTQ persons who challenged and expanded my theological and cultural boundaries. Warm relationships, not cold logic, transformed me.

For example, at the covenant ceremony of two lesbian friends in Atlanta in 1996, the presence of grace and holiness in that ceremony and later at their dinner table was undeniable.

Additionally, I facilitated in 2011 the founding of The Open Church of Maryland, a congregation in Baltimore committed to radically inclusive love, courageous social justice activism, and compassionate interfaith collaboration. A gay friend accepted my invitation to serve as the first chair of the congregation's board of directors. He fulfilled the role ably for more than a year and has served as the vice chair of the board for several years. Two lesbian friends also join him on the congregation's board. Thus, the six-person board is balanced between people who identify as LGBTQ and those who identify as heterosexual, respectively.

The outstanding leadership and winsome interpersonal skills of these LGBTQ congregational leaders have substantially enhanced the congregation's worship life, community engagement, and governance structure. Witnessing the powerful ministries of these colleagues and friends, I realize that "right heart orientation," not "straight sexual orientation," is God's prerequisite for service in the church, and their hearts are rightly oriented toward God.

At the intersection of relationships, I made a U-turn and set my face toward inclusion. Human transformation has mysterious dimensions that transcend theoretical analysis and rationality.

Stories go where statistics cannot. People can easily ignore "facts," but human faces are not as easily dismissed. Faces are doorways to people's hearts. The adoption of more inclusive approaches will entail more than a mind game. It will require heart transplants—not on operating tables but around fellowship tables, as friends of diverse gender identities and sexual orientations recognize the face of God in one another.

Face-to-face encounters create vulnerability and blur the boundaries of neat theological doctrines and tidy ecclesial politics. These encounters are risky and do not always lead to positive outcomes. A 2007 controversy revealed the challenge and complexity of genuinely "facing" inclusion.

The Broadway Baptist Church, a moderate, predominantly white congregation in Fort Worth, Texas, was known for its quiet acceptance of lesbian and gay members. However, things became "noisy" as the congregation prepared for its 125th anniversary in 2007. In celebration of the historic moment, church leaders wanted to create a pictorial directory of congregants with photographs of families. Controversy erupted when gay couples in the congregation wanted to have their pictures in the directory. While some members welcomed the pictures of gay couples, others felt that placing these photographs in the directory crossed the line of welcome to the unacceptable position of actually affirming gay persons as *gay persons*.[13]

Eventually, church leaders resolved the dispute by creating a directory with photographs of church groups but not families. The pictures of gay couples would have placed an explicit frame around diversity. Such photographs for some congregants would have been too much *to face*. How often have congregations, irrespective of ethnicity or denomination, ignored or deleted sacred pictures of family because the photographs displayed diversity in all its stunning beauty?

Nearly a decade after this incident, I, too, experienced an episode illustrating the difficulty some people have facing inclusion. An association of black ministers in Baltimore invited me in 2015 to facilitate a seminar at a local preaching conference. The president of the association is a longtime pastoral colleague.

Although he is more moderate than I theologically, he is respectful of my progressive views on LGBTQ equality.

Our similarities or differences on LGBTQ issues were not germane to his invitation. The conference aimed to provide professional development resources to improve the preaching skills of a group of Baltimore ministers, some of whom had not attended seminary. I readily accepted the invitation. News about my participation in the forthcoming conference circulated informally through the community.

A few weeks before the event, the president of the association asked for my headshot photograph to accompany my brief biography in the flyer announcing the event. I sent the photograph, and the flyer with my photograph was distributed to the wider membership of the association. Chaos erupted.

The informal circulation of my name had not ostensibly disturbed anyone. However, when the flyer associated my face with my name, apparently some ministers realized that the keynote presenter at the conference was going to be "that preacher—Brad Braxton—the one who started the Baltimore church with all the LGBTQ people."

Even though I am ordained in a Baptist denomination and have taught in seminaries for more than a decade, some of the Baptist ministers refused to attend a preaching conference where someone like me was a featured presenter. Their protest was swift and decisive.

Thus, a few days before the event, the president of the ministers' association called me and reluctantly rescinded the invitation. In 1949, the renowned theologian Howard Thurman wrote his influential book, *Jesus and the Disinherited*. I was honored in 2015 to join a distinguished group, *Jesus and the Disinvited*. If the promotion of radical inclusion in Jesus's name requires my name—and face—to be excluded from some "guest" lists, let it be so!

Many black people know the painful realities of racial politics where certain white people "welcome" black people as long as they reject or mute their cultural identity markers. In the face of this dehumanizing racism, James Brown declared these defiant lyrics, "Say it loud: I'm black and I'm proud!" The disruption of racism requires more than just black bodies. It requires *proud* black bodies.

Similarly, the disruption of dehumanizing heterosexism requires more than the quiet presence of LGBTQ bodies.[14] It, too, requires *proud* LGBTQ bodies. God's inclusive love calls LGBTQ persons to offer a creative remix: "Say it loud: I'm LGBTQ and I'm proud!" The courage and compassion needed for congregations to hear, face, and embrace this kind of diversity will surely make Jesus proud as well.

Preaching a Progressive Word: Sacred Use of the Sacred Desk

"Sticks and stones may break my bones, but words will never hurt me." This cute proverb cannot hide the ugly truth: words can hurt! Linguistic lacerations can inflict wounds on the psyche that linger beyond any physical fracture.

Thankfully, however, words can also heal. For example, gracious, thoughtful sermons are acts of "linguistic hospitality." Through the creative use of language, sermons provide God a hospitable place to meet with and transform listeners. As a professor of homiletics—the art of sermon creation, delivery, and evaluation—words are my world. Thus, my question is, How might black Christian preaching advance inclusive theologies of sexuality? A brief discussion of black preaching will facilitate answers to this question.

Preaching is a preeminent feature of black Christianity. The poetic name describing the black pulpit—*the sacred desk*—reveals the reverence that preaching commands. Black Christian preaching has provided some of the world's most powerful examples of rhetorical virtuosity.[15] Thus, it stands alongside other significant black contributions such as the spirituals, the blues, and jazz. I focus on two features of black preaching: (1) the preacher's authority and (2) the preacher's style.

Typically, black churches grant preachers a generous amount of authority. This authority consists of a communally derived sanction for preachers to speak on behalf of the congregation to the external "powers that be." Black congregations also expect their preachers to speak boldly to the congregation itself. Since spiritual authority comes through the congregation, humility in the preacher is appropriate. Yet most black congregations have no tolerance for timidity in the pulpit. The preacher must wed a silver tongue to nerves of steel, taking parishioners to theological depths and heights they would not experience otherwise.

Philosophically, the authority given to the black preacher reflects the primacy of the spoken word in many African rhetorical traditions. Certain African traditions emphasize *Nommo*. Nommo, a word from the African tribe Dogon, conveys "the generating and sustaining powers of the spoken word"—powers that permeate "every department of life."[16] Because of Nommo, "vocal expression reigns supreme" in most African cultures.[17]

Nommo requires the right persons and circumstances to convert its potential into power. In traditional African cultures, tribal chiefs and other religious leaders are catalytic agents. Since the preacher is the agent and embodiment of Nommo for many black Christians, Nommo is conveyed to the community through the preacher's presence and words. The authority of the preacher is a rhetorical umbilical cord connecting black ministers with Mother Africa.

Second, black Christians believe that style is a vital component of preaching.[18] Distinctive aspects of sermon delivery—gestures, tone of voice, rate of speech, picturesque language—are channels for Nommo and the gospel. Some preaching traditions regard the emphasis on style as an inappropriate focus on the messenger instead of the message. While it is true that a preacher can employ style for improper purposes, the lack of emphasis on style is also problematic.

The gospel transforms people in their emotional as well as their cognitive dimensions. The homiletician Henry Mitchell insists, "The opposite of 'entertaining' is not 'educational' but boring. Unless the gospel is engaging it is hardly heard, much less remembered."[19] Style is the preacher's antidote against sermonic amnesia, the inability of congregants to remember a sermon shortly after it is preached. Considering these two features of black preaching, let us explore briefly (1) the ethics of preaching and (2) the potential of imaginative preaching to sponsor healthier conversations and progressive theologies of sexuality.

The Ethics of Preaching

The considerable authority enjoyed by many black ministers should motivate them to achieve the highest standards of speech ethics. Since black Christians revere sacred speech (Nommo), the pulpit microphone is arguably the most significant (and potentially dangerous) symbol of human power in congregations. An "open mic" should never be open season for preachers to take aim at persons with hatred and sarcasm, especially when addressing the mysteries of sexuality. For example, the crass phrase "God made Adam and Eve, not Adam and Steve" is undignified language unfit for any pulpit. Instead, care and compassion should characterize all sermons, regardless of preachers' theological perspectives.

The Bible is concerned about the ethics of how Christians communicate. For example, the book of James warns believers, and especially leaders, about the lethal consequences of an unholy tongue: "Not many of you should become teachers, my brothers and sisters, for you know that we who teach will be judged with greater strictness. . . . The tongue is a small member, yet it boasts of great exploits. How great a forest is set ablaze by a small fire! And the tongue is a fire . . . and is itself set on fire by hell" (Jas 3:1, 5–6).

On those rare occasions when sexuality is addressed, too many sermons fuss about the sinful use of genitals, even as those sermons ironically ignore the sinful use of the tongue—the body part often injuring the body of Christ through callous discussions of sexuality. Jesus never condemned LGBTQ persons. He, however, was explicit about God's intolerance for careless speaking: "On the day of judgment you will have to give an account for every careless word you utter; for by your words you will be justified, and by your words you will be condemned" (Matt 12:36–37). Considering Jesus's admonition, I present a sobering reminder to fledgling ministers in my preaching courses in seminary: "There is a heavenly stenographer assigned to every preacher who records every word that comes from your mouth in the pulpit. At God's judgment bar, you will have to answer for every time you opened your mouth to bless or curse someone."

Many professions—such as medicine, law, and business—regulate the ethics of their practitioners. A failure to abide by the code of ethics can result in the loss of a license or disbarment. Preachers one day will stand before the Ultimate Chief Justice in Heaven's High Court. It would be tragic for any minister to be disbarred on judgment day for reckless endangerment with a lethal weapon—the tongue.

Preaching with Imagination

The emphasis on style should empower black ministers to preach about sexuality with greater imagination. Sermons can facilitate constructive dialogue when preachers are "poets" and "spoken-word artists." Poetic preaching can supply compelling images that exemplify the breadth of diverse forms of sanctified sexuality.

Jesus is an excellent tutor for homiletic creativity. He did not avoid sensitive, controversial subjects. He sometimes approached issues directly. For example, his initial sermon in Nazareth about justice and social boundaries incited a riot that nearly led to his death (Luke 4:16–30). However, on many occasions, Jesus's homiletic purposes were better served by the poetic indirection of parables—short stories with common elements that led to uncommon meanings. The pastor and theologian Eugene Peterson discusses the subversive nature of parables: "Parables sound absolutely ordinary: casual stories about soil and seeds, meals and coins and sheep, bandits and victims, farmers and merchants. . . . As people heard Jesus tell these stories . . . they relaxed their defenses. They walked away perplexed, wondering what they meant, the stories lodged in their imagination. And then, like a time bomb, they would explode in their unprotected hearts. . . . Parables aren't illustrations that make things easier; they make things harder by requiring the exercise of our imaginations."[20] Preachers should imitate Jesus's creative style when seeking to promote healthier dialogue concerning sexuality, especially given the discomfort and defensiveness caused by sexual topics. I offer two examples.

The first example occurred when I spoke as a guest preacher several years ago in a Sunday worship service focusing on ministry with men in Christian congregations. During the sermon, I inserted this sentence: "Let this be a house where heterosexual Christian men and gay Christian men can peacefully break bread even as they break down stereotypes." This sentence created a perceptible shift in the spiritual energy in the sanctuary. It was as if some congregants were asking, "Did he just put the words 'gay' and 'Christian' in the same sentence?" Maybe others were envisioning diverse groups of men engaged in peaceful dialogue, a promising image considering the epidemic of violence sending so many black men to cemeteries. Moreover, some might have considered the reference about "breaking bread" as an invitation to think about holy communion and its implications for genuine hospitality.

Like a poem or parable, that simple sentence was designed to imply as much and hopefully more. Amid a sermon of more than two thousand words, I smuggled in twenty-three words to explode preconceived assumptions about the boundaries of the church. It was not a frontal attack on exclusion but instead guerilla warfare for an inclusive gospel.[21]

A second example involves my presiding at holy communion. The biblical scholar Margaret Aymer helped me recognize the profound theological connections between the symbolic "blood" at holy communion and the blood issues affecting millions through HIV/AIDS.[22] Now when inviting persons to the Lord's table, I remind them that the body of Christ has AIDS. Therefore, if they drink the "blood of Jesus," they, too, will have AIDS and must show compassion and solidarity with those infected with this disease that is spread frequently through heterosexual activity. Jesus's broken body becomes an instrument for further reflection and action concerning our sexualized bodies. The table in the church house and the beds in our houses are connected.

Rules of Engagement: Promoting "Public Safety"

Christians should seek to influence practices not only inside faith communities but also in the larger society. By referring to his followers as the "salt of the earth" and the "light of the world," Jesus believed that faith in God had consequences beyond religious borders (Matt 5:13–16). The social dimensions of the gospel call persons in Christian circles to enter the public square. The goal is not to invade the public square with Christian imperialism disguised as evangelism. Rather, our calling as believers is to improve public conversation and conduct through distinctive, if not unique, values and practices.

The ethicist Ellen Marshall outlines the extensive and informal boundaries of the public square: "The 'public square' is not a neatly circumscribed area that we enter only at a specified time for a preplanned discussion. . . . [The public square] denotes a circumstance more than a place, a circumstance marked by a plurality of views and by discussion of issues that affect people beyond the discussants. In this sense, the public square is everywhere, even though we are frequently surprised by its appearance around us."[23] Diverse people with different perspectives who seek and even compete for seemingly dwindling resources are often a formula for social contexts that are contentious, inhospitable, and potentially violent. Many television news programs provide striking examples of public incivility. Inflammatory rhetoric from political opponents can heat up ratings but does little to illumine a path toward the transformation of public values and public policies.

Spirited debate and disagreement are signs of healthy public life in a congregation or an entire country. Yet when public arguments become arsenals for dehumanization, a "public safety" crisis emerges. We have witnessed in recent years horrific incidents where snipers shoot people in public places, such as churches, schools, and grocery stores. Tragic examples include the shootings at Mother Emanuel AME Church (Charleston, South Carolina) in 2015, Pulse nightclub (Orlando, Florida) in 2016, Marjory Stoneman Douglas High School (Parkland, Florida) in

2018, a Walmart store (El Paso, Texas) in 2019, Aromatherapy Spa and Gold Spa (Atlanta, Georgia) and King Soopers grocery store (Boulder, Colorado) in 2021, and Tops grocery store (Buffalo, New York) and Robb Elementary School (Uvalde, Texas) in 2022. The moral outrage at such events is swift and insistent.

We must become equally adamant about the safety of public conversations, refusing to tolerate character assassinations by the tongues of rhetorical snipers. The election of Donald Trump as president of the United States in 2016 contributed to the downward spiral in our speech ethics. Rather than offer examples of the power of language to lift downtrodden hearts, former president Trump's divisive rhetoric often fueled a cultural climate that normalized character assassinations and other forms of hostility.[24]

Christian communities can aid and abet new life by promoting and demonstrating values that ensure safe spaces for courageous public dialogue. If adopted more broadly, these values could transform the current climate of partisan rancor and move us toward more constructive discussions of critical issues in the public square. Whether we are talking about human rights for LGBTQ persons, immigration reform, or national security strategies, we need an enhanced ability to air legitimate differences of opinion without the divisiveness that diminishes a sense of the common good. In this age of expanding social diversity, Christian congregations might best serve the body of Christ and the body politic by seeking to improve the character of public conversations. The way we talk in public about complex moral issues is itself a moral issue.

More Christian congregations might consider adopting three "rules of engagement" to govern their actions, especially in matters of significant public consequence. Typically, "rules of engagement" refer to the principles governing army or police use of violent force to subdue enemies or lawbreakers. I redeploy the term to depict principles for unleashing a nonviolent "soul force" that triggers the retreat of hostility and the advancement of mutual understanding, even if genuine differences remain. These rules are not novel, nor are they unique to Christianity. Their value lies in the ability to foster what the theologian Victor Anderson calls "creative exchange" or a deep commitment to religious and moral openness that enlarges the truths derived in our limited social contexts.[25]

As a practical theologian, I value these rules because of their proven ability to promote safer and more courageous conversations about sensitive topics like sexuality. In large public conversations, congregational discussion groups, and small academic seminars, I have employed these rules, and they have kept me and others safe as we sought to speak the hard truths that can lead to more tender hearts.

1. Demonstrate Intellectual Charity

The word "charity" is a synonym for unconditional love, or *agape*. When expressing the demanding morality needed to foster the beloved community, Jesus said, "Love your enemies" (Matt 5:44). In this verse, the Greek verb "to love" (*agapaō*) is used, hence the term *agape*.

The true test of unconditional love is our ability to treat well those who are opposed to us. Removing love from the sphere of emotions and placing it in the sphere of the will, Jesus suggests that love for opponents is a love we must think about. Thus, it is an intellectual form of love. This kind of love will neither come naturally, nor will it necessarily "feel good." It is a love that comes into existence through our will and intentionality. Intellectual charity requires a toughness of mind and a dogged determination that allow us to bestow goodwill on people without discrimination.

Furthermore, by intellectual charity, I also mean a generous attempt to understand and depict the perspectives of our opponents. Too often in public conversations, we listen superficially to the opinions of others just long enough to create a caricature that we dismiss with haste and hostility. The philosopher Iris Murdoch suggests that love is the "nonviolent apprehension of difference."[26] Consequently, we approach different perspectives not to do violence to those perspectives or the people holding them. Rather, we honor difference as a moral demonstration that something other than our perspective is also real.[27]

2. Show Compassion

The word "passion"—a significant part of the word "com*passion*"—is related to the Greek verb *paschō*, which means "to suffer" or "to endure." Compassion involves a willingness to endure vulnerability and risk in order to enter imaginatively into the experiences of other people. Compassion often begins with a simple question: Why does this person or group hold certain perspectives? Compassion may not produce kindred spirits about difficult topics, but it will produce kinder speech as people wrestle with difficult topics. Mother Teresa insisted, "Kindness has converted more people than zeal, science, or eloquence."[28]

In the Bible, kindness is referred to as a "fruit of the Spirit," a virtue arising in people who humbly seek God's guidance (Gal 5:22). Like other spiritual fruit, kindness infuses individual bodies and the body politic with a sweetness that enables us to endure the bitterness of social inequities, even as we struggle for a more equitable society. Compassion is the root that supports kindness, which is the fruit.

If kindness is supported by compassion, what then supports compassion? Patience is the fertile soil that nourishes compassion. We will not be consistently compassionate until we subdue the knee-jerk, psychological reflex to aggressively defend ourselves when we are offended by what someone has said, done, or failed to say or do.

My wife, Lazetta, and I are the parents of a beautiful teenage daughter, Karis. Parenting is the equivalent of a PhD course in patience. When there is tension or miscommunication between Karis and me, it is typically the result of impatience on my part, her part, or our part. Occasionally, our hurried pace causes us to assume that the other person possessed vital information that was never shared.

As my progeny, Karis possesses some of my genetic code. Furthermore, since we live in the same house and share many daily experiences and cultural rituals, I have also contributed to her cultural DNA. Even as relatives who share biological and cultural DNA, Karis and I must exercise patience if we are to genuinely hear, and be heard by, the other. If an abiding commitment to patience is necessary for healthy communication between blood relatives, how much more patience will be required for healing communication with more distant "kinfolk" in local and global communities?

My Buddhist and Jewish friends and other practitioners of mindfulness meditation are deepening my understanding of patience and its link to compassion. As the scholar Jon Kabat-Zinn observes, to be patient is to "'die on purpose' to the rush of time while you are still living. . . . By 'dying' now in this way, you actually become more alive now."[29]

My earlier agricultural metaphor and Kabat-Zinn's death metaphor are congruent. We must "bury" impatience in the soil of patience. This fertile soil nourishes and irrigates the hard shell of that seed, thereby allowing the root of compassion to break forth. Eventually, compassion becomes the sturdy stalk that gives life to the fruit of kindness. Patience nurtures compassion. Compassion nurtures kindness. If we infuse our speech ethics with values such as patience, compassion, and kindness, our public conversations about weighty moral matters such as sexuality will be exponentially more valuable and effective.

3. Practice Hospitality

Hospitality involves the gracious honoring of one's neighbors, and especially strangers. A compelling gesture of hospitality is contained in the Sanskrit greeting used in India when people meet one another, "Namaste." This simple salutation carries a profound meaning: "The sacred in me greets the sacred in you." Even as people stand firm on their differences of opinion, their spirits can bow with reverent hospitality. When we encounter others, we host the sacred significance of every life.

What accounts for the disturbing lack of hospitality in many spheres of American public life and discourse? The short answer is fear. In the United States, the body politic is suffering from an acute case of xenophobia. Xenophobia is fanatical fear of the stranger or the "other," and this fanatical fear frequently manifests itself when people of diverse sexual identities encounter one another.

In Greek, the word *xenos* means "stranger" or "other." The word *phobos* means "fear." Thus, xenophobia is the fear of people who are different. Sometimes this fear drives people to homicidal and suicidal mania or to hateful, divisive speech that violates people's emotional and psychological wellness.

In the Bible, an early Christian writer explored the ethical consequences of hospitality: "Let mutual love continue. Do not neglect to show hospitality to strangers, for by doing that some have entertained angels without knowing it" (Heb 13:1–2). In this passage, the Greek word translated "mutual love" is *philadelphia* (the word used to name various ancient and contemporary cities). This word connotes the bond that people share in a community.

According to Hebrews 13, believers also have moral obligations to persons outside their community. The biblical writer urges the community to embody an ethic of hospitality toward strangers. The Greek word translated "hospitality" is *philoxenia*. This word means "love of strangers." In the cosmology of ancient Christianity, a porous boundary was thought to exist between the worlds of humans and divine beings. Consequently, believers were instructed to practice hospitality enthusiastically, since at any time, they might unwittingly be hosting angelic visitors disguised as humans.

If we approached public discussions about complex issues such as sexuality with Hebrews 13 in mind, our public speaking would seek to edify, not vilify, even amid intense disagreement. According to Hebrews 13, every person we encounter is potentially an "angel." It is not necessary to conjure images of otherworldly beings for this teaching to have real-world ethical impact.

In this biblical text, the word translated "angels" (*aggelos*) literally means "messenger." We should not consider people who differ from us, or with whom we disagree, as villains or even worse. Instead, we grow in moral stature when we consider such persons to be "messengers" and even "friends" who have something to teach us. This discussion recalls a poignant aphorism from an unknown source, which I adapt slightly for the sake of gender inclusion: "Three people are my friends: the one who loves me, the one who hates me, and the one who is indifferent to me. The one who loves me teaches me tenderness. The one who hates me teaches me caution. The one who is indifferent to me teaches me self-reliance. Three people are my friends."

Hospitality is the gracious acknowledgment of the sacredness of another person's humanity. This acknowledgment is not purely altruistic. There is benevolent self-interest involved as well, since the one who offers hospitality also benefits. The persons to whom we offer hospitality are "messengers," and even "friends," with lessons to teach us if we are humble enough to listen and learn.

A Matter of Death and Life

As noted above, words can wound. Thankfully, however, words can also heal. The scholars Rosemarie Harding and Rachel Harding rightly assert that we "need to create a larger atmosphere of healing and wellness at the level of human relations and social structures."[30] People from different religious, spiritual, and ethical backgrounds should model these healing practices in their speech ethics and especially as we explore the deep mysteries of our diverse sexual identities.

As a nation of laws, we have well-defined legal statutes prohibiting people from using their hands to harm other people. If we also want to be a nation of love, we must be equally concerned about the use of the tongue when speaking, especially about sexuality in the public square. A sage in ancient Israel conveyed the urgent and ultimate significance of speech ethics: "Death and life are in the power of the tongue" (Prov 18:21).

It is my hope that when Christians come before God on the Day of Judgment, God will find irrefutable evidence that we aided and abetted new life. Based on this conviction, I pray that the Great Judge will mercifully toss out other offenses and sentence us to life eternal.

5

Baptism and Holy Communion

Affirming That Black Lives Matter

Jesus of Nazareth is a troubling—and troublesome—figure, and it seems to me the church has never known what to do with him.

—VERNA J. DOZIER, *THE DREAM OF GOD: A CALL TO RETURN*

My Trip(s) to the Holy Land: The Jordan River and Jerusalem

I have touched the Jordan River, the location of Jesus's baptism.* I have gazed at Golgotha, also known as Calvary, the site of Jesus's execution in Jerusalem. Through the generosity of the Baltimore Jewish Council, I traveled to Israel in 1997.

My US passport facilitated the trip to Israel. Close inspection of my "spiritual passport" reveals that I traveled to the Jordan and Jerusalem long before 1997. Concerning nationality, I am a grateful citizen of the United States. Concerning spirituality, I am a grateful citizen of the commonwealth of emancipatory

* This chapter was originally published in *T&T Clark Handbook of African American Theology*, edited by Antonia Michelle Daymond, Frederick L. Ware, and Eric Lewis Williams (New York: T&T Clark, 2019), 197–211. T&T Clark is an imprint of Bloomsbury Publishing Plc. Reprinted with permission of T&T Clark.

black churches that the womanist theologian Delores Williams calls the "black church invisible."

Williams employs the illustrative phrase "black church invisible" to delineate the liberating practices of African American religious communities from the oppressive practices in those communities that promote, for example, sexism, heterosexism, and classism: "The black church is invisible, but we know it when we see oppressed people rising up in freedom. It is community essence, ideal and real as God works through it on behalf of the survival, liberation and positive, productive quality of life of suffering people."[1]

Decades before my feet touched Zion in 1997, the "black church invisible"—as manifested at the First Baptist Church in Salem, Virginia—strapped wings on my soul and transported my religious imagination to the Jordan and Jerusalem. In this loving congregation, where my father served as pastor and my mother as a lay leader, black Christians practiced baptism and holy communion with grace-filled gusto.

Baptism and Holy Communion: The Terms of Engagement

The word "baptism" comes from the Greek word *baptizō*, meaning "to dip or immerse in water." For Christians, baptism affirms a person's relationship with God through Jesus Christ. While often associated with John the Baptizer in the Bible, baptism is—in the most radical sense—a willingness to join Jesus in death (e.g., Mark 10:38; Rom 6:3). John's baptism anticipated the Messiah to come. Christian baptism honors the Messiah who has come and awaits the Messiah who is coming again.[2]

My childhood spiritual community transported me to the Jordan River through baptism. More than forty years have passed since my father baptized me. Yet I still hear the voices surrounding that moment. The choir sang about the Jordan River that was "chilly and cold," and its water "chilled the body but not the soul." As the choir lowered their voices, my father raised his: "On the profession of your faith, and in the presence of God, the angels, and this company, I now baptize you." He lowered me into the water and lifted me into a new life of Christian discipleship.

Holy communion is a Christian ritual meal consisting of the simple elements of bread and wine (or grape juice). Yet the meal possesses a complex constellation of theological meanings.[3] The ritual commemorates Jesus's last meal with his disciples on the evening before his execution. The meal enables believers to partake ritually in Jesus's death, thereby reminding them of the promise of everlasting life. The biblical scholar Stephanie Crowder remarks, "The various designations of holy communion include: the Lord's Supper, the Last Supper, and the Eucharist. The term 'Eucharist' is derived from a Greek verb meaning 'to give thanks' (*eucharisteō*). Across the centuries, Christians have come to the communion table with great gratitude for Jesus's ultimate sacrifice at Calvary."[4]

My childhood spiritual community transported me to Calvary through holy communion. On holy communion Sundays (every first Sunday), the lay leaders dressed alike in dark suits and white dresses, and my father donned a gleaming white clerical robe with velvet crimson panels. On the wings of spirited communion hymns, the choir lifted the congregation and placed us "down at the cross where my Savior died."[5]

The lay leaders handled the communion elements with priestly precision. After receiving the communion elements, people waited so that the entire congregation could eat and drink together. The grape juice in the thimble-sized glasses was barely enough to wash down the chalky residue from the white communion wafers. Nevertheless, the community approached this sacred meal with heightened zeal, believing that this monthly, mythic trip to Calvary made all the difference in this world and in the world to come. As the meal concluded, the congregation sang exuberantly the chorus of the hymn "At Calvary":

Mercy there was great and grace was free,
Pardon there was multiplied to me,
There my burdened soul found liberty—
At Calvary.[6]

Ritual Renewal: Ancient Practices in Contemporary Contexts

Rituals are a powerful language. By rituals, I mean ceremonial, symbolic actions by which people express their deepest convictions.[7] Yet rituals can lose their efficacy if they are not conversant with contemporary social issues. As black Christians practice baptism and holy communion, what contemporary issues must be engaged so that these rituals can speak afresh to the present?

Many recent events have impacted local and global cultures. Notable examples include the historic election and reelection of former president Barack Obama, the Great Recession, and the rise of international terrorism. The emergence of another recent phenomenon—the Black Lives Matter movement—provides salient opportunities to renew baptism and holy communion.

Social activists Alicia Garza, Patrisse Cullors, and Ayo Tometi (formerly known as Opal Tometi) created the social media hashtag #BlackLivesMatter in 2013. The hashtag was a response to the 2012 death of Trayvon Martin, an unarmed black teenager in Florida, and the 2013 acquittal of his armed killer George Zimmerman. These activists were seeking to raise public consciousness concerning the protection and valuing of black people.[8]

This social media hashtag has become a rallying cry of a new movement, especially in the light of the recent onslaught of lethal interactions of black people and law enforcement. The infamous and growing list includes, but is not limited to, the following: Rekia Boyd (Chicago, Illinois); Michael Brown (Ferguson, Missouri); Tanisha Anderson (Cleveland, Ohio); Eric Garner (New York, New York); Freddie Gray (Baltimore, Maryland); Sandra Bland (Prairie View, Texas); Alton Sterling (Baton Rouge, Louisiana); Philando Castile (St. Paul, Minneapolis); Ahmaud Arbery (Brunswick, Georgia); Breonna Taylor (Louisville, Kentucky); and George Floyd (Minneapolis, Minnesota).[9] The seeming inability to compile comprehensive lists of black people recently killed by law enforcement is "damning evidence of the level of violence against black bodies in America."[10]

We must add to this grim social portrait the dilemma of "black-on-black" violence. Baltimore, Maryland, is an epicenter of this epidemic. In April 2015, Freddie Gray, a twenty-five-year-old black man, was killed while in the custody of Baltimore police officers. This event blazoned Baltimore onto the national consciousness as both the site of another police-related black death and the site of significant civil unrest that engulfed the city for several weeks.[11] In the years since these incidents, Baltimore has struggled with escalating homicides, and most of the victims have been black people.

In addition to being the president of Chicago Theological Seminary and a senior program adviser at the Smithsonian Center for Folklife and Cultural Heritage in Washington, DC, I serve as the founding senior pastor of The Open Church of Maryland, a theologically progressive and predominantly black congregation in Baltimore. A front-page story in the *Baltimore Sun* remarked, "Baltimore suffered 343 homicides in 2017—the second most in a single year, and the most per capita in city history. More than 1,000 people were shot last year."[12] In Baltimore, and many other American cities, there are passionate conversations—from social media to barbershops and beauty salons—about the ugly dilemma of violence, especially violence involving black people.

Embodiment: Embracing the Body

We must not ignore embodied realities such as violence or economic impoverishment when considering the contemporary relevance of baptism and holy communion. When we fail to embrace the body, we eviscerate these rituals of their social potency. These rituals were, and are, bodily.

In Jesus's baptism, John immersed Jesus's body in the Jordan River. Bodies are also involved in our diverse baptism practices, whether through sprinkling water on babies' foreheads or immersing adults in baptismal pools. Additionally, the final meal that Jesus shared with his disciples was a bodily affair, involving the ingesting of bread and wine. Likewise, the contemporary administration of holy communion is bodily. Beyond the obvious ingesting of bread and wine, holy communion in some traditions incorporates additional bodily gestures.

Some gestures are modest, such as congregants tracing a symbolic cross on their heads and torsos using a hand. Other gestures are more majestic, such as congregants genuflecting noticeably before high altars, washing their hands in basins of water, and wiping their hands on white towels to ensure that pure hands handle the holy elements.

These pious gestures to "sanitize" the meal, while rooted in sincere piety, might also reveal a subconscious attempt to avoid the ghastly details of Jesus's execution. The biblical scholar Neil Elliott depicts the grotesquery of ancient crucifixion: "As a means of capital punishment for heinous crimes, crucifixion was the 'supreme Roman penalty' yet almost always inflicted upon the lower class. . . . Crucifixion was 'the typical punishment for slaves.' . . . In the Roman practice, 'whipping, torture, the burning out of the eyes, and maiming often preceded the actual hanging.'"[13]

The New Testament depicts the mob mentality and brutality that surrounded Jesus's arrest and trial before Pontius Pilate (e.g., Matt 26:36–27:23). The four Gospels also provide glimpses of the torture inflicted upon Jesus during the crucifixion. While it had psychological dimensions, Jesus's fatal suffering was undoubtedly bodily.

The Gospel of John supplies a unique detail about Jesus's crucifixion. This Gospel depicts a Roman soldier lancing Jesus's side, allowing blood and water to flow from Jesus's dead body (John 19:31–37). Some patristic and medieval thinkers interpreted this graphic detail as a symbolic allusion to holy communion (blood) and baptism (water).[14] In other words, Jesus's execution was the spiritual fountain for these rituals.

While this interpretation is theologically plausible, it underscores a problematic tendency in the ritual imagination. Some religious communities move too rapidly to "symbols" without also adequately embracing the embodied "substance" upon which many rituals are founded. Deeper and different symbolic meanings might emerge from our rituals if we paid more attention to embodiment.

By embodiment, I mean a robust appreciation for the full dimensions of corporeal existence. In the example above from the Gospel of John, an interpretation rooted in embodiment might attend more carefully to the tangible details surrounding this gruesome, state-sponsored execution of an innocent African Jewish man in approximately 30 CE in a colonized outpost of the Roman Empire.[15]

Embodied interpretation would notice the four courageous women at the cross including Jesus's "mother, and his mother's sister, Mary the wife of Clopas, and Mary Magdalene" (John 19:25). In the violent, male-dominated world of this ancient empire, the presence of female witnesses at an execution should not be ignored. Another noteworthy feature is the embodiment of intimate relationships as the dying Jesus implores his mother and one of his closest disciples to embrace each other as family (John 19:26–27). The juxtaposition of tenderness and torture is palpable.

Embodiment enhances symbolic analysis by anchoring interpretation in the tangible specifics of human experience. At Calvary, a body—a young, black, male, economically vulnerable Jewish body made in the image of God—was decimated. In the eyes of the empire, Jesus's black life did not matter. Before examining pragmatic ways that embodiment can enhance baptism and holy communion, a brief exploration of political theology will be helpful.

Political Theology: Politics in the Pews

Baptism and holy communion can affirm embodiment, especially when these rituals are interpreted in the light of political theology. For some persons, the phrase "political theology" is oxymoronic and joins two supposedly separate worlds: politics and religion. Instead of being oxymoronic, political theology critiques the ironic nature of versions of Christianity that seek to domesticate, if not eradicate, the political symbols and semantics of Christianity.

The Roman Empire executed Jesus on a charge of political sedition. This crucifixion, like countless other Roman crucifixions, conveyed a tangible warning to political pretenders: Rome was intolerant of insurrection. Yet upon the news of Jesus's resurrection, his earliest followers cast their gospel proclamation in overtly *political* language: Christ is *Lord!*

Early Christian leaders such as the apostle Paul defined religion in ways that included politics. The biblical scholar N. T. Wright suggests that when some of the earliest Christians affirmed that Jesus was Lord, they simultaneously were affirming that Caesar was *not* Lord.[16] Wright imaginatively accentuates the political nature of early Christianity: "Since Paul's proclamation clearly carried a political message at its heart. . . . Perhaps Paul should be taught just as much in the politics departments of our universities as in the religion departments."[17]

While some might question including early Christian beliefs in a university politics course, I, as a proponent of political theology, want to heighten the political consciousness of people sitting in church pews. The theologians William Cavanaugh and Peter Scott characterize political theology in this way: "The task of political theology might then be to expose the ways in which theological discourse reproduces inequalities of class, gender or race, and to reconstruct theology so that it serves the cause of justice. . . . What distinguishes all political theology from other types of theology or political discourse is the explicit attempt to relate discourse about God to the organization of bodies in space and time."[18] Political theology avoids "pie in the sky" rhetoric in favor of serious analysis about how God-talk empowers or disempowers bodies on earth. The embodied rituals of baptism and holy communion can raise awareness about just or unjust political arrangements and the ways those arrangements devalue or value black lives.

The Politics of Baptism

I reflect below on Matthew's account of Jesus's baptism. These reflections will be followed by pragmatic observations concerning how baptism can affirm that black lives matter.

In Matthew 3:13–17, Jesus's baptism declares his readiness for the revolution represented by the "kin-dom" of heaven.[19]

In the synoptic Gospels, only Matthew presents a curious dialogue between Jesus and John prior to the baptism. Recognizing Jesus's "superiority," John urges a role reversal, protesting that Jesus should baptize him. John eventually concedes and baptizes Jesus.

Matthew likely uses this dialogue to address a "messianic embarrassment" troubling some followers of Jesus. Some early Christians may have inquired, "Why would Jesus, a sinless messiah, submit to John's baptism, which was for the repentance of sins?" According to Matthew, Jesus is baptized not to repent of sin but rather to "fulfill all righteousness" (Matt 3:15).

The word "righteousness" evokes thoughts of personal piety. Some Christian traditions have emphasized the *personal* dimensions of righteousness to the exclusion of its *political* dimensions. Therefore, the politically provocative characteristics of John and Jesus are often ignored.

The Greek word for "righteousness" (*dikaiosunē*) can be translated as "justice." Righteousness encapsulates God's passionate commitment to set right the things that are wrong in society.[20] Thus, righteousness is also a matter of *social justice*. Through baptism, Jesus says in effect, "I join this populist, political movement whereby God's justice will be manifest for *all* God's children, not just the powerful and the elite. I am ready for the revolution because my life, and the lives of people like me, matter!"

The emphasis on repentance in the preaching of John and Jesus also indicates their radicalism. Sentimental moralizing has blunted the sharp edge of the word "repentance." Repentance involves more than an admission of wrong. The Greek word for "repentance" (*metanoia*) connotes a change of mindset and the embodiment of a new identity.

Perhaps this is why the heavenly voice after the baptism refers to Jesus as the "son" and "the beloved" (Matt 3:17). This is not an announcement of Jesus's divine uniqueness but instead a divine affirmation of Jesus's political boldness. God is pleased with Jesus's attachment to a radical political movement that calls for radical repentance.[21]

Repentance is a revolutionary action creating new ways of imagining the world. Both John and Jesus assert that only those who embody new mindsets will be fit for the new "kin-dom." Furthermore, the means by which John and Jesus meet their deaths should convince even the most hardened skeptics about the revolutionary nature of their ministries. Neither prophet dies of old age or natural causes. Both are the victims of government-sponsored execution.

The Practice of Baptism: Troubling the Waters

The black spiritual "Wade in the Water," sung often in black baptism services, insists that God is "gonna trouble the water." In the spirit of this troublesome God, our baptism services should be more politically provocative. In other liturgical moments, we can soothe people's "souls" with images of God, the Eternal Shepherd, who leads us beside still waters (Ps 23:2). Baptism, however, is an opportune time to remember a God who champions oppressed people and struggles alongside them. This God troubles the waters of the Red Sea in order to enable the oppressed to be free. The theologian James Cone poignantly characterizes the God of the oppressed: "Unlike the God of Greek philosophy who is removed from history, the God of the Bible is involved in history, and [God's] revelation is inseparable from the social and political affairs of Israel. . . . Yahweh is known and worshipped as the Lord who brought Israel out of Egypt and raised Jesus from the dead. [Yahweh] is the political God, the Protector of the poor and the Establisher of the right for those who are oppressed."[22]

To baptize people in the name of this God is to immerse them in politically turbulent waters. Baptism services should not be polite. On the contrary, they should create a guttural awareness in those about to be baptized, and in those already baptized, that following God will at times be costly. A major currency for payment of that cost is struggle, and this struggle may exact a toll from our bodies.

When baptizing children, and especially when christening babies, I congratulate families for their desire to inaugurate a child's life with a spiritually significant ritual. Yet baptism is vacuous if it morphs into a genteel moment to acknowledge godparents, provide a gilt-edged baptism certificate with filigree font, and share an after-church baptism brunch for family and friends at an upscale restaurant.

It is incumbent upon me pastorally to puncture the politeness of the moment with politics. I remind families, or the candidates for baptism if they are old enough to comprehend, that when Jesus stepped into the Jordan River to be baptized, he signed his death certificate. I then tell the families, or the baptism candidates, that in addition to baptism certificates, we should also provide them with death certificates. To serve God is to be willing to struggle for our freedom and the freedom of others, even to the point of death. Baptism is not a cleansing of our souls from sin; it is a marking of our bodies for struggle!

At baptisms, we should call the names of those who have been martyred in movements for righteousness and especially in the arduous, ongoing movement to affirm that black lives matter. Imagine a baptism service where before the baptism occurs, the names of martyrs are interspersed throughout the spirited singing of "Wade in the Water."

The roll call obviously would include names such as John the Baptizer and Jesus. The roll call also might include the names of Addie Mae Collins, Denise McNair, Carole Robertson, and Cynthia Wesley. These four precious black girls were attending Sunday school on a September morning in 1963 at the 16th Street Baptist Church in Birmingham, Alabama, when a terrorist bomb revealed that America was still savagely judging black children by the color of their skin and *not* by the content of their character.[23]

In that same baptism service, it would also be fitting to call the names of the Rev. Clementa Pinckney, Cynthia Hurd, the Rev. Sharonda Coleman-Singleton, Tywanza Sanders, Ethel Lance, Susie Jackson, Depayne Middleton Doctor, the Rev. Daniel Simmons, and Myra Thompson. These nine Christians were slaughtered by a white supremacist on June 17, 2015, at Mother Emanuel AME Church in Charleston, South Carolina, as they read scripture in what they thought was a sacred, and safe, place.[24]

The Birmingham Four and the Charleston Nine are embodied reminders that in the fight to make black lives matter, "we have come over a way that with tears has been watered; we have come, treading our path through the blood of the slaughtered."[25] Salty water flows in our baptism fonts and pools. The water contains the saline tears shed by those who mourn the martyrs of the movement. God's tears are also mixed in those baptismal waters. We present our bodies in baptism in the hope that one day God will wipe away all our tears and that we will wipe away all God's tears. When we finally put an "end to the very culture that has declared war on innocent, young black bodies," God will weep no more.[26]

The Politics of Holy Communion

I reflect below on a scandal during holy communion in 1 Corinthians. These reflections will be followed by pragmatic observations concerning how holy communion can affirm that black lives matter.

The Corinthian church included Jews and Gentiles as well as social elites and economically vulnerable persons who were enslaved or recently emancipated (1 Cor 1:26–28; 7:17–24). First Corinthians depicts a community encountering the opportunities and challenges of diverse bodies attempting to coalesce into "the body of Christ."

In 1 Corinthians 11:17–34, divisive social stratification is occurring at holy communion. Paul's indignation is evident: "When you come together, it is not really to eat the Lord's supper. For when the time comes to eat, each of you goes ahead with your own supper, and one goes hungry and another becomes drunk. What! Do you not have homes to eat and drink in? Or do you show contempt for the church of God and humiliate those who have nothing? What should I say to you? Should I commend you? In this matter I do not commend you!"

Economic inequity is at the root of the schism. The inequity manifests itself ironically during holy communion, the community's sacred meal symbolizing a shared history and destiny. More specifically, as the community gathers for holy communion, certain wealthier members also bring elaborate "picnic dinners" and eat in front of the economically impoverished members who lack resources for such meals. The flaunting of class differences demonstrates an inexcusable lack of concern for the community.

Chastising this classism, Paul recalls Jesus's institution of holy communion (1 Cor 11:23–26). By remembering Jesus, Paul hopes to "re-member" the body of Christ, which is always "dismembered" when one part of the body exerts power and privilege over other parts of the body.

In 1 Corinthians 11:27–29, Paul implores the community to engage in discernment that will restore solidarity among believers from different economic classes: "Whoever, therefore, eats the bread or drinks the cup of the Lord in an unworthy manner will be answerable for the body and blood of the Lord. Examine yourselves, and only then eat of the bread and drink of the cup. For all who eat and drink without discerning the body, eat and drink judgment against themselves." By parading their social status before the rest of the church, these wealthier Christians are liable to the judgment of Jesus, who died so that barriers among diverse people might be dismantled.

Pietistic interpretations have obscured Paul's searing, social critique in this text. Many Christian traditions have fixated narrowly on identities or behaviors that constitute taking holy communion in an "unworthy manner." Consequently, sanctimonious gatekeepers have placed "fences" around communion tables, barring "unworthy" people from sharing the meal. Across the ages, the "unworthy" deemed unfit to share the meal have included persons from different religious denominations, divorced persons, unmarried mothers, and LGBTQ persons.

In an attempt to create a "rigorous Christian purity system" enacted liturgically at the communion table, many Christians have unwittingly defiled the body of Christ by exclusion.[27] If we connect Paul's words about taking holy communion in an "unworthy manner" (1 Cor 11:27) with his exhortation about communal discernment (1 Cor 11:28–29), the theme of inclusion and social cohesion is abundantly clear.

Paul urges the community to engage in probing self-examination (1 Cor 11:28) and warns about the danger of not "discerning the body of the Lord" (1 Cor 11:29). The body of the Lord is the gathered community. The unworthy partaking of holy communion occurs when the ritual disregards or excludes people. If we share this meal without concern for who is present—and concern for who is absent because of our exclusion—we eat and drink judgment upon ourselves.

Believers should examine themselves at holy communion. The examination should include more than personal piety. The belief that "sin" is primarily a matter of individual piety is a symptom of the sin of classism. Donna Langston observes, "Preoccupation with one's self—one's body, looks, relationships—is a luxury working-class women can't afford. . . . The middle class has the leisure time to be preoccupied with their own problems, such as their waistlines, planning their vacations, coordinating their wardrobes, or dealing with what their mother said to them when they were five—my!"[28]

At the communion tables of middle-class black churches, have we become so preoccupied with our class-based privileges that we have failed to "discern the body of the Lord"? The body of the Lord—not white wafers on the communion table but black people in underserved neighborhoods struggling to put food on their kitchen tables. Discrimination based on class status and social identity is a violation of the inclusive principles of the "kin-dom" for which Jesus lived and died.

The Practice of Holy Communion: Creating Welcome Tables

The black spiritual/folk song "I'm Gonna Sit at the Welcome Table" is often sung at holy communion services in black churches. One stanza declares,

All God's children gonna sit together.
All God's children gonna sit together one of these days,
    hallelujah.

All God's children gonna sit together.
All God's children gonna sit together, one of these days, one of
   these days.

Civil rights protestors sang these words in defiance of a segregated social system preventing different races from sitting together at lunch counters in the United States. Lunch counters were desegregated in the 1960s through valiant struggle and historic legislation. Yet many communion tables remain segregated. Some black churches passionately protest racial discrimination while remaining eerily silent about oppression based on economic class and other types of social stigma. We must break the silence to enable communion tables to become authentic welcome tables for black lives from all segments of society.

At The Open Church of Maryland, where I serve as the founding senior pastor, holy communion on one occasion became a radical object lesson about classism and inclusive welcome tables. As an entrepreneurial church start, The Open Church benefited economically from attracting middle-class persons who were early adopters of the ministry. These persons made generous financial contributions that enabled the congregation to establish a firm footing.

Amid this financial generosity, signs began to emerge that some in the congregation were becoming preoccupied with material concerns. The congregation was renting space in a beautiful Lutheran church in Baltimore. Yet the passion for "buying our own space" appeared to be more important for some than establishing partnerships with communities experiencing social and economic marginalization.

Additionally, a spirit of entitlement began creeping into the congregation. Some congregants seemed to feel that their financial contributions gave them a "right" to religious "goods and services" (i.e., worship services and sermons) being delivered according to their "preferences." It felt as if the relationship between some congregants and me had morphed from partnership to patronage. These congregants seemingly presumed that they were the "patrons," and I, as the "client," was expected to implement their wishes.

To employ a different metaphor, the congregation had contracted a case of "affluenza," which the homiletician Dale Andrews defines as "a cultural disease of excess—an excess that seldom satiates the desire for more." When affluenza is present, "our daily appetite increases as we normalize privilege. Yesterday's privilege becomes today's expectation."[29] As the congregation's resident doctor of the soul, I diagnosed the situation and prescribed an antidote.

On the First Sunday of Advent in 2013, we were scheduled to serve holy communion after my sermon. I preached a sermon titled "The Toughest Examination" that was based on 1 Corinthians 11:17–34. I reminded the congregation that the communion table brings us to Calvary, the Christian shrine of revelation. The divine light emanating from Calvary's darkness illumines our probing self-examination, which is the toughest examination. Whenever we approach the communion table, we should plead in the words of the gospel song: "Search me, Lord. . . . Shine the light from heaven on my soul."

As I concluded the sermon that appeared well received by the congregation, and as the congregation was eagerly preparing to share holy communion, I administered the antidote for classism and affluenza. Like any "flu shot," it was initially painful, but the potential long-term benefits outweighed, in my estimation, any short-term discomfort.

I issued my sermonic conclusion and supposed invitation to the communion table with these words:

> As we come to the table today, I do not have time to be concerned about your individual moral transgressions. What I am concerned about are the attitudes and actions that perpetuate the sin of social inequity.
>
> Because of your social status, do you secretly feel superior to the homeless sex worker who might come to our church from a "rough neighborhood" looking for assistance for her sick child? Examine yourself.
>
> Do you have time to luxuriate in the latest gossip at The Open Church? Instead of gossiping about who said a curse

word in a church meeting recently, what about the obscenity of a middle-class church nestled comfortably in a luxurious, half-empty house, eating a symbolic meal of bread and wine with thousands of poor people within miles of this comfortable house?

We have yet to invite these economically vulnerable friends to our feast. Examine yourself. Discern the body. It is the toughest examination.

The examination is not about us bathing our conscience so that we can eat the meal. Rather, the examination may involve a *refusal* to eat the meal until more of our economically vulnerable sisters and brothers have a seat at the table with us. The dinner bell is ringing, calling us to the communion table. Or is that the school bell ringing, calling us to take an examination. Amen.

I then came from the pulpit and addressed the congregation: "As your pastor, I love you too much to allow us to take holy communion today. There is not enough class diversity in this congregation. We have not worked hard enough to invite economically marginalized people to the feast. If we eat this meal today, it is simply a middle-class snack, and according to scripture, we will eat and drink judgment upon ourselves. Thus, holy communion will *not* be served today!"

I pronounced the benediction. The service was over, but the "scandal" had only begun. Many congregants sat with their mouths ajar as if to say, "Did he just do what I think he did?" Other congregants smiled as they realized that my spoken sermon had been a "setup" for the real sermon, the dramatic demonstration of *not* serving holy communion. Still, other congregants were offended because my action had tampered with their "right" to take holy communion.

Whether my audacious action was right or wrong, it inaugurated an ongoing dialogue in a middle-class congregation concerning how class-based privileges and "rights" oppress and exclude others, and oppression is always wrong. In the quest to affirm that black lives matter, the womanist theologian Keri Day challenges black religious communities to consider how their practices impact economically vulnerable black people and especially black women: "Religious institutions can provide leadership in developing a moral consensus on the blight and plight of our poor. Specifically, black churches can begin to rethink antipoverty strategies, prosperity theologies, and policy activism in order to participate in a project of hope and thriving with and for poor black women and other poor persons within an American underclass."[30] Taking holy communion "in remembrance of Jesus" should involve remembering, including, and partnering with persons who are economically oppressed. Long before his last supper with disciples, Jesus provided etiquette for inviting people to a meal: "But when you give a banquet, invite the poor, the crippled, the lame, and the blind. And you will be blessed, because they cannot repay you, for you will be repaid at the resurrection of the righteous" (Luke 14:13–14). When we invite as Jesus taught us, communion tables become welcome tables. At welcome tables, irrespective of creed or class, black lives matter.

The Benediction: A Communal Rallying Cry

Baptism and holy communion are liturgical acts that can heighten the social and political consciousness of black Christians. Most liturgies conclude with a benediction. I wrote this benediction to send us forth as we radicalize our practices of baptism and holy communion:

> **Leader:** A first-century freedom fighter named Jesus, living in colonized Israel, once declared, "You will know the truth, and the truth will make you free."
>
> **People:** A twentieth-century freedom fighter named Assata Shakur, living in colonized America, once declared, "It is our duty to fight for our freedom. It is our duty to win."
>
> **Leader:** Sacred Spirit, through baptism and holy communion, teach us and trouble us until we not only *know* the truth but also *do* the truth. In *doing* the truth, we, too, are set free. Righteous action is radical abolition.

People: "We must love each other and support each other. We have nothing to lose but our chains."

Leader: "It is our duty to fight for our freedom. It is our duty to win. We must love each other and support each other. We have nothing to lose but our chains."[31]

All: Since black people were brought to America in chains, it will be heaven—or heaven on earth—when all bodies, *and especially black bodies*, are unshackled, and we are free, indeed! Amen.

6

Policy *and* Poetry

The Black Religious Imagination and Social Transformation

What is poetry? It is the human soul entire, squeezed like a lemon or a lime, drop by drop, into atomic words.

—LANGSTON HUGHES, "DRAFT IDEAS"

The African "Drumbeat" in a Corporate Boardroom

Jacob Olupona, professor of African religious traditions at Harvard Divinity School, invited a group of scholars in 2018 to present at a Harvard University conference about the public role of religion in African and African diasporic communities. After accepting the invitation to the conference, I immediately knew the topic for my presentation. My presentation would reconnect with some theoretical work I had done during my service as the program officer for religion in the public sphere at the Ford Foundation.

The Ford Foundation, a philanthropic institution whose annual grant-making activities typically exceed $500 million, is well known for supporting progressive social justice initiatives in the United States and around the globe. As Ford's program officer for religion, I reviewed all faith-based grant proposals and recommended to the foundation's senior leadership the disbursement of grant awards. Additionally, I served as Ford's thought leader on religion.

The theoretical framework for my presentation at the Harvard conference and this chapter emerged at a meeting during my time as a grant-maker at Ford. The recounting of that meeting below will reveal the intellectual commitments and spiritual energy animating the forthcoming exploration of the public role of religion in African diasporic communities.

In March 2014, dozens of senior leaders at the Ford Foundation, including vice presidents and program officers, gathered in a conference room in Ford's office building in Midtown Manhattan. As the meeting ensued, one of the vice presidents graciously introduced me to the group. I had begun my employment at Ford only a few days earlier. Thus, this was my first official group meeting.

Since I was one of the newest members on Ford's team, my plan was to quietly observe the meeting and orient myself to the organizational culture. Brilliant scholars, policy and educational analysts, and attorneys were assembled, and the atmosphere was replete with cogent examinations of public policy issues. I was honored to be in the room and delighted to witness my new colleagues approach complicated social issues from their respective disciplines.

Yet the longer I listened to the dialogue, the more uncomfortable I became. I began having "auditory hallucinations." In my "third ear," I was hearing the driving, polyrhythmic beats of the African drum. Some spiritual traditions speak of a "third ear" and/or a "third eye," which are metaphors for keen moral discernment and spiritual intuition that penetrate beneath the surface to expose the deeper truths of any situation. I was in a New York City corporate boardroom. There was no way I was hearing the drum. Yet the drum—the African drum that talks—would not leave me alone.[1] It was as if the drum were saying to me, "As a person of African descent, you come from a people who were the original architects of religion, art, culture, and commerce. The policy conversation your colleagues are having is not *incorrect*. The conversation, however, is *incomplete*. Although this is your first meeting, this is no time for feigned humility or timidity. Raise your hand and speak *your* truth."

I raised my hand. The Ford vice president moderating the meeting called on me, and I said, "I appreciate this keen policy analysis, but where is the 'poetry'? Where is the 'music'? In this discussion thus far, is there anything that 'hums'? There is a West African proverb that says, 'Where there is no music, the Spirit will not come.' If we are going to change the world for the better, there must be some music. There must be some poetry."

(Theo)Poetic Musings

In professional philanthropy, grant-makers often discuss their "theory of (social) change."[2] In my first meeting at the Ford Foundation, I summarized my theory of change in a sentence: "Where there is no music, the Spirit (that emboldens freedom fighting and social transformation) will not come."

To substantiate my theory of change and facilitate the pragmatic aspects of grant-making, I eventually wrote a concept paper at the Ford Foundation concerning the intertwining of public policy *and* poetry in religiously motivated social transformation. When potential grantees visited me at the Ford Foundation to present ideas for grant proposals supporting social transformation, my initial questions to them often were "What 'hums' in your grant proposal? Is there any 'music' here?"

These poetic questions highlighted my expectation for a collaborative vision-casting process with potential Ford grantees that was as passionate as it was precise. The emphasis on the heart as well as the head in fostering social transformation enlivened the conversations with potential grantees. This integrated approach inspired a dynamic interplay between the cognitive and emotive dimensions. Thus, whether or not the conversations led eventually to funding, "poetry" enriched our approaches to social transformation.

I will explore more fully below the connotations of "poetry" and its role in social change. I preface that discussion by noting that what I refer to as poetry other scholars call "theopoetics."

This term arises from a creative mingling of two Greek words. The Greek word *theos* means "god" and gives us the English word "theology." The Greek verb *poieō* means "to create" and gives us the English word "poetry." Thus, theopoetics involves diverse attempts to understand and embody the sacred (or all that is good and beautiful) through creative acts and the arts.

These creative acts seek to impact not only our cognitive dimension but also our emotive dimension and sensory perceptions. Theopoetics realizes that rational logic on its own cannot fully plumb the heights and depths of our complex interactions with each other and with the natural and social environments. Another logic—aesthetics—is also needed.

Aesthetics is the unapologetic appeal to feelings, intuitions, and sensory perceptions in the creation and appreciation of all that is good and beautiful. Feelings are a bridge, not a barrier, to deeper, more nuanced knowledge. The word "aesthetics" is derived from a Greek word (*aesthēsis*) that means "insight" or "discernment." By utilizing creativity and aesthetics, theopoetics excavates deeper truths and motivations.

Although theopoetics is a relatively new term, the phenomena described by the term are as old as the Jewish and Christian scriptures, and even older. For example, Genesis, the first book in the Jewish and Christian scriptures, introduces the main character—God—not by philosophical principle but rather through a poetic chronicle of the creation of the cosmos. The first thing we learn about God in these scriptures is that God is creative and concerned about the good and the beautiful.

God frequently uses the term "good" to describe the creation in Genesis 1. The Hebrew word translated as "good" (*tôb*) connotes things, experiences, and creatures/beings that are desirable or pleasing. God's statement about the creation's goodness "carries the sense of achieving the divine intention, which includes elements of beauty, purpose, and praise."[3] In the Greek translation (i.e., the Septuagint) of Genesis 1:1, God (*theos*) creates (*poieō*) the heavens and the earth. The Jewish and Christian scriptures begin, etymologically speaking, in a theopoetic way.

Further investigation of Genesis 1:1 indicates that creativity is a key strand of God's divine DNA. In Genesis 1:1, the Hebrew verb "to create" is *bārā*. Throughout the Jewish scriptures, only God is the subject of this verb, since creativity is the special province of God. The verb *bārā* refers to "the fundamental newness and uniqueness of what God brings into being. . . . [Consequently,] no analogy from the human sphere can exhaust the meaning of God's creative activity."[4]

Although Genesis insists that there is a unique form of creative power reserved only for God, God also bestows derivative powers of creativity and imagination upon humans (Gen 1:26–28). The biblical scholar Terence Fretheim observes, "From the beginning God chooses not to be the only one who has or exercises creative power."[5] Humans are perhaps most godlike when we create, or contribute to, the good and the beautiful in personal, public, and environmental spheres.

(Theo)Poetic Manifestations: Black Churches

People of African descent have embodied a deep cultural commitment to cocreating with God across the millennia. The creative impact of Africans on world civilization is well documented.[6] Africans have created, and contributed to, many aspects of global culture from commerce to cuisine. Religion has been at the center of these African contributions. For many Africans, religion is not a separate sphere but the context in which life occurs.[7] Some scholars suggest that a "religious consciousness among African peoples constitutes their single most important common characteristic."[8]

Even during the ineffable horrors of transatlantic slavery, the theopoetic creativity of Africans remained indomitable. Millions of enslaved Africans came forcibly to the United States not as *immigrants* seeking a better life but as slave-ship *inventory* already considered socially dead.[9]

During the fifteenth through the nineteenth centuries, the criminal shipping of Africans to the Americas and the Caribbean by white Christian nations created the conditions for new, revolutionary, theopoetic communities—black churches. These exiled Africans, like the exiled Israelites in Babylon (Ps 137), eventually learned how to sing the Lord's song in strange diasporic lands such as the United States. Across the centuries, black churches became a "refuge of resistance" where oppressed people "assembled to be renewed in the spirit, to be fortified in the mind."[10] Were it not for the fervent prayers and fiery preaching, the impassioned singing and ecstatic dancing of those early, faithful Africans in the United States, black churches would not be what and where they are today.

The religious studies scholar James Hill defines this extraordinary black creativity amid extreme crisis as "theopoetics": "When I use the term theopoetics to describe the black Christian experience in America, I am referring to the ability of black religious communities to imaginatively express their faith convictions through art, song, poetry, oral witness, and other embodied practices. Key to understanding the rich theopoetical tradition of black religious communities is the manner in which their theopoetic practices were used to inaugurate alternative worlds of anti-colonial, socio-political possibility; worlds that were often sequestered from them by the necropolitical forces surrounding them."[11] In immeasurable ways, people in the United States and around the world are indebted to Africa for its role in creating black churches—these theopoetic communities whose prophetic witness redeemed distorted versions of white "Christianity" and white "democracy." The sacred fire of black churches has illumined the pathway for the journey to justice and ignited deep moral reflection about the true meaning of freedom.

Defining Progressive Black Religion

As I examine religion's public role in African diasporic communities such as the United States, I want to advocate for progressive approaches to black religion in general and black Christianity in particular. Progressive black religion realizes that sacred texts and authoritative religious traditions must be continually reinterpreted for those texts and traditions to remain relevant.

Flexibility and an appreciation for pluralism and nuance, rather than a rigid adherence to narrowly defined dogmas, should characterize the ethos of progressive black religion.

This discussion, however, should not romanticize black religion. There are problematic contemporary manifestations of black religion that must be subjected to rigorous critique. For example, after more than twenty years of serving as an educator and religious leader, I am dismayed by how many black churches remain enslaved to antiquated scriptural hermeneutics and colonial theologies. These hegemonic hermeneutics and theologies oppress women, girls, LGBTQ persons, persons who are economically vulnerable and differently abled, and persons from different religious traditions or those with no religious affiliation.

I made a momentous shift in my work as a scholar, religious leader, and activist eleven years ago. I decided to stop obsessing about what was wrong with religion. Instead, attempting to channel the creativity and courage of past and present artists and activists, I rededicated my life to building theoretical and pragmatic alternatives that model inclusive community and the democratic sharing of power.

Consequently, in addition to my work as the president of Chicago Theological Seminary and a senior program adviser at the Smithsonian Institution, I have spent the last eleven years establishing The Open Church of Maryland, a progressive and predominantly black religious community in Baltimore. This community is committed to radically inclusive love, courageous social justice activism, and compassionate interfaith collaboration.[12]

When I talk about theopoetics in progressive black religion, I am not simply opining about the theoretical. I am "tangibilitating" in the practical. The tangible yield of this practical, collaborative work with other committed leaders has resulted in the creation of a small and stable religious congregation whose membership is balanced between heterosexual persons and LGBTQ persons. From its inception, the congregation has endorsed my officiating of LGBTQ weddings. The congregation also engages regularly in interfaith collaboration with persons from diverse religious, spiritual, and ethical traditions.

Civic engagement is also important at The Open Church. The congregation has participated in various social justice initiatives, including community events to promote health equity for older adults and persons affected by HIV/AIDS, public advocacy for the moral and civic equality of LGBTQ persons, support for youth in Baltimore's foster care system, and strategic financial investments in a congregation in Kenya.

The Open Church is also striving to be a community where power is shared, especially the power associated with the pulpit. In black Protestant churches, the pulpit microphone is arguably the most visible and important symbol of communal power. Consequently, the ways a congregation permits or prohibits certain people from "taking the mic" indicate a great deal about the community's explicit and implicit values.

At The Open Church, congregants who were interested received a seminary-level introduction to preaching course from me. I have taught homiletics, the art and science of preaching, in several divinity schools and seminaries. These congregants are as likely to preach the sermon on Sundays as I am. Additionally, examples of "sacred siblings" from diverse traditions who have spoken in our pulpit recently include, but are not limited to, a Humanist professor, a Muslim rap artist, a Jewish visual artist, a Zen Buddhist priest, an imam, a Yoruba priest, a Catholic priest, and a Buddhist lama. The sexual and gender identities of these speakers ranged from LGBTQ and gender nonconforming to heterosexual and cisgender. The congregation received all these speakers gladly and engaged them in respectful and provocative dialogue.

In establishing The Open Church, we have drawn inspiration from the pioneering work of progressive black luminaries such as Howard Thurman, Zora Neale Hurston, and Cecil Williams. Howard Thurman was a theologian, pastor, and writer who cofounded the Church for the Fellowship of All Peoples in San Francisco, the first fully racially integrated congregation in the United States. Zora Neale Hurston was a writer and anthropologist who famously chronicled the distinctive folk idioms and religious sensibilities of black people in the United States in the early twentieth century. Cecil Williams is a theologian, pastor, and community activist who led the Glide Memorial United Methodist Church in San Francisco in implementing a theology of radical hospitality.[13]

The purposeful embrace of theopoetics has aided The Open Church's ongoing experiment of radical religious openness. For example, theopoetics played an invaluable role in a sermon on "biblical authority" that I preached in the congregation's earliest days. This sermon enabled the congregation to replace rigid, conservative notions of biblical authority with more Spirit-infused, African-derived approaches that value Spirit and embodied experiences as "texts" that are as sacred as the scriptures.[14]

The fifty-five founding members of The Open Church were eager to explore progressive ways of being religious. Yet the conservative approaches to biblical interpretation that many of them learned in their formative years made some of them fearful of critiquing problematic aspects of the Bible, such as its endorsement of patriarchy, slavery, and genocide.

A pedagogical intervention was clearly needed to enable congregants to think more expansively about the positive and negative roles of the Bible in past and present quests for social liberation. Thus, I preached in 2012 a sermon titled "Interpretation for Proclamation: Working with the Book" only a few weeks after the congregation had begun meeting regularly for worship services. The sermon was filled with academic teaching and insisted that not everything in the "Good Book" is necessarily good news. Consequently, the sermon encouraged congregants to wrestle with—and question—the Bible.

According to the reports of congregants, theopoetics dramatically enhanced the sermon's effectiveness. Before launching into the sermon's more conceptual teaching, I arrested the congregation's attention through dramatic acts. After reverently placing the Bible on the pulpit, I genuflected before the pulpit and began passionately "worshipping" the Bible. I bowed my face repeatedly to the ground with my hands raised, giving unashamed devotion to the Bible as if the Bible were a "deity" sitting upon the "throne" of the pulpit.

Then using small bungee cords, I bound my feet, my neck, and finally my hands. The cords symbolized the shackles that white colonizers brutally employed to enslave millions of Africans in the transatlantic slave trade. With my limbs bound and mobility severely limited, I began hopping in front of the same Bible on the pulpit that had been worshipped moments before. My movements were intended to dramatize the laborious movements of shackled Africans as they were cruelly marched onto slave ships bound for the Americas and the Caribbean.

These dramatized actions were not simply a prelude to the sermon. They were a sermon unto themselves. This was the message conveyed by my movements: slavish, literal readings of the Bible by white colonizers in the fifteenth through nineteenth centuries facilitated the enslavement of Africans and the grand larceny of land and other wealth. Or as the famous mantra declares, "When the Europeans came to Africa, the Europeans had the Bible, and the Africans had the land. When the Europeans left Africa, the Africans had the Bible, and the Europeans had the land."

I then declared to the congregation that "worship" of the Bible is a form of idolatry that some scholars rightly call "bibliolatry"— ascribing ultimate authority to a sacred book instead of courageously wrestling with the book to discern contemporary, liberating meanings emerging from the book. With my neck, hands, and feet still bound, I insisted that churches cannot speak prophetically (our necks are bound), embrace diverse groups lovingly (our hands are bound), or run swiftly to address social challenges (our feet are bound) because of our enslavement to conservative readings of the Bible.

At that point in the dramatized sermon, Vincent Stringer—a congregant, vocal studies professor, and professional singer— began singing a mesmerizing version of the black spiritual "O Freedom."

O Freedom! O Freedom!
O Freedom over me!

An' before I'd be a slave,
I'll be buried in my grave,
An' go home to my Lord,
An' be free.

As his sonorous baritone voice echoed across the sanctuary, I released my hands, feet, and neck from the bungee cords and emphatically threw the cords at the pulpit. My dramatic actions were a tangible response to the singing of the spiritual, and the spiritual was a sonic interpretation of my emancipation from the cords. Although I continued to preach a sermon with words after these dramatic actions, the theopoetic portion of the sermon had set the stage and delivered the message: individual and social freedom—especially for black Christians—will require manumission from conservative religious approaches and the embrace of progressive approaches to religious texts and cultural traditions.

In promoting progressive religion, The Open Church has employed theopoetics in other ways. For instance, we have occasionally sponsored a rotating art gallery in the main hallway of The Open Church's facility. Vincent Stringer, who is also a poet and visual artist, serves as the curator. The gallery displays beautiful and provocative renderings from Baltimore artists. Some of the artwork transgresses cultural orthodoxies, thereby inviting people to reflect more deeply on topics such as gender identity, sexual identity, and religious affiliation. Some of the artists have visited The Open Church to discuss their attempts to channel creativity in the service of social justice.

The black religious imagination, with its innovative use of theopoetics, is sorely needed at this moment to challenge and change systems of domination. This imagination is also needed to exhort some black religious communities to confess and repent their complicity in the same systems of domination they seemingly protest. Furthermore, these black religious communities can signal the authenticity of their confession and repentance by creating progressive, inclusive, and equitable communities where people embody Jesus's revolutionary plea in the prayer that he taught his disciples (Matt 6:9–13): "God's *kin*-dom come. God's will be done, *on earth* as it is in heaven."[15]

Mapping the Public Square

When progressive black religious communities endeavor to bring the inclusion and social justice of God's *kin*-dom to earth, they are doing public theology. The theologian Andrew Bradstock provides an expansive understanding of public theology: "Public theology is concerned with bringing a theological perspective to bear upon contemporary debates in the public square. . . . In the delightful words of the prophet Jeremiah (Jeremiah 29:7), public theology seeks first the 'welfare of the city,' wanting to use the resources at its disposal to support the task of building a decent and fair society and foster human flourishing. . . . Always its concern will be the ongoing transformation of society in the direction of justice and peace."[16]

Instead of fixating endlessly on pews, offering plates, and worship services, public theology realizes that street corners are also sanctuaries where grace is present and justice and forgiveness are needed. Some of the most incisive and spiritually adept people whom I have met are not in elite universities or stately cathedrals but in "public squares"—those shifting social sites of cultural commentary, political critique, and "no-nonsense" common sense.

Public squares occur in coffee shops and barbershops, community improvement meetings and protest rallies. In such settings, the intellectual work is not beholden to the professorial politics of university tenure and promotion policies. Rather, straight talk and street knowledge put flesh and blood on skeletal theories. In many public squares, people are geographically closer to the pain and anxiety of ceaseless violence and lethal poverty. Consequently, people in public squares keep their rhetoric real to keep people alive.

Furthermore, some of the most compelling interpretations of Scripture I have ever encountered have come from so-called working-class people in the congregations I have served and on the streets of the cities in which I have lived, such as New York City, Chicago, and Baltimore. For example, there was a man in the first church I served in Baltimore who worked at the funeral home around the corner from the church. One of his responsibilities was to wash the funeral home's fleet of cars in the alley behind the funeral home. As I traveled around the neighborhood fulfilling various pastoral duties, I had frequent conversations with him. His straightforward wisdom was so illuminating that I affectionately called him the "alley philosopher."

The "alley philosopher" and many other people like him—custodians, cafeteria workers, and postal carriers—have convinced me that I must be more than an academic. Their incisive thinking has motivated me to be a public intellectual—that is, a thinker whose analyses are informed and transformed by the pragmatic concerns of "everyday people." John Hope Franklin, the towering historian who chronicled the creativity and heroism of black people, championed the importance of intellectual accessibility. He suggested that if intellectual discourse is worthwhile, "it should be placed within the reach of all."[17]

Policy *and* Poetry: A Dialectical Tension

The overturning of unjust public policies and the promotion of just public policies are crucial aspects of any theory of change. Therefore, progressive black religion should concern itself with policy. Measurable policy wins, however, do not exhaust the capacity of progressive black religion to sponsor social change.

A sobering truth emerging from many civil and human rights movements is that legislation cannot combat all dimensions of injustice and prejudice. Some of the worst manifestations of injustice and prejudice remain locked behind the steel doors of the most gated house—the human heart. The doors in that fenced fortress are rarely breached by protests that lead to new policies. Rather, these doors are often pried open slowly by the persuasive dimensions of theopoetics. Progressive black religion ought to be as concerned with poetry as it is with policy.

Black religion's unashamed appeal to the poetic dimensions of social transformation distinguishes it from many other modalities of social change. Theopoetics can move hate-clenched hands to unlock and open the doors of the heart, enabling love to rectify injustice and transform prejudice into never-before-imagined partnerships. A redeemed United States and a transformed world will require investments in both righteous policies and robust poetry.

Policy work is crucial and can articulate effectively what the problems are and what the potential solutions might be. Yet the most contested ground in social transformation is often the space between head and heart. Frequently, we *know* what to do, but we need the power of poetry to enliven our *will* to do it.

Black religion understands that often before we can become politicians, we must first be artists. As the inimitable artist Paul Robeson once mused, "The purpose of art is not just to show life as it is, but to show life as it should be."[18] In other words, social justice work is not exhausted by the indicative mood, which is the grammatical mood that tells us *what is*. Social justice work also requires the subjunctive mood, which is the grammatical mood that tells us what *may be*. A theory of change rooted in black religion welcomes the creative tension between policy and poetry.

The necessity for poetry to accompany policy was illustrated vividly at former president Bill Clinton's first inauguration. During his inauguration on January 20, 1993, President Clinton invited Maya Angelou, poet extraordinaire, to recite a poem. As the poet who taught us why caged birds can still sing, Angelou realized that the cosmic possibilities of "morning" always extend beyond the occasionally lackluster language of public policy. As powerful as policy makers are, we still need prophetic poets to envision the higher possibilities the universe intends for us. Angelou titled her poem "On the Pulse of the Morning."

Twenty-eight years later, during the inauguration of President Joe Biden on January 20, 2021, Amanda Gorman, another black female poet extraordinaire, mesmerized the world with "The Hill We Climb," a poem about the possibilities of the morning.

Gorman's intervention was especially timely as she uttered her inspiring words a mere two weeks after a brazen insurrection on the United States Capitol on January 6, 2021. This insurrection created deep distress in the body politic and cast a menacing shadow on a world already grappling with the suffering of the Covid-19 pandemic. Nevertheless, as a prophetic poet of morning-like possibilities, Amanda Gorman, as her predecessor Maya Angelou had done, refused to let nightfall have the last word.

Policy makers will come and go, but prophetic poets must always remind us of the morning. On the horizon of hope, there is the morning star, the astronomical sign announcing morning's arrival. This star provides assurance that in a world where love lives, night cannot last forever. The morning will always come.

(Theo)Poetic Pedagogy: The Classroom and Cosmological Power

I conclude by reflecting on the connection between theopoetics and pedagogy. Theopoetics can provide students and teachers with a significant pedagogical resource—the transcendent power of the ancestors. In my teaching experiences, students have responded positively to the prospect of transcendent power, irrespective of their religious affiliation or lack thereof. I have witnessed even among secular students a hunger for mysticism that bestows a greater sense of purpose in their educational pursuits and social activism.

According to African cosmology, there are dimensions of Spirit and power available to us beyond what our finite senses can detect. The visible and invisible dimensions of existence are connected by Spirit—the eternal life force animating the cosmos with divine purpose. The theologian Gayraud Wilmore vividly describes African cosmology: "African religions know nothing of a rigid demarcation between the natural and the supernatural. All of life is permeated with forces or powers. . . . The Supreme Being, ancestors, spirits resident in or associated with certain natural phenomena, and living humans who possess gifts of healing or of making mischief, were all united in one comprehensive, invisible system that has its own laws which sustain the visible world and ordinary life for the good of all."[19]

The ancestors are a key component of an African-derived cosmology. When honorable members of an African tribe die, they continue to live as spirits. These ancestral spirits provide guidance to those who are still physically alive.[20] African-derived ways of knowing acknowledge and humbly access the wisdom and power of the ancestors in all endeavors, including the rigorous pursuit of knowledge in classrooms.

Theopoetics is a mechanism to invoke and provide hospitality to the cosmic presence and power of the ancestors in classrooms. This lesson was indelibly etched into my psyche when I delivered the Bray Lectures in 2006–7 as part of the two hundredth anniversary of the abolition of the transatlantic slave trade in the British Empire. As the Bray Lecturer, I was invited by two British religious organizations to explore the contemporary social justice consequences of Britain's colonialism and complicity in the slave trade. The first set of lectures was given in Ghana and the second set in England.

One of the Ghana lectures was delivered at St. Nicholas (Anglican) Seminary in Cape Coast. For more than two hours, I led a graduate-level seminar on postcolonial biblical hermeneutics in a lecture hall filled with several dozen seminary students and faculty. Midway through the seminar, the dean of the seminary called for a brief break.

As a seasoned teacher, I was accustomed to the practice of a break in the middle of a seminar to allow students and faculty to refresh themselves. In the United States, my students frequently retreat to vending machines for snacks during the break. However, the African students at St. Nicholas Seminary approached the break in a different manner. They irrevocably transformed my understanding of theopoetics and pedagogy.

Unbeknown to me, many of these African students had small musical instruments inside their desks and around the room. When the seminar break began, they seized their instruments and immediately broke into the most marvelous music. With their bodies swaying, hands clapping, and voices ringing, they sang unashamed praise to God. In the middle of a sophisticated seminar on postcolonial hermeneutics, theopoetic African praise burst forth!

This was a profound pedagogical lesson for me: precise theology and passionate doxology can be mutually reinforcing. Adoration of God and acknowledgment of the ancestors are expressions of gratitude and a humble entreaty for divine guidance into the deepest dimensions of learning where *knowledge* is transformed into *wisdom*. When we restored "order" in the classroom and returned to the theoretical work in the seminar's second half, the intellectual insights shared among all of us were even more acute than the insights shared before the "praise break."

In addition to enriching my pedagogy, these African students motivated me to interrogate more carefully the cultural assumptions of various epistemologies—the principles and practices undergirding how we create and disseminate knowledge. In the epistemologies of certain white cultural frameworks that colonized the world and continue to colonize many classrooms, dispassionate detachment supposedly facilitates the life of the mind. Yet this detachment in my experience often leaves students and teachers void of an animating energy that connects knowledge with real-world relevance and larger meaning.

In African-derived epistemologies, passionate employment of the body through song and ritual enlivens the cognitive, emotive, and volitional dimensions of students and teachers. This integrated approach creates a more porous atmosphere in the classroom and enables the sharing and vulnerability that foster lasting transformation of the head, the heart, and the will. Theopoetics can decolonize epistemological frameworks and pedagogical practices, thereby aiding what the womanist theologian Linda Thomas calls the process of "reconstructing knowledge": "Reconstructing knowledge means tearing down myths that have paralyzed communities, and re-creating truths that have been buried in annals containing vast sources of knowledge. . . . It may be knowledge based on human experience as well as theory, and it decidedly involves the inclusion of the ideas, theories, orientations, experiences, and worldviews of persons and groups who have previously been excluded."[21] As we educate students to solve pressing problems in the public square, the inclusion of African-derived worldviews can enhance our pedagogy.

During my more than twenty years of teaching in divinity schools and universities, I have begun most class sessions with the proverb "Where there is no music, the Spirit will not come." After the proverb, I then sing some black spiritual or freedom song.[22] Diverse groups of students have embraced warmly this simple, theopoetic gesture. The musical beginning has infused the classroom with pedagogical power that has had a lasting impact on students and me. When teaching with the transcendent power of the ancestors, classrooms have become even more provocative and productive sites of transformation.

I road tested my theopoetic pedagogy on one occasion at Harvard. The results were positive. As an adjunct lecturer, I taught a Harvard Divinity School course in 2016 titled "Preaching, Healing, and Justice." A section of the syllabus described the course's purpose: "Suffocating poverty, police brutality, gang violence, racist and heterosexist hate speech and crimes (to name but a few) constitute serious 'public health' threats to the body politic. In the face of such threats, there is an urgent need for competent 'doctors of the soul' who dispense healing balm through careful and courageous religious rhetoric and imaginative religious rituals." In the course, students witnessed firsthand the social significance of performing cultural and religious practices with intellectual sophistication and artistic finesse.

In the final assignment of the course, students were asked to deliver a eulogy and create a funeral liturgy for one of the recent victims of police-related lethal force: Rekia Boyd (Chicago, Illinois), Michael Brown (Ferguson, Missouri), Tanisha Anderson (Cleveland, Ohio), Eric Garner (New York, New York), and Freddie Gray (Baltimore, Maryland). If I were to teach the course now, I would add other tragic examples, including Breonna Taylor (Louisville, Kentucky) and George Floyd (Minneapolis, Minnesota). Many students acknowledged how the relevance and specificity of the final assignment plumbed the depths of their cognitive and emotive intelligence as well as their artistic imagination.

A key contributor to the course's success, in my estimation, was the infusion of Spirit and cosmological power unleashed through theopoetics. On the first day of class, staying true to my long-standing pedagogical practice, I introduced myself to the students and then remarked, "There is a West African proverb that says, 'Where there is no music, the Spirit will not come.'" I then began singing a black spiritual/freedom song, using a version of the lyrics that was inclusive and respectful of the diverse students in the course:

> *I woke up this morning with my mind stayed on freedom.* . . .
> *Hallelu . . . Hallelu . . . Hallelujah!*

After singing it through the first time, I invited the students to join me. We lifted our voices joyfully and sang the song a few more times. Some students seemed pleasantly surprised that a professor in a Harvard classroom would begin a course in such an unorthodox way.

Since this was my first teaching experience at Harvard, my wife, Lazetta, joined me in the classroom to provide moral support. Lazetta is a nationally respected certified financial planner with an undergraduate degree from the University of Virginia and an MBA from Wake Forest University.[23] She loves to learn and is inspired by university students. Thus, she was eagerly anticipating the two-hour seminar.

In addition to her impressive professional pedigree, Lazetta possesses a deep and dexterous spirituality. She practices Christianity and is conversant with certain practices of African Traditional Religions, especially the veneration of the ancestors. On my first day of teaching at Harvard, Lazetta became a spiritual medium through whom the ancestors visited the classroom. The ancestral visitation she facilitated at Harvard on a cold afternoon in January 2016 had spiritual roots in a mystical encounter that she and I shared on a hot African beach in June 2001.

Lazetta and I visited Benin in 2001 as part of a cultural exchange trip sponsored by Wake Forest University, where I at the time was a divinity school professor. During the trip, we prayed on the beach at Ouidah, a coastal town in Benin, which is both the center of the African religion Vodun and an infamous port from which approximately one million Africans were shipped into slavery. Ouidah is an exceedingly "porous" place spiritually, where centuries of the positive energy of African religious worship intersect the negative energy of enslavement and degradation.

As we prayed, remembered, and mourned the nearly one million lives decimated by slavery from that very beach, Lazetta for the first time started "speaking in tongues."[24] She began speaking a fluid set of Spirit-inspired utterances or languages. The tone of her utterances was hauntingly mournful. We were convinced then, and remain convinced now, that Lazetta was giving linguistic witness to the horrendous pain that remains in the cosmic atmosphere at Ouidah.

Even centuries later, the screams and torment of countless Africans, as their families were separated and bodies brutalized, still play like a melancholy cosmic soundtrack on repeat. Occasionally, the ancestors enable certain people to serve as mechanisms for unmuting those sounds and allowing them to enter our ears and pierce our hearts. We believe that Lazetta was selected that day by the ancestors for that purpose. This mystical encounter was a commissioning for us to serve as agents of remembrance, restorative justice, and reconciliation.

Since then, Lazetta has regularly manifested the "gift of tongues" and served as a medium through whom certain African ancestors communicate. When Lazetta and I visited Ghana in 2006, she had her first visitation with the ancestral spirit of Yaa Asantewaa, the eighteenth- and nineteenth-century African (Ashanti tribe) queen who valiantly led a rebellion to overthrow British colonialism.[25] Lazetta continues to have occasional visitations with Yaa Asantewaa.

I now return to the first day of my 2016 Harvard course. As the students and I sang "I woke up this morning with my mind stayed on freedom," Lazetta sat in the classroom quietly observing. With the repetition of every chorus, her body began moving subtly but perceptibly, and tears flowed from her eyes. Having witnessed these embodied signs before, I knew that we were on the verge of an ancestral visitation.

Moments later, Lazetta began softly chanting in tongues and giving expression to the spirit who had just entered the room. The students observed this mystical encounter with openness and amazement. As I interpreted the event for them, I wanted them to take heart because we were not alone in the classroom. In the language of the New Testament, we were "surrounded by so great a cloud of [invisible] witnesses" from the outset of the course (Heb 12:1). When the visitation began, I had a premonition of the primary spirit whom Lazetta was channeling. Lazetta subsequently confirmed that my premonition was correct: Yaa Asantewaa graced us with her ancestral presence.

In a Harvard course designed to equip students with diverse tools for careers of healing and justice in the public square, theopoetics conjured the spiritual presence of Yaa Asantewaa—a regal African freedom fighter—to accompany us on the journey. Every seminar session throughout the semester teemed with transcendent power that facilitated compelling demonstrations of cognitive and emotive intelligence among students. In the course evaluation, a student wrote, "Dr. Braxton created a unique classroom culture where students brought their whole selves, not just their minds but also their hearts and spirits. By modeling courage and spiritual depth in his own lectures, Dr. Braxton encouraged students to share deeply of themselves, creating a brave space for constructive and sometimes challenging but necessary class discussions." I was heartened by this student's gracious evaluation. I was also mindful that the Spirit, Yaa Asantewaa, and other ancestral freedom fighters were really the professors in the course. I was simply a willing teaching assistant with a wide-open theopoetic imagination.

"Lift Every Voice and Sing"

In a poem that would eventually become the "Negro National Anthem," James Weldon Johnson imagined an equitable social order where every voice would sing,

> *Lift ev'ry voice and sing,*
> *Till earth and heaven ring,*
> *Ring with the harmonies of liberty.*[26]

When Johnson wrote this poem in 1900, the United States was a deeply segregated society. The racial terrorism of lynching was acute and would eventually compel another artist—Billie Holliday—to lament the "strange fruit" of black bodies hanging on southern trees as thousands of black people were lynched.

From a policy standpoint, Johnson's depiction of social inclusion seemed unobtainable at the time. Yet the scholar Soyica Diggs Colbert rightly insists that aesthetic production possesses "the capacity to imagine the unreasonable and impossible in order to open political possibility to reason and to what western episteme may categorize as unreason."[27] In the decades since Johnson penned those words, the "unreason" in his exhortation has inspired many freedom fighters in the public square to protest and picket, to strategize and organize, for justice and peace. Langston Hughes was right. The songs and verses of poets possess "atomic" power!

In a poignant manifesto about the black scholar's responsibility to the community, Vincent Harding, an activist and key adviser to the civil rights movement, identified theopoetics as an indispensable part of the scholar's vocation: "I think that a part of this responsibility is to sing, constantly to sing, to and with the people; in other words, to affirm the people, to celebrate the people, to clarify all those elements of their life that have been built through the pain of the land, all those elements of their life that have been built on the way to a new life. . . . And of course, to sing to them, scholars must sing to themselves."[28] Cue the music. I am ready to clear my throat and "sing" until the world is filled with more justice and love!

7

Sanctification and Proclamation

Walking with God

Spirituality is a holistic and continuous process of becoming. . . . It enables me to look at others with mutual respect. Spirituality is always coupled with justice. The more I grow spiritually, the more I am concerned with justice and taking action for justice.

—Mercy Amba Oduyoye, quoted in
Dwight N. Hopkins, *Being Human:
Race, Culture, and Religion*

The Connection between "Sacred Talking" and "Sanctified Walking"

Maria Stewart, a nineteenth-century abolitionist, offered a stirring petition for moral purification.* With poetic imagery alluding to the call of the prophet Isaiah, she invoked God's sanctifying presence upon her life, her church, and her preacher:

O thou King eternal, immortal, invisible, and only wise God, before whom angels bow and seraphs veil their faces, crying holy, holy, holy, is the Lord God Almighty. True and

---

* This chapter was originally published in *A Spiritual Life: Perspectives from Poets, Prophets, and Preachers*, edited by Allan Hugh Cole Jr. (Louisville, KY: Westminster John Knox, 2011), 231–41. Copyright © 2011 by Brad R. Braxton. Reprinted with permission of Brad R. Braxton.

righteous are thy ways, thou King of Saints. Help me, thy poor unworthy creature, humbly to prostrate myself before thee, and implore that mercy which my sins have justly forfeited. O God, I know that I am not worthy of a place at thy footstool; but to whom shall I go but unto thee? Thou alone hast the words of eternal life. . . .

Bless the church to which I belong, and grant that when thou makest up thy jewels, not one soul shall be found missing. Bless him in whom thou hast set over us as a watchman in Zion. Let not his soul be discouraged. May he not fail to declare the whole counsel of God.[1]

Stewart recognized that sanctification was indispensable for authentic discipleship and an effective ministry of proclamation. Pulpit power was linked to the quest for holiness for many of our forebears in the faith. Yet in contemporary Christianity, I wonder if we have neglected the wisdom of the ancestors and need to reclaim some timeless truths.

One timeless truth is that the quest to embody the holy attributes of a holy God provides power for the holy act of preaching a holy word so that we become holy people prepared for holy living. In this chapter, I pursue a straightforward theme: the sanctification of the messenger is a crucial aspect of the proclamation of the message. Homiletics and holiness are inextricably linked, and by exploring the link in a robust manner, preachers avail themselves of valuable resources for pulpit excellence. While my reflections are aimed primarily at preachers, persons from many different walks of life can benefit from this conversation about spiritual life and walking with God.

Homiletics is the art of sermon creation, proclamation, and evaluation. The term "homiletics" comes from the Greek verb *homileō*, which means "to talk." Thus, homiletics deals with "sacred talking." I contend that "sacred talking" must always be connected to "sanctified walking." When "sacred talking" divorces itself from "sanctified walking," preachers open themselves up to homiletic flunking and moral failing.

The brief story of Enoch in Genesis 5:22–24 accentuates the centrality of sanctified walking: "Enoch walked with God after the birth of Methuselah three hundred years, and had other sons and daughters. Thus all the days of Enoch were three hundred sixty-five years. Enoch walked with God; then he was no more, because God took him." Enoch is noteworthy, not because of the *quantity* of his years but rather for the *quality* of his life. Enoch receives a stellar compliment. The writer says twice that Enoch "walked with God." The verb "to walk" (*halak* in Hebrew) connotes a way of life or a person's conduct in the world. To say that Enoch "walked with God" is to say that he conducted his life in ways that pleased God. Enoch had an intimate connection with God.

Can the same be said of many preachers? A master of divinity degree, required for ordained ministry in many Christian traditions, does not necessarily ensure a sanctified life. The homiletician Noel Schoonmaker says it well: "It is possible to have a Master of Divinity without being in relationship with *the* Master of Divinity."[2]

Public victories in the pulpit usually have some grounding in the preacher's quest to embody God's amazing work of sanctification. In the pulpit, God uses us in spite of us. However, by pursuing a vibrant spiritual life, we ensure that God has the sharpest tools with which to work. Charles Spurgeon, the nineteenth-century British prince of the pulpit, emphasized the importance of giving God sharp tools: "It will be in vain for me to stock my library, or organize societies, or project schemes, if I neglect the culture of myself; for books, and agencies, and systems, are only remotely the instruments of my holy calling; my own spirit, soul, and body, are my nearest machinery for sacred service; my spiritual faculties, and my inner life, are my battle axe and weapons of war."[3]

Spurgeon's phrase "the culture of myself" deserves further exploration. Effective preachers pay as much attention to their interior culture as they do their exterior culture. In recent years, there have been numerous ministry conferences highlighting the need for "prophetic preaching." Prophetic preaching involves an intense critique of the social order. However, some preachers fail to examine their interior culture, much less critique it, with the same probing intensity.

A holistic prophetic ministry involves an investigation of the exterior culture in which a preacher lives and cultivation of the interior culture within a preacher's soul. Too often, prophetic preachers talk about the devil in the exterior culture while giving consent for the devil to preside at the altar in their souls. As preachers and pastors, we tend altars in our public sanctuaries. The question is, Who is tending the private altar in our souls? A failure to set proper boundaries in the interior world can quickly contribute to a transgression of boundaries in the exterior world. Consequently, conversations concerning prophetic preaching are incomplete apart from a prophetic spirituality. Prophetic spirituality keeps in creative tension the external culture in the street and the internal culture in the soul.

In spite of our failures, God still uses us. If that's not grace, I don't know what is. God's willingness to use us in spite of us calls to mind a comment from William A. Jones Jr., the late, legendary pastor of Bethany Baptist Church in Brooklyn, New York. He once suggested that some ministers have such marvelous preaching gifts that you hope that they will never leave a pulpit once they enter one. And some of these same ministers have such messy lives that you hate to think they will ever enter a pulpit when they are outside of one.

In these tough times, the world desperately needs a new-found commitment to integrity among preachers—an earnest attempt to close the gap between our marvelous gifts and our messy lives. What would happen to our preaching if we spent as much time cultivating our spirituality as we did preparing to preach? God would be pleased, the church would be stronger, and the world would be more loving.

Coming to Terms with Spirituality, Holiness, and Sanctification

Clarifying important terms will facilitate this consideration of the spiritual life. These terms include (1) "spirituality," (2) "holiness," and (3) "sanctification."

Spirituality

The Latin word *spiritus* means "breath" or "wind" and, by extension, "life force."[4] *Spiritus* is the life force existing in individuals and communities. The creation story in Genesis 1 emphasizes the life force that hovers over the unruly waters, transforming chaos into creation. In Genesis 1, the Hebrew word for divine breath is *ruach*, and the Latin word is *spiritus*. If *spiritus* is the divine breath animating creation and all its creatures, then *spirituality* is an acknowledgment that breath comes from God and that breath will lead us back to God.

In other words, spirituality entails personal and communal stewardship over the breath—the life force—that God has breathed into us. To preachers, matters of breath should be of utmost concern, especially since preaching is heavily dependent on the breath. No matter how melodic your voice or poetic your prose, preaching is impossible without breath. Spirituality involves giving an account to God and others concerning the use of our breath, our life force, both inside and outside the pulpit.

The womanist ethicist Emilie Townes presents a definition of spirituality worthy of embrace: "Womanist spirituality is not grounded in the notion that spirituality is a force, a practice separate from who we are moment by moment. It is the deep kneading of humanity and divinity into one breath, one hope, one vision. . . . It is a style of witness that seeks to cross the yawning chasm of hatreds and prejudices and oppressions into a deeper and richer love of God as we experience Jesus in our lives. This love extends to self and others. . . . This understanding of spirituality seeks to grow into wholeness of spirit and body, mind and heart—into holiness in God."[5] Spirituality involves an assortment of attitudes and actions—some as regular and unnoticeable as breathing—that propel us toward God's holiness.

Holiness

When considering spirituality, Emilie Townes ultimately locates holiness in God. This is instructive because all understandings of holiness will miss the mark until we realize that holiness is

primarily not something we do; it is who God is. Holiness, first
and foremost, is an attribute of God, not a human action.

   One task of prophetic ministry is reasserting the centrality
of God's holiness in our conceptions of prophetic preaching. For
evidence, I summon the prophet Isaiah to the witness stand. In
his unforgettable call story, Isaiah receives a glimpse of God's
glory in the heavenly temple, and this prophet is confronted
with the chief characteristic of God—*holiness*: "In the year that
King Uzziah died, I saw the Lord sitting on a throne, high and
lofty; and the hem of his robe filled the temple. Seraphs were in
attendance above him. . . . And one called to another and said:
'Holy, holy, holy is the Lord of hosts; the whole earth is full of his
glory'" (Isa 6:1–3).

   A redemptive rendezvous with a holy God was the precur-
sor to Isaiah's prophetic ministry. God is so holy that seraphs
had to hit the repeat button on their celestial soundtrack: "Holy,
holy, holy." Their repetition was a rhetorical attempt to plumb
the unsearchable sanctity of God.

   Holiness is a significant attribute of God's character. The biblical scholar Walter Brueggemann observes, "The term *holiness* . . .
refers to the radical otherness of Yahweh, who may not be easily
approached, who may not be confused with anyone or anything
else, and who lives alone in a prohibitive zone where Israel can
enter only guardedly, intentionally, and at great risk."[6] Thus, the
term "holiness" expresses the unique nature of God. The difference between God and humans is more than quantitative. God is
not simply a supersized version of us. To speak of God as holy
is to affirm that there is an infinite qualitative difference (to recall
the philosopher Søren Kierkegaard's observation) in God's being.
Holiness is an attestation of God's difference from us.

   However, the womanist theologian Kelly Brown Douglas
reminds us that alongside the radical otherness of God, there
exist other radical impulses: divine love and passion, which create an "insatiable desire to foster life" and an "unquenchable thirst
for that which is not yet."[7]

   Douglas enables us to perceive more clearly the marvelous
mystery of God's holiness. Simultaneously, holiness involves

God's *infinite difference* from us and God's *insatiable desire* for us. God is so dramatically unlike us, and at the same time, God so desperately wants to be with us. Even though God is radically other, there is a quality in God's character that compels God to be in relationship with us. Holiness encapsulates divine difference and divine desire.

God's *difference* sets the standard for the relationship, reminding us of God's transcendent presence and power. God's *desire* invites us into relationship with God, reminding us that God passionately seeks to bestow on us love and life. Thus, holiness is God's insatiable desire to transform our relationship with God and all other relationships in our lives. A radically other God seeks to initiate with us radically transformed relationships so that all our relationships lead to life.

Holiness is not an outdated puritanical concept. Holiness is the ultimate social justice category. Holiness encompasses God's relationship with us. Yet God does not allow holiness to remain solely on the vertical register. Holiness becomes horizontal when God says to Israel, and to us by extension, "Sanctify yourselves therefore, and be holy, for I am holy" (Lev 11:44). At the horizontal level, holiness is our attempt, made possible by God's Spirit, to seek right relationships with others because God has graciously decided to seek right relationship with us.

Since God is holy and desires transformed relationships, we should be holy and seek transformed relationships. Holiness is not simply a priestly concept; it is also a prophetic concept. Anyone who would dare to preach prophetically must come to grips with God's command for us to be holy.

Sanctification

The ethicist Barbara Holmes recasts sanctification in a compelling fashion: "The holiness that Jesus describes has less to do with pious character traits and more to do with the hosting of God's abiding presence. It is not effort but invitation that opens the human spirit to the possibility that God may sojourn with us."[8] If God chooses to abide with us, even for a little while, the anointed aroma of God—the same aroma that overflowed in the temple with Isaiah—surrounds us. This aroma is so thick and pervasive that even on some of our worst days, the aroma covers us, and we appear to the world as much better people than we are.

Sanctification is not the onerous effort to avoid scarlet letter sins. Sanctification is the ongoing invitation to host God's presence—a presence that radically transforms all our relationships, if we would only submit to it and let it have its way. Sanctification is ultimately not asceticism (denying ourselves to death), nor is it athleticism (working ourselves to death). Sanctification is acceptance, allowing God's Spirit to love us into new life, abundant life, and finally, everlasting life!

Practice, Practice, Practice: Resting, Embracing, Meditating

Some skeptics might ask, "What does all this have to do with preaching?" My response is, "Everything." More ministers need to prioritize the Holy Spirit and sanctification in their overall discipleship and in their preparation and delivery of sermons.[9] In an essay on preaching that I coauthored with Martha Simmons, we contend that "the Holy Spirit must constantly remind each proclaimer of the gospel . . . that to preach a *life-changing* word requires a preacher with a *changed life*."[10] Thus, I now explore three practices than can help preachers (and many other people too) change their lives and become better conduits for God's life-changing power.

Resting

Walking with God involves resting. Exodus 20:8 clearly commands us to remember the Sabbath day and keep it holy. Yet instead of following that biblical commandment, too many preachers read the noncanonical books of "First and Second Hesitations" as it relates to Sabbath keeping.

In his book *Rest in the Storm: Self-Care Strategies for Clergy and Other Caregivers*, the ethicist Kirk Byron Jones chronicles why preachers hesitate and eventually fail to keep Sabbath. First, some preachers succumb to the myth of indispensability. We feel that the ministry or the church service will not run effectively unless we are there all the time. The myth of indispensability fosters a "messianic complex," the idolatrous belief that we are omnipotent and omnipresent and must do what everyone asks and make every appointment.

The need to be needed can be dangerous and addictive, and it leads us to believe the myth of indispensability. The myth often sounds like this among some pastors: "I can't take a vacation because if I go away for a couple of weeks, I may not be the pastor when I get back." Let's be honest—if you won't be the pastor after two weeks of vacation, then you really aren't the pastor now.

Second, some preachers confuse activity for productivity. We live in a world of constant motion. The culture coaxes us into doing many things, and we rarely pause to ask if the activity is worth doing in the first place. Catholic contemplative Thomas Merton challenges our "holy hyperactivity": "There is a pervasive form of contemporary violence . . . [and that is] activism and overwork. . . . To allow oneself to be carried away by a multitude of conflicting concerns, to surrender to too many demands, to commit oneself to too many projects, to want to help everyone in everything, is to succumb to violence."[11] Self-neglect is a form of violence. Irrespective of the size of our church memberships and annual budgets, if we are unable to cultivate other congregational leaders such that we can take off twenty-four or forty-eight hours each week and rest from our labors, we have been professionally negligent as it relates to equipping the saints (Eph 4:11–13).

As Rabbi Abraham Heschel suggested, we should keep Sabbath as a continual reminder that God created the world and that God can handle the world for twenty-four hours (or maybe even forty-eight hours) without our help.[12] Furthermore, my wife, Lazetta, insists that I should keep Sabbath since there has been no expansion in the Trinity. God is God, and God can handle things while we rest.

Embracing

Walking with God involves embracing our shadow side. For this wisdom, I am indebted to Gardner Taylor, the late venerable dean of American preachers and pastor emeritus of the Concord Baptist Church of Christ in Brooklyn, New York. In 2007, I sat for nearly two hours in his living room gleaning homiletic wisdom from him and learning great lessons about life. Toward the end of the conversation, he said that preachers, and all of us, are like a coin being held up to the light. One side of the coin is in the light, and the other side is in the shadows. It is important, he said, to recognize the shadow side as well.

We are genuinely on the path to sanctification and walking with God when we recognize and embrace our shadow side. On the underside of the coin of our character are impulses, tendencies, and memories that are not in the best interests of anyone, including our families, our congregations, and ourselves, and certainly not in the best interests of the commonwealth of God. Yet to deny the shadow side is to eventually set up circumstances where the shadows can be overcome by dense darkness.

I am no physicist, but I believe that shadows only exist where light is present. So embracing our shadow side means acknowledging those disturbing aspects of our character and keeping them in some modicum of light. As long as the underside of our character is somewhat in the light, the possibility for further conversion exists. When we fail to embrace our shadow side and turn the underside of our character away from the light, our demonic impulses will devour us in the deep darkness.

Embracing the shadow side requires a willingness to examine the depths of our character. It is serious work, not for the fainthearted. The poet Annie Dillard underscores the diligence required: "In the deeps [of our personality] are the violence and terror of which psychology has warned us. But if you ride these monsters deeper down . . . you find what our sciences cannot locate or name, the substrate, the ocean or matrix of ether which buoys the rest, which gives goodness its power for good, and evil its power for evil, the unified field: our complex and inexplicable caring for each other, and for our life together here."[13] Dillard is right. In order to care for ourselves and others, we must embrace our shadow side and travel into the depths of those parts of us that disturb us. By communing with them, we will prevent those parts of us from destroying us.

Meditating

Walking with God involves meditating. Meditation is a practice by which we embody the words of Psalm 46:10: "Be still and know that I am God!" There is a connection between stillness and the proper acknowledgment of God. As long as we are constantly moving, we can fool ourselves into believing that our activity is ultimately what matters. But stillness, the distant cousin of death, reminds us that some cemetery will eventually bring all our movement to a halt.

Stillness moves us to consider our mortality and God's eternality. In stillness, we realize afresh that we are simply walking dust. The theologian Howard Thurman creatively described the process of meditating: "How good it is to center down! To sit quietly and see one's self pass by!"[14] When was the last time you were still enough to watch yourself go by? And when you saw yourself, did you like what you saw? To meditate is to gather all our emotional and intellectual faculties to a point of "holy focus."[15] When there is a holy focus, our "third eye" will be blessed with homiletic sight, moral insight, and prophetic foresight.

So meditate. Take a walk and meditate. Pray and meditate. Sit by a body of water and meditate. Shut off your cell phone and meditate. Stop texting, tweeting, and emailing, and meditate. Let some of those deacons, trustees, and elders handle their own meetings, and go meditate. Recommend someone else to do some of those speaking engagements you get offered and go meditate!

Resting, Embracing, Meditating—Spiritual REM

REM, which in medical terminology stands for "rapid eye movement," is the creative, restoring form of sleep. Scientists believe that REM is important for declarative memory, which is the memory that stores facts. REM is also important for memory consolidation. By memory consolidation, scientists mean the removal of "certain undesirable modes of interaction in networks of cells in the cerebral cortex," a process called "unlearning." Consequently, during REM sleep, "those memories which are relevant . . . are further strengthened, whilst weaker, transient, 'noise' memory traces disintegrate."[16] If our REM sleep is disturbed, our creative capacity is diminished.

Preachers without "spiritual REM" (Resting, Embracing, Meditating) are not really walking with God; we are sleepwalking on the job because our creativity has been dulled. When we are REM deficient, our words come out slow and stagnant because we are sleepwalking. We get a great idea but can't turn it into a great sermon because we are REM deficient. We find an amazing sermon illustration, but we can't make it fit because we are REM deficient. We want to be more prophetic but end up throwing up our hands and feeling overwhelmed.

But when we get enough spiritual REM, the eyes of our souls are wide open. Our senses are heightened. Our creativity crescendos, and people know. When we are in the grocery store, people know. When we are at the airport, people know. When we are at the barbershop or the beauty salon, people know. When we are on the phone, people know. When we are in the pulpit, people know. What do they know? They know that they are in the presence of a preacher who has been in the presence of "the Presence."

To walk with God ultimately is to be in the presence of the Presence. When we as preachers walk with God, people will walk by us and say, "The presence of the Lord is here, the presence of the Lord is here, I feel it in the atmosphere, the presence of the Lord is here!"[17]

Part 2

Sermons

8

Beyond Control but within Reach

Sermonic Background

The initial inspiration for this sermon occurred during an international experience in 1997. During my pastorate at Douglas Memorial Community Church in Baltimore, Maryland (1995–2000), the Baltimore Jewish Council (BJC) invited several Baltimore civic leaders, including me, to participate in its annual ten-day mission trip to Israel in May 1997. The trip was designed to expose civic leaders to the cultures, customs, and political complexities in Israel. Informed by this experience, participants would be better equipped to foster intercultural collaboration. During the trip, we toured sites from Jerusalem to Tel Aviv to the Dead Sea, visited Arab Muslims residing in northern Israel, and engaged in dialogue with political and educational leaders throughout the country.

A signal moment on the trip was the "counterpart experience." BJC arranged an opportunity for each participant to meet with a professional counterpart, namely, a person living in Israel who had similar professional duties as each of us in the United States. For instance, Baltimore business leaders on the trip met with Israeli business leaders. Since I am a Christian minister, BJC arranged for me to meet with a Christian minister who was working in a small Christian congregation in Jerusalem. The meeting with my Christian counterpart in Israel was both instructive and explosive.

This Christian minister in Jerusalem offered me gracious hospitality as our meeting began. However, as the meeting progressed, and we shared our respective theological positions, hospitality gave way to tension. My Christian counterpart in Israel was deeply troubled to learn that I was a progressive Christian committed to interfaith collaboration. The more I talked about religious openness and respect for other religious traditions, the more vehemently he stressed the necessity of converting people from other traditions to Christianity. I eagerly informed him of my unwillingness to "evangelize" people from other religious traditions because these people already possessed the "good news" and "salvation" within their traditions.

As if those words from my mouth were an intolerable heresy, the minister said that I was a "disgrace" to the Christian faith. Sensing the escalating hostility in the room, I asked the minister if we could pray together. He adamantly refused to pray with me. We exchanged our goodbyes as pleasantly as was possible in that heated moment, and the meeting ended.

During a trip that took me nearly six thousand miles from my home, I had more in common with various people from other religious traditions whom I encountered in Israel than I did with a conservative Christian minister in Israel with whom I supposedly "shared" a religious tradition. It was especially intriguing to me that this fellow Christian considered me a "disgrace." I wrote in my journal shortly after the meeting:

> If openness to otherness makes me a disgrace to the faith, then let me be a disgrace. If the ability to struggle with—and accept—people with different viewpoints makes me a disgrace, then let me be a disgrace.
>
> If advocating for the validity, beauty, and importance of differences in race, class, gender, religion, physical ability, and sexual orientation makes me a disgrace, then let me be a disgrace. If critically challenging those who want to "control" God makes me a disgrace to the faith, then let me be a disgrace.
>
> I will continue to be a disgrace until there is no longer breath in my body. Then, on the great day of judgement, I will place my life in the hands of the living God, who is beyond control, and with dignity and courage, I will suffer any consequences associated with my commitment to honoring differences.

Upon returning to Baltimore, I wrote the sermon "Beyond Control but within Reach" and preached it initially at Douglas Memorial Community Church on Sunday, June 1, 1997. I have subsequently preached a version of this sermon in other settings, including a Unitarian Universalist Fellowship (Winston-Salem, North Carolina) in 2003, Vanderbilt University Divinity School (Nashville, Tennessee) in 2007, McCormick Theological Seminary (Chicago, Illinois) in 2010, Southern Methodist University's Perkins School of Theology (Dallas, Texas) in 2011, The Open Church of Maryland (Baltimore, Maryland) in 2012, and Pittsburgh Theological Seminary (Pittsburgh, Pennsylvania) in 2016.

Joel 2:28-32

[28]Then afterward I will pour out my spirit on all flesh; your sons and your daughters shall prophesy, your old men shall dream dreams, and your young men shall see visions. [29]Even on the male and female slaves, in those days, I will pour out my spirit. [30]I will show portents in the heavens and on the earth, blood and fire and columns of smoke. [31]The sun shall be turned to darkness, and the moon to blood, before the great and terrible day of the Lord comes. [32]Then everyone who calls on the name of the Lord shall be saved; for in Mount Zion and in Jerusalem there shall be those who escape, as the Lord has said, and among the survivors shall be those whom the Lord calls.

Acts 2:16-21

[16]No, this is what was spoken through the prophet Joel: [17]"In the last days it will be, God declares, that I will pour out my Spirit upon all flesh, and your sons and your daughters shall prophesy, and your young men shall see visions, and your old men shall dream dreams. [18]Even upon my slaves, both men and women, in those days I will pour out my Spirit; and they shall prophesy. [19]And I will show portents in the heaven above and signs on the earth below, blood, and fire, and smoky mist. [20]The sun shall be turned to darkness and the moon to blood, before the coming of the Lord's great and glorious day. [21]Then everyone who calls on the name of the Lord shall be saved."

In the summer of 1986, I was on top of the world. I was a seventeen-year-old high school senior. More importantly, I was a senior with a 1972 green Dodge Dart car! My parents had recently purchased this vintage used car for my siblings and me. Of course, I did what any red-blooded high school boy would do. I used my summer earnings to install a car stereo in that Dodge Dart that cost twice as much as the car. That stereo was "off the hook!"

As I cruised in my car in the summer of '86, I kept playing a hot new track by Janet Jackson titled "Control." The lyrics of this now iconic R&B song declared,

> Got my own mind. I wanna make my own decisions.
> When it has to do with my life, I wanna be the one in control.

These are strong words: "I wanna be the one in control." This song was a hit among teenagers in the late 1980s who were seeking to carve out space for themselves in a grown-up's world: "When it has to do with my life, I wanna be the one in control."

The desire to be in control was not just my generation's youthful fantasy about gaining power. The desire to control is a deep longing in the human heart. Most people want to be in control of their lives in some meaningful way. Why is control such an important thing for so many? I claim no expertise in psychology, but my theology tells me that the desire to be in control is often a coping mechanism.

Everything around us tells us how insignificant and out of control we are. Earthquakes on the West Coast remind us that our foundations are not as firm as we think. Wildfires, which refuse to be tamed, torch a neighborhood in Texas in twenty minutes. Tornadoes in Tennessee destroy in thirty seconds homes with mortgages it took thirty years to pay.

Everything around us tells us that we are *not* in control. We sit helplessly in a hospital room, looking at a loved one lying in a bed hooked up to a machine. We pray and pace and pace and pray. Yet despite our piety, the death angel slips into the room and snatches that loved one from us without ever asking permission.

So much of our existence is beyond our control. We did not ask to be born, and we cannot cancel our reservations for the cemetery. Our lives are riddled with chaos and insecurity. Chaos and insecurity left unchecked can create fear, and fear can immobilize. Thus, in an attempt to deal with chaos and insecurity, we exercise control over the smaller areas of our lives, and this provides us with a modicum of confidence and some equilibrium to move forward with our lives.

Control can be good or bad depending on how one understands and uses it. I would contend, however, that a notion of human control may be problematic concerning the life of faith and the practice of religion. When religion is at its best, and not merely the servant of the status quo, religion creatively reminds us that there is an ultimate being who is absolutely beyond human control.

A god whom we control ceases to be God and becomes an idol subject to our whims. A god whom we control ceases to be God and mutates into a personified religious ideology, which merely places a divine stamp of approval on our provincial opinions and parochial viewpoints. A god whom we control can be put into our pint-sized boxes. Such a god makes no serious demands on us. A god whom we control is not the biblical God; for Jewish and Christian scriptures declare that God is beyond control.

The Hebrew Bible prophet Joel communicates this message in the second chapter of the book bearing his name. Joel offers the inhabitants of the southern kingdom of Judah a compelling and chilling depiction of the impending judgment of the Lord. Because of the moral lapse of the people, God spoke through Joel to alert the people that the hand of judgment would no longer be withheld.

Joel poetically declares that when God comes, the earth will quake, and the heavens will tremble. When God comes, the sun and the moon will be darkened, and the stars will withhold their shining. God will come like a general leading an army. The God of judgment, the true and living God, is beyond human control.

Contrary to what the psychoanalysts may say, God is not wish fulfillment superimposed upon the canvas of the psyche.

Contrary to what the Marxists may say, God is not ideological cocaine administered by the ruling class to quiet the protests of the underclass. Contrary to what the white supremacists may say, God is not a blond, blue-eyed Caucasian. Contrary to what the black nationalists may say, God does not have dreadlocks and wear kente cloth. Contrary to what the sexists may say, God is not a man. Contrary to what some Christians may say, God has not granted the Christian Bible a copyright on sacred truth.

Contrary to what some progressive theologians may say, not only is God concerned about social justice, but God also wants us to strive for personal holiness. Contrary to what some conservative theologians may say, God is not a red-state Republican who watches Fox News.

God is a moving, living Spirit, existing in space but not limited by space, existing in time but not limited by time. God is beyond control—the control of our sectarian labels and academic ideologies. God is beyond the control of our religious and cultural barriers and philosophical musings. God is attentive to our self-interests but is not bound by them.

God is beyond the control of any religion and any religionist. No priest, no pastor, no bishop, no rabbi, no imam, no monk, no nun, no elder, no deacon, no steward, and no missionary can ultimately legislate when, where, and how God will show up and whom God will redeem. This is the prophetic message of Joel 2.

Yet there is another significant lesson that Joel teaches us. After dealing with judgment, Joel offers words laced with grace. Joel informs his hearers then and now that if we repent, sanctify ourselves, and live according to God's plan, God will bring an abundant harvest for God's people. The threshing floor will be full of grain; the fig tree will bloom again, and its sweet fruits will satisfy our hunger. After judgment, there is mercy. God declares, "I will pour out my spirit upon all flesh; your sons and your daughters will prophesy. Your old men shall dream dreams, and your young men shall see visions. Even on the male and female slaves . . . I will pour out my spirit. . . . Then everyone who calls on the name of the Lord shall be saved."

We who are Christians believe that Joel's prophecy was ful-filled on the day of Pentecost, when the Holy Spirit was poured out. Consequently, in Acts 2 when Peter preaches on Pentecost, he quotes the prophecy in Joel. Both Joel 2 and Acts 2 offer us hope. While God is beyond control, God is within reach through God's spirit. I can live with a God whom I cannot control. But to live, I need a God whom I can reach.

Good news! Even though we cannot control God, we can surely reach God! God says, "I will pour out my Spirit on all flesh." If we want a relationship with the divine, it can be made available to us.

Did you hear God's open and affirming language? "I will pour out my Spirit on *all flesh.*"

All flesh—female clergy striving to be ordained amid opposi-tion in the "old boys' country club" that some people mis-takenly call a "church."

All flesh—those who grew up in trailer parks on the wrong side of the tracks and those living in high-rise luxury towers.

All flesh—senior citizens moving cautiously on canes and walkers, teenagers scurrying in sneakers on skateboards, and hip-hoppers wearing Sean John shirts.

All flesh—lesbian, gay, bisexual, transgender, queer, and het-erosexual people.

All flesh—undocumented workers who do not speak English as well as those with official passports. *All flesh!*

No one can control God, but everyone can have access to God and God's saving power. I do not know what you need today, but if you call on the Lord, the Lord will be there. The "call center" in heaven works around the clock. Everyone who calls on the name of the Lord will get through. The Lord is within reach. Call the Lord!

The Lord may not deliver you from the mess, but the Lord can grant you peace amid the mess. The Lord may not cure the sick-ness, but the Lord can give you the strength to bear the sickness.

The Lord may not change the situation, but the Lord can change you. God is within reach. Call the Lord!

There was a song we sang in my childhood that conveyed our ready-made access to God:

> *Jesus is on the main line; tell him what you want; call him up and tell him what you want.*
> *If you want more power, tell him what you want. . . .*
> *If you want the Holy Ghost, tell him what you want. . . .*
> *Call him up and tell him what you want.*

In an age of text messages and voice mail, where we rarely talk with another living voice, it is good to know that we can establish a holy hookup with heaven. To talk with the Lord, we do not need to enter our username, password, account number, social security number, date of birth, or zip code. We can reach heaven directly with a simple, sincere word of prayer asking the Lord for assistance.

And if God or Jesus is not your Lord, that is fine because heaven has plenty of other sacred operators—diverse deities, angels, and ancestors—upon whom you can call to get help. Just call on somebody, or something, sacred to help you. The God whom I serve is beyond control. But I am so glad that God is within reach! "Everyone who calls on the name of the Lord shall be saved."

"Everyone"—this is a word dripping with grace. There is more than enough grace in the word "everyone" to include you and even a "disgraceful," unorthodox nonconformist like me.

9

The Battle Cry of a New Revolution

Sermonic Background

I preached this sermon initially on Thursday, April 3, 2003, at the Crown Forum Induction Service at Morehouse College in Atlanta, Georgia. During the service, which occurred in Morehouse's iconic Martin Luther King Jr. International Chapel, I was inducted with a cadre of other leaders into the Martin Luther King Jr. Board of Preachers, Board of Sponsors, and Collegium of Scholars. Morehouse College bestows this honor annually upon a group of leaders who are striving to embody Martin Luther King Jr.'s legacy.

In October 2001, the United States, along with a coalition of other nations, began a military offensive against Afghanistan in response to the terrorist attacks in the United States on September 11, 2001. By March 2003, the United States' war effort had expanded to include a preemptive attack on Iraq to supposedly capture Iraq's "weapons of mass destruction." Consequently, a foreboding sense of conflict and violence saturated the atmosphere throughout the United States and other parts of the world in 2003.

After accepting the invitation from Lawrence Carter Sr., dean of the chapel, to preach at Morehouse's 2003 Crown Forum Service, I thought that a sermon about nonviolence based on Luke 22:47–51 would be fitting—both for the cultural climate at that time and for the enduring tradition of nonviolent struggle that was a salient feature of Martin Luther King Jr.'s ministry.

Four years after the Crown Forum Service, as those wars continued, I traveled in 2007 to England in my capacity as the Bray Lecturer. Two British organizations—the United Society for the Propagation of the Gospel (USPG) and the Society for Promoting Christian Knowledge (SPCK)—sponsored this lectureship that enabled a scholar of religion to examine the aftermath of British colonialism. The first part of the lectureship occurred in Ghana and the second part in England.

Christopher Rowland, my University of Oxford mentor, and Clare Amos, the theological resource officer of USPG, informed the leaders at Westminster Abbey in London, England, of my role as the Bray Lecturer. Robert Wright, subdean of Westminster Abbey, invited me to preach at the 11:15 a.m. Sung Eucharist Service at Westminster Abbey on Sunday, March 11, 2007. The service was part of the bicentennial commemoration of the abolition of the transatlantic slave trade in the former British Empire.

Galvanized by the sermon's enthusiastic reception at Morehouse College in 2003, I preached a version of this sermon at Westminster Abbey in 2007. The sermon also resonated with that historic British congregation. I have subsequently preached a version of this sermon in other settings, including The Riverside Church (New York, New York) in 2008 and Ebenezer Baptist Church (Atlanta, Georgia) in 2019.

Luke 22:47-51

[47]While [Jesus] was still speaking, suddenly a crowd came, and the one called Judas, one of the twelve, was leading them. He approached Jesus to kiss him; [48]but Jesus said to him, "Judas, is it with a kiss that you are betraying the Son of Man?" [49]When those who were around him saw what was coming, they asked, "Lord, should we strike with the sword?" [50]Then one of them struck the slave of the high priest and cut off his right ear. [51]But Jesus said, "No more of this!" And he touched his ear and healed him.

Revolutions have littered the landscape of civilizations the globe over. Revolutions are decisive turning points ushering in immense consequences, and revolutions transpire for many reasons. Regardless of their origins, revolutions require a mixture of the right people, the right time, and the right ideals.

Revolutions often create slogans—brief, easily remembered phrases that capture the highest principles of the movement. These slogans function as linguistic billboards, announcing the aims of the revolution to all who pass by. Thus, investigating slogans can be an entrée to a revolution's main philosophy.

Revolutions create slogans. In the eighteenth century, as American colonists cast off the chains of British imperialism, irate revolutionaries exclaimed, "No taxation without representation!" Revolutions create slogans. In the nineteenth century, as American women cast off the chains of sexism, the pioneering feminist Elizabeth Cady Stanton declared, "All men *and women* are created equal!"[1]

Revolutions create slogans. In the twentieth century, as civil rights protestors cast off the chains of racism, the audacious social activist Fannie Lou Hamer declared, "I'm sick and tired of being sick and tired!"[2] Revolutions create slogans. In the twenty-first century, as diverse communities are casting off the chains of unjust systems that continue to oppress women, LGBTQ people, and people of color, social media influencers are declaring, "Me too" and "Black Lives Matter." In times of controversy, slogans are more than mere words. Slogans are the battle cry of a revolution!

A revolution is in full swing in Luke 22. In this text, a conflict occurs between the power politics of this world and the mysterious reign of God. The seeds of this revolution were sown earlier. In Luke 9, Jesus, with steely determination, set his face toward Jerusalem. Jerusalem, with its massive temple, was the center of Jewish life. Jerusalem had the special attention of Rome. Lest some deluded messianic imposters upset the imperial equilibrium, Tiberius Caesar gave the governor Pontius Pilate special orders to keep Jerusalem under control.

When Jesus set his face toward Jerusalem, he committed himself to a revolutionary struggle against conservative religionists and imperial henchmen. After an arduous trek, Jesus and his followers finally made it to Jerusalem, the holy city where unholy things would soon occur. In Jerusalem, the question of violence emerges again.

Earlier in Luke 22, Jesus's followers misunderstood his instructions to purchase "swords." He had in mind symbolic swords of spiritual resistance. They, however, had in mind steel swords of bodily destruction. Jesus invited them to embrace the sword of the Spirit and to put away their swords of steel. Surely, his followers *heard* Jesus's renunciation of violence, but whether they *heeded* it remained an unanswered question.

The scripture text, Luke 22:47–51, takes us to a Thursday night prayer meeting in an ominous garden. Jesus scales the Mount of Olives to pray and receive final orders from heaven's command post. Some intruders rudely interrupt the prayer meeting to apprehend Jesus.

In the white-hot heat of this charged moment, followers of Jesus raise a question: "Jesus, should we strike them with the sword?" Before waiting to receive a response, one of Jesus's disciples whips out his sword and amputates the ear of the slave who was representing the high priest. This disciple had heard Jesus's earlier renunciation of violence, but he obviously decided not to heed it.

With violence swirling like a tornado and the blood of that slave drenching Gethsemane's ground, Jesus hollers,

No more of this! No more of this violence! I told you to put away the swords of steel. No more of this!

Yes, the other day I turned over some tables in the temple. That was *civil disobedience* resulting from my *spiritual obedience* to God's purposes. The temple incident was *not* my endorsement of violence. Soldiers who join my revolution must accept this battle cry: "No more of this!"

In that garden, Jesus gave his followers then and now the battle cry of a *new* revolution: "No more of this!"

To further emphasize his rejection of violence, Jesus heals the ear of that slave. Had Jesus endorsed violence, he might have considered that maimed slave as "collateral damage." A revolution that comes to give life, and give it more abundantly, does not proceed by taking life. Healing—not destruction—is the order of the day in the new revolution.

This first-century story is relevant for a twenty-first-century world stained with tangible bloodshed and the intangible carnage of other forms of violence. As we courageously embrace an ethic of nonviolent resistance and restorative justice, let us solemnly remember the countless victims of violence.

We remember with remorse the African holocaust of chattel slavery and the Jewish holocaust and displaced and oppressed Palestinians. We remember the atrocities of South African apartheid and abused migrant workers in South America and Asia and tortured prisoners of war across the world.

We remember families and communities torn apart by police brutality and gun violence and despondent children in detention centers in the borderlands of the United States who have been separated from their parents by our country's inhumane immigration policies.

We remember the many victims and survivors of sexual harassment and assault who are sometimes forced to be in the same residence or job alongside their victimizers. We also remember the many maimed and murdered from our prolonged military exploits in Iraq and Afghanistan, where we have spread as much death as democracy. To our obsession with violence in all its forms, Jesus says, "No more of this!"

Permit me to highlight two details in the text that can facilitate a new revolution. First, the disciple who wielded the sword asked a question but failed to let Jesus answer it. Before Jesus could respond, this disciple made a unilateral decision to embrace violence. Violent approaches to revolution tend to create a dangerous impatience. Patience may not always be a virtue. Yet when impatience prevents serious dialogue, fatal consequences can occur.[3]

In this text, the embrace of violence is the termination of dialogue. Notice that it is the slave's *ear* that is amputated. The ear is an organ for receiving the opinions of others. Had Jesus not intervened in this mayhem, even more persons might have become "earless" and unable to heed the voice of peace.

Second, in addition to Jesus's *verbal reaction* to violence, notice his *physical response* to violence. He heals the wounded slave with a restoring touch. Yes, Jesus's revolution is about healing! Perhaps the United States can more effectively achieve its purposes if we become more concerned about healing. Maybe more countries will respect us if we are more committed to healing.

As a political and economic superpower, the United States can facilitate a considerable amount of healing. We should start by doing more healing at home. We have talked piously about bringing democracy and justice to the world. Nevertheless, many state legislatures in our country are enacting laws to make voting more difficult, especially in locations heavily populated by people of color. Furthermore, many marginalized communities in the United States live with the constant threat of overzealous policing, where certain police officers seem more eager to punish innocent citizens than to protect and serve them.

Before policing the world and searching sand dunes for nerve gas, we should have spent more time cleaning up the mess in our own land. We have spent trillions of dollars to fight ill-defined wars in Afghanistan and Iraq while idly watching aspects of our social and economic infrastructure deteriorate. If the United States is really concerned about peace and prosperity domestically and internationally, let us spend trillions of dollars mounting a global war on poverty. As James Forbes Jr., the senior minister emeritus of The Riverside Church, has often declared, "Poverty is the real weapon of mass destruction."

Jesus pleads with us, "No more of this! No more military violence; no more economic violence; no more religious violence. In the name of the new revolution, stop all violence."

"No more of this!" No more military bombing of bridges in other countries when people experiencing homelessness are sleeping under bridges in our own country. "No more of this!"

If we prosecute small misdemeanors in the streets, we must also prosecute gigantic Wall Street felonies in corporate suites. "No more of this!" No more violence against LGBTQ persons, whether that violence is perpetrated by a baseball bat or the slings and arrows of hateful religious rhetoric that demonizes diversity in sexual identity and gender expression. "No more of this!" This is the battle cry of a new revolution.

For the sake of this new revolution, Jesus took up arms at Calvary's cross. Not bombs and bullets but a different, more personal kind of arms. Yes, at Calvary, Jesus took up arms. He raised his right arm, and he raised his left arm as they nailed him to that blood-soaked tree.

At Calvary, God's nonviolent, five-star general took up arms: "God, forgive them for they know not what they do." At Calvary, Jesus took up arms: "Into your hands I commit my spirit." For the sake of justice, Jesus willingly surrendered his life, but God was so pleased with Jesus's nonviolent revolution that three days later, God gave Jesus brand-new life!

We need a new revolution. A new United States, a new Afghanistan, a new Iraq, a new you, and a new me will only emerge with a new revolution. A new battle cry must break forth: "No more of this!"

To accompany the *new* battle cry, the black ancestors offer us an *old* song. In a black spiritual birthed in racial injustice, the ancestors sang, "I'm gonna lay down my sword and shield, down by the riverside . . . to study war no more." As cadets for peace, we must lay our swords and shields down by the riverside:

Lay them down by the Tigris River and the Euphrates River.
Lay them down by the Amazon River and the Nile River.
Lay them down by the Yellow River and the Ganges River.
Lay them down by the Chattahoochee River and the Mississippi River.
Lay them down by the Hudson River and the Potomac River.

Lay them down to study war no more. "I ain't gonna study war no more . . . study war no more." *"No more of this!"* This is the battle cry of a *new* revolution!

10

A Gift for Mother Earth

Clean Your Room!

Sermonic Background

April 22, 2020, marked the fiftieth anniversary of Earth Day. In 1970, the fledgling Earth Day campaign heightened the awareness of millions of people in the United States about environmental contamination. The campaign also advocated for people to be more responsible in their partnership with the earth's diverse species and natural resources. In subsequent decades, the Earth Day movement has galvanized a global network of activists and agencies dedicated to preserving the environment.[1] This watershed anniversary in 2020 highlighted the positive possibilities of consciousness raising, grassroots activism, and global coalitions when addressing a worldwide dilemma.

Yet the history of the contemporary environmental movement is brief when compared to the length of time that many religious traditions have prioritized care for the earth as a sacred commitment. Across centuries and millennia, religious communities have trumpeted in their texts and traditions the importance, and even sanctity, of the environment. For example, in one of the creation stories in Genesis, God is a "cosmic artist" who steps back after each creative masterpiece and perceives with delight that the creation is "good." One can infer from this story that the environment is not a tool to be manipulated but instead a divine treasure to be appreciated.

At the conclusion of this creation story, God commands humans to "have dominion" over the creation (Gen 1:28). A significant nuance in this divine command should not be missed. The Hebrew verb "to have dominion" (*radah*) connotes a relationship with the earth rooted in respect, reverential care, and stewardship. The theologian Walter Burghardt offers cogent insights about humanity's role as stewards in light of this command in Genesis: "A steward is one who manages what is someone else's. A steward cares, is concerned, at times agonizes. Stewards may not plunder or waste; they are responsible and can be called to account for their stewardship. Yes indeed, 'The earth is the Lord's, and all that is in it'" (Ps 24:1).[2]

Several centuries after Genesis was written, the apostle Paul reflected on the creation stories in Genesis and the suffering inflicted upon the creation by malevolent forces. He likened the ecological or cosmological body of creation to a pregnant woman who was in the throes of labor pain. Paul suggested that something beautiful was being born throughout creation. Yet the birthing process was riddled with enormous struggle. To examine humanity's role in alleviating creation's suffering and promoting ecological justice, I initiate in this sermon a creative conversation between Paul's ancient maternal image in Romans 8:18–22 and contemporary feminist theology.

I initially preached this sermon on Sunday, May 3, 2009, for the Eco-Justice Celebration at The Riverside Church (New York, New York). As part of this service, holy communion was served. The maternal image in the sermon also foreshadowed Riverside's commemoration of Mother's Day on the following Sunday that year. I subsequently adapted the sermon for a presentation on ecological justice at the Greening the Earth Summit at Trinity United Church of Christ (Chicago, Illinois) in 2015.

Romans 8:18–22 (Common English Bible)

[18]I believe that the present suffering is nothing compared to the coming glory that is going to be revealed to us. [19]The whole creation waits breathless with anticipation for the revelation of God's sons and daughters. [20]Creation was subjected to frustration, not by its own choice—it was the choice of the one who subjected it—but in the hope [21]that the creation itself will be set free from slavery to decay and brought into the glorious freedom of God's children. [22]We know that the whole creation is groaning together and suffering labor pains up until now.

When you were growing up, how many times each week did your mother tell you to clean your room? If she told you once, she told you a thousand times. Except for the words "I love you," the phrase "clean your room" might be mothers' most uttered words to their children.

Did your mother tell you to clean your room because you forgot to hang up your clean clothes, and your dirty socks fell short of the hamper, which you used as a makeshift basketball hoop? Did she tell you to clean your room because puzzle pieces and stuffed animals had turned your floor into a treacherous obstacle course? Did she tell you to clean your room because dirty dishes on your desk from a late-night study session with your friends had become a dinner table for the ants and their friends? "Clean your room!"

In 2015, my wife, Lazetta, and I bought a home after several years of renting a home. My mother came to visit and assisted us in organizing and decorating our new home. Although I at the time was in my midforties, my mother was still telling me to clean my room. Why are so many mothers concerned about their children's rooms—the spaces where their children live, play, and rest? Is it simply a maternal need for external neatness, or might there be a more subtle, internal reason?

As I pondered my mother's many exhortations for me to clean my room throughout my life, it occurred to me that my mother was my first room. The walls of her womb enveloped the embryonic me. Mothers are concerned about children's rooms because mothers are rooms for their children. Mothers are sources of life and shelter for life. A mother's womb is our first room.

The apostle Paul understood the communicative power and intercultural appeal of the metaphor of childbirth. In the exploration of creation's journey from suffering to hope in Romans 8, Paul employs this image and depicts creation as a lady in labor. While the word "creation" (*ktisis*) in Romans 8:18–22 likely connotes more than just planet Earth, we will focus on our planet in this sermon. On another occasion, we can extend our gaze to galaxies beyond ours.

According to this scripture, Earth is a woman in labor. Mother Earth is eager to continue giving birth to a variety of life-forms. She realizes that the health of all her children—trees and tundra, rivers and rocks, humans and herbivores—is dependent upon the well-being of her womb, that space where we live and are nurtured.

Feminist theologian Sallie McFague develops the maternal metaphor in her classic book *The Body of God: An Ecological Theology*:

> A theology of embodiment takes space seriously, for the first thing bodies need is space to obtain the necessities to exist—food, water, air. Space is not an empty notion from an ecological perspective ("empty space"), but a central one, for it means the basic world that each and every creature inhabits. . . . The category of space reminds us not only that each and every life-form needs space for its own physical needs, but also that we all exist together in one space, our finite planet . . . within the nurturing matrix of God's body. We are all enclosed together in the womblike space of our circular planet.[3]

Since the earth is our mother's womb—and our first and final room—cleaning our room is a task of planetary proportions. Cleaning our room is no longer a routine chore but a redemptive choice to enable life to abound in myriad ways on this magnificent planet. If we fail to make ecological justice a priority, our mother's womb will become our tomb!

The biblical image of our planet as a pregnant woman is appropriate as a framework for ecological initiatives. In labor, the unity between mother and child is tangible. Mother and child are united by an umbilical cord—a tangible tunnel through which life-giving resources pass.

As it relates to ecological justice for Mother Earth, we seemingly have amnesia concerning this anatomical reality. If we remembered the image of an umbilical cord, we would recognize that poison and pollution in the mother's womb will inevitably pass to the child.

Mother Earth is eager to nurture us in her womb. Yet she is crying out to us, "Clean your room! You are ruining my womb. You are polluting my life-sustaining possibilities."

In the metaphor of creation as a woman in labor, the apostle Paul suggests that a life-and-death struggle is occurring. Creation is straining to give birth to life. Yet creation is in bondage to decay. At the very point that life attempts to come through the birth canal, death is lurking at the door.

Decay threatens the delivery. Death desires to devour life. Mother Earth is frustrated because this slavery to decay—this ecological deterioration—is not the result of her own doing. This bondage to decay is the consequence of the deadly decisions of others.

Throughout Romans, Paul grapples with people's propensity to make bad decisions that inflict harm on themselves and others. Paul often employs a simple word for this complex dilemma—sin. I hope that "left-leaning" religion has not become so progressive that we expunge the word "sin" completely from our theological vocabulary. Although the word "sin" does not appear explicitly in Romans 8:18–22, sin has left its fingerprints on this text.

For Paul, the foundational story of sin occurs in the early chapters of Genesis. Our contemporary, faith-based ecological efforts would be negligent if we ignored Eden's ancient garden. Eden is the mythological symbol of divine goodness and the culmination of cosmological creativity. The echoes of Eden reverberate in Romans 8.

As Paul writes Romans 8:18–22, he is surely remembering the repeated affirmation in Genesis 1 that the creation is *good*:

> *A blazing sun and burnings stars. It was good.*
> *A celestial ceiling and a silvery moon. It was good.*
> *Rustling rivers and peaceful ponds. It was good.*
> *Daffodils and daisies; red wood trees and black-eyed peas. It*
> *   was good.*
> *Giraffes and gazelles; inchworms and iguanas. It was good.*
> *Six-legged praying mantises and two-legged praying people.*
> *   It was good.*

But perhaps the praying mantises in Eden were more in tune with God than those praying people. People—symbolized in Genesis by the mythic characters Adam and Eve—at some point stopped praying and willfully made a deal with the devil, resulting in decay and death for the creation.

God gave Adam and Eve wide latitude to enjoy Eden's abundance. The Creator simply asked them to not eat from one tree. The temptation to transgress limits crawled on its belly and spoke through the hiss of a mythic serpent. The serpent placed before Eden's first human tenants a choice to disregard sacred boundaries, and Adam and Eve willfully chose to violate those boundaries. Through humanity's sin, the creation was subjected to frustration and ecological deterioration.

Sallie McFague offers a poignant explanation of the sin that enslaves Mother Earth to decay: "In the common creation story, we are not sinners because we rebel against God or are unable to be sufficiently spiritual: our particular failing . . . is our unwillingness to stay in our place, to accept our proper limits so that other individuals of our species as well as other species can also have needed space."[4]

In short, what mess up Mother Earth's womb are greed, selfishness, and the unwillingness of humans to stay in our designated lane. Ecological decay is the consequence of anthropological arrogance—the mistaken belief that we are the center of creation instead of us realizing that we are one species among millions in Mother Earth's womb. Mother Earth is saying to us,

For the sake of your generation and generations yet unborn, stop ruining my reproductive capacity. Your acid rain is eating up my uterus. Cases of cancer inevitably will abound if you inject carcinogens into my umbilical cord.

My human children, don't you realize that we are connected? My womb wants to support you. But if you do not clean up chemical spills and prevent them in the first place, my breasts will not flow with life-giving nutrients. Consequently, you will be forced to suckle a lethal soup.

If you continue deforestation, I will be short of breath because of a limited oxygen supply. If you refuse more rigorous regulation of fossil fuel emissions, the smog in my womb will prevent you humans from paying attention to the countless other creatures next to you in my womb.

Like a mother dispensing tough love, Mother Earth is pleading with us,

My human children, because of your inflated ego, you think that you are independent and isolated from other human and nonhuman siblings in my womb. As I mourn with you the horrific suffering and losses of the Covid-19 crisis, I pray that the pandemic's lessons will not be lost on you.

This disease, which may have originated with animals, moved rapidly to the human population. Your missiles, tanks, and closed-border immigration policies were no match for this microscopic invader that decimated the entire world. I hope the pandemic will compel you to reconsider global interdependence and ecological connectivity.

I am your mother, and if you want to give me a perpetual Mother's Day gift, clean your room. Stop ruining my womb. Recycle your plastic bottles and cell phones. Take shorter showers and reuse towels. Print double-sided copies if you must print copies at all.

Do not pour old prescription medicine down the drain, and fix leaky faucets. Protest until your cities and towns manage properly all sewage treatment plants and clean up abandoned waste sites and dilapidated row houses. Demand that corporations and governments stop targeting underserved communities of color as illegal dumping grounds for toxic waste.[5]

If we are serious about cleaning our room and respecting the life-generating wonders of Mother Earth's womb, we must reject insatiable consumption and the corporate lust for endless growth. Steven Rockefeller, an ally of the ecological movement, commends the attempt to move from a mindset of conspicuous consumption to an ethically balanced framework of sustainability: "Patterns of production and consumption are considered to be ecologically sustainable if they respect and safeguard the regenerative capacity of our oceans, rivers, forests, farmlands, and grasslands. . . . Sustainability includes all the interrelated activities that promote the long-term flourishing of Earth's human and ecological communities. . . . Finding our way to a truly sustainable way of living together is our hope for the future. It is the path to building a culture of nonviolence and peace."[6] The planet upon which we live is a pregnant woman eager to sustain diverse life-forms in all their stunning vibrancy. Yet the womb of Mother Earth is being contaminated by our callousness.

Nevertheless, the gospel always provides us an opportunity to repent, which entails a purposeful reorientation of our perspectives and practices. Accordingly, even as the creation experiences frustration, the creation maintains a hope that it might be emancipated if humans change their ways. A key site and symbol of repentance in Christian theology is the communion table. Holy communion is a food ritual that involves bread and wine (i.e., harvested wheat and crushed grapes). My reference to the communion table calls to mind a portion of a Swedish communion prayer:

> We break this bread for our wounded earth,
> for fields, forests, and seas,
> as a sign that we belong together
> with the whole of God's creation

*and want to take responsibility for the healing of the earth's
        wounds.*[7]

Let me expand that last line slightly: "And (we) want to take
responsibility for the healing of the earth's wounds" ... and the
healing of Mother Earth's *womb*.

Henceforth, when we come to the communion table to eat bread
and drink wine, may we also take a moment—call it a ... pregnant
pause if you will—and consider how this meal will strengthen us
to clean our room. By cleaning our room, we would make Mother
Earth extraordinarily proud.

11

On Purpose

Sermonic Background

I celebrated in 2021 the thirtieth anniversary of my ordination in Christian ministry. Across the decades, I have preached in numerous pulpits throughout the United States. My ministry has also afforded me speaking opportunities in Benin, Canada, England, Ghana, and South Africa. Although I have written hundreds of sermons, this sermon—"On Purpose"—is perhaps my favorite of them all. A challenging professional episode set in motion the inspiration for this sermon.

After prayerful deliberation and a yearlong employment candidacy, I accepted the call to serve as the sixth senior minister of The Riverside Church in New York City in September 2008. Yet within several months of serving that congregation, longstanding congregational tensions about the senior minister's role began to severely hinder progress in implementing the church's mission and vision.

My pastoral predecessors at Riverside—including Ernest Campbell, William Sloane Coffin, and James Forbes Jr.—also grappled with these issues. During my Riverside pastorate, both Ernest Campbell and James Forbes Jr. shared with me their stories about the perils associated with the senior minister position at Riverside. Rather than force the issue and create additional strife, I voluntarily resigned from the pastorate of Riverside in hope that all parties would benefit from a time of rebooting.

On a computer, the boot device is a part of the technology that helps the computer's operating system load. Sometimes, there are system issues or technical glitches that keep the operating system from functioning at full capacity. When this happens, the instruction manual recommends a "soft reboot"—a process of momentarily powering down the computer in order to power it back up at full functionality. Performed correctly, rebooting enables you to preserve the work you have already completed and empowers you to press forward with new work.

My resignation from Riverside was official in August 2009. In September 2009, I moved with my family to Chicago for a year of spiritual renewal and professional discernment. During this sabbatical, the love and laughter of my family and the compassionate counsel of friends facilitated the rebooting process.

Several friends invited me to use the rebooting process to carefully consider my purpose. Upon the recommendation of friends, I read, among other inspirational writings, two brilliant books about purpose during the rebooting process: (1) *Holy Play: The Joyful Adventure of Unleashing Your Divine Purpose* by Kirk Byron Jones and (2) *Real Power: Stages of Personal Power in Organizations* by Janet Hagberg. The uploading of these new "files" to my mental hard drive profoundly impacted my thinking about the role of purpose in fulfilling my destiny.

Both books are replete with pertinent, practical insights. For instance, in *Holy Play*, Jones writes, "Purpose is not something that we passively receive from God, but something that we actively cocreate with God."[1] In *Real Power*, Hagberg insists that discerning one's purpose requires a "long inner struggle of definition and self-acceptance—which takes years for some and a lifetime for most," and people who live with purpose are empowered to "concentrate on essentials, the things that give meaning to them and to the lives of others."[2]

As I delved more deeply into my purpose through reading, contemplation, and dialogue with family and friends, I eventually crafted a paragraph that encapsulated my purpose: "In Old English, 'Brad' means 'broad meadow.' Thus, my goal in life is to live into my name. My ministry strives to create broad spaces where people from diverse backgrounds with divergent beliefs can peacefully probe their differences and celebrate their similarities for the sake of a better world." I also inventoried afresh my talents, skills, and interests and renewed my long-standing commitment to connecting the precision of ivory-tower classrooms with the passion of grassroots communities.

During a generative period between 2010 and 2014, my pursuit of purpose produced significant fruit. McCormick Theological Seminary in Chicago invited me to serve from 2010 to 2012 as a distinguished visiting scholar, enabling me to reconnect with my love for teaching and research. During this period, I wrote an extensive vision essay for what would eventually become The Open Church of Maryland. Moreover, a cadre of courageous people in Baltimore joined me in founding The Open Church of Maryland in October 2011, thereby translating the "ink" of that vision essay into the "flesh and blood" of a living, growing congregation.

Furthermore, as my visiting faculty position at McCormick Seminary was ending, God's providence and the pursuit of purpose once again opened other doors and windows. In November 2011, I was offered a tenured faculty position as the Lois Craddock Perkins Professor of Homiletics (Preaching) at Southern Methodist University's (SMU) Perkins School of Theology in Dallas, Texas. When negotiating the employment offer with William Lawrence, the visionary dean at Perkins at that time, I purposefully shared with him my deep commitment to my professorial and pastoral callings. Furthermore, I informed him of the recent founding of The Open Church just weeks earlier.

As a scholar and ordained United Methodist minister, Dean Lawrence embraced my dual commitments and understood the intellectual rigor and entrepreneurial savvy required to establish a new congregation. Furthermore, he considered my church-planting efforts to be a valuable dimension of my work with Perkins's students, faculty, staff, and community partners. Thus, Perkins School of Theology allowed me to live in Baltimore to facilitate my ministry at The Open Church, and I commuted to Dallas weekly to fulfill the bulk of my professorial duties on Tuesdays through Thursdays.

I was privileged to serve on the Perkins faculty from 2012 to 2014. External assessments—including excellent course evaluations from my students and performance evaluations from Dean Lawrence—indicated that this arrangement was successful. Moreover, since my salary and employment benefits were provided by SMU, this innovative arrangement alleviated fiscal constraints from The Open Church in its earliest days.

In its first nine months, The Open Church raised more than $140,000 through donations from its members. The congregation gladly defrayed the cost of my weekly travel to Dallas as a tangible testimony of its support of theological education in general and my teaching ministry at SMU in particular. In negotiating my employment covenant with The Open Church's board of directors, the directors and I mutually agreed to insert this statement into the covenant: "The Open Church endorses Dr. Braxton's teaching ministry at Southern Methodist University (SMU) in Dallas, Texas and considers his service as Lois Craddock Perkins Professor of Homiletics to be an extension of his pastoral ministry at The Open Church."

When we seek to accomplish positive things on purpose, creative opportunities and innovative solutions will emerge. As a celebration of the role of purpose in my life and in the development of The Open Church, I preached this sermon initially on Monday, December 31, 2012, for the New Year's Eve service at The Open Church. I have subsequently preached it in other settings, including Tabernacle Baptist Church (Milwaukee, Wisconsin) in 2015, Loudon Avenue Christian Church (Roanoke, Virginia) in 2015, New Beginnings Christian Fellowship (Kent, Washington) in 2020, and St. Peter United Church of Christ (Houston, Texas) in 2022.

Luke 16:1-9 (Common English Bible)

[1] Jesus also said to the disciples, "A certain rich man heard that his household manager was wasting his estate. [2] He called the manager in and said to him, 'What is this I hear about you?

Give me a report of your administration because you can no longer serve as my manager.'

[3]"The household manager said to himself, What will I do now that my master is firing me as his manager? I'm not strong enough to dig and too proud to beg. [4]I know what I'll do so that, when I am removed from my management position, people will welcome me into their houses.

[5]"One by one, the manager sent for each person who owed his master money. He said to the first, 'How much do you owe my master?' [6]He said, 'Nine hundred gallons of olive oil.' The manager said to him, 'Take your contract, sit down quickly, and write four hundred fifty gallons.' [7]Then the manager said to another, 'How much do you owe?' He said, 'One thousand bushels of wheat.' He said, 'Take your contract and write eight hundred.'

[8]"The master commended the dishonest manager because he acted cleverly. People who belong to this world are more clever in dealing with their peers than are people who belong to the light. [9]I tell you, use worldly wealth to make friends for yourselves so that when it's gone, you will be welcomed into the eternal homes."

The story is told of a community of people who lived on a dangerous seacoast where shipwrecks often occurred. Considering the frequency of these shipwrecks, some townspeople decided to invest time, effort, and money into creating a rescue operation. A small lifesaving station was built, and the devoted members of the rescue team kept an ongoing watch over the sea, ready to use their little boat to search for survivors in case of a shipwreck.

As a result of this volunteer operation, the town became famous because many lives were saved. People increasingly joined the rescue team. After a while, a new rescue building was constructed. It was much larger than the first little building, and it was beautifully furnished and decorated. As more amenities were added for the members' pleasure and comfort, the new building was slowly transformed into a clubhouse. Consequently, some members began to lose interest in the rescue operation.

One fateful day, a major shipwreck occurred, and many survivors were rescued and brought into the clubhouse for first aid. During this significant rescue operation, the frenzied activity resulted in extensive damage to the clubhouse. Blood from the survivors stained the lush carpeting, and furniture was broken in the attempt to fix battered people.

At the next clubhouse meeting, there was a contentious split in the membership. Most members felt that the lifesaving operation had become a hindrance to the social life of the organization. Those who disagreed were told that they could build another lifesaving station farther down the coast. As the years passed, this cycle repeated itself. Today, in that town, the seacoast has a number of exclusive clubhouses dotting the shore. However, no one in the area is passionately concerned any longer about rescue operations.[3]

As I scan the ecclesial "coastline" in our country, there are many finely adorned congregational clubhouses adjacent to churning seas where desperate people are drowning in drug addiction, dilapidated housing, and death-dealing violence. The members in some of these clubhouses seem strangely idle in the face of desperately needed rescue operations. Why do lifesaving stations often become comfortable clubhouses? I have an answer. We have too many purposeless churches whose pulpits and pews are filled with purposeless people.

Do not misunderstand me. Many of the people in these churches mean well, but they have not done the painstaking work of defining their purpose.

Purpose—your fundamental reasons for existing.
Purpose—my primary rationales for being on the planet.
Purpose—our individual and collective goals to enhance our lives and the lives of others.
Purpose—not the duties in your job description but rather the positive destinies to which the universe is calling you.

Many of us lack purpose because we confuse *fate* and *faith*. Fate is a weakhearted resignation to allow things to continue as they are. Fate has many other faces: *"C'est la vie.* That's life. If it is meant to be, it will be." When we surrender to fate, we stop seeking our purpose.

On the other hand, faith is a tough-minded determination to change things in spite of the evidence and seemingly insurmountable odds. Thank God that courageous freedom fighters across the centuries did not confuse fate and faith. Those who struggled for the abolition of slavery or for women's right to vote or for labor unions to create safe working conditions did not throw up their hands in futile resignation. Instead, with faith, they put their hands to the plow to churn up political agitation that led to a harvest of positive social transformation.

Positive change will only happen on purpose: a change in gun laws; a change in immigration policy; a change in racist structures, patriarchal patterns, and homophobic attitudes; a change in the mass incarceration crisis; a change for nuclear disarmament; a change for safer streets, cleaner water, and fresher air. Changes such as these only happen on purpose. We need more courageous people engaged in creative struggle on purpose. People doing good stuff, not by accident but on purpose!

Purpose was a central feature of Jesus's ministry. Jesus called disciples *on purpose.* He created enemies *on purpose.* He traveled to Jerusalem *on purpose,* knowing full well that the trip might result in his death. Jesus knew that righteousness "never rolls in on wheels of inevitability."[4] The necessity of purpose for disciples is illustrated in a controversial parable Jesus tells his disciples in Luke 16:1–9.

In the parable, there was a very wealthy businessman. We might liken him today to a CEO of a Fortune 500 company. This rich man owned plenty of real estate and employed a vast number of people to oversee his business dealings. In particular, the rich man hired a manager to account for the profits accrued from his vast financial portfolio. The manager who was chosen to monitor the rich man's accounts must have been competent because a responsible CEO would not turn over the corporate checkbook to just anybody.

The CEO eventually learned that his manager was wasting profits. Troubled by this development, the CEO called for an audit of the company's books and fires the manager. The looming loss of employment created a crisis for the manager. This crisis prompted serious introspection in the manager. In Luke 16:3, the manager said to himself, "What will I do now that my [boss] is firing me as his manager? I'm not strong enough to dig and too proud to beg."

The first step toward purpose is *introspection*, which raises the question, What shall I do? In the manager's question, there is urgency, accountability, and responsibility. The manager did not fixate on the crisis, which, by the way, he created. Rather, he focused on the question.

If we are going to live on purpose, we cannot get stuck looking backward at the crisis. We must move forward to ask the question, What shall I do? Whether you created the crisis, or it came through no fault of your own, do not let a crisis block you from your purpose. There are so many crises that can cause us to become stuck: "I know she cheated on you. I know he abused you. I know you messed up on the job. I know your boss is 'Satan in the flesh.' I know you inherited a genetic trait for diabetes. I know you got 'baby mama' or 'baby daddy' drama. I know your arthritis flares up at night. I know your grandchildren are crazy. I know city council is sometimes unproductive. I know Congress is often in a gridlock." There are crises of all kinds. However, at some point, we must take our eyes off the external situation and go deep inside and ask, What shall *I* do?

In discerning what he should do, the manager assessed both what he *could not* do and what he *would not* do. In Luke 16:3, the manager says, "I'm not strong enough to dig (that is what I cannot do) and too proud to beg (that is what I will not do)." In the search for purpose, we must honestly assess our talents and skills. Samuel Weber, my former colleague at Wake Forest University, always says, "Do what you can, not what you can't." Purpose comes from eliminating what we cannot do and embracing what we can do.

May I please offer myself as an example? I have no manual dexterity whatsoever. My mother jokingly suggests that God put all my talent in my mouth, which meant that there was nothing left for my hands. I am not going to transform the world through my hands. There will be no piano concertos or picturesque portraits created by these hands.

However, with words from my mouth, I have become a verbal virtuoso playing in the key of rhetorical creativity. I paint kaleidoscopic portraits of human possibility with pronouns and participles. One of my purposes is to use my gifts of imaginative language and eloquent speech to empower others. Rather than lamenting what I cannot do, I have walked confidently into my purpose by joyfully embracing what I can do.

Furthermore, the introspection that leads to purpose involves maintaining our standards. The manager said, "I am too proud to beg." Not only did he know his skills, but he also asserted his standards. No matter how desperate my situation might be, I refuse to compromise my standards or relinquish my dignity. Sometimes crises come to remind us of what is truly valuable. Dignity cannot be measured in dollars. Preserving your sanity is so valuable that it cannot be computed on a spreadsheet.

As we follow the manager's journey in the text, we witness how his *introspection* then resulted in *ingenuity*. Before the termination took effect and his company key card and password were voided, the manager took the initiative to call in various account holders who owed debts to the CEO.

The manager called in the first account owner who owed the CEO nine hundred gallons of olive oil. The manager said to that debtor, "Take your contract and write four hundred fifty gallons." In other words, the manager cut the debtor's bill in half. The manager then called in the second account owner who owed the CEO one thousand bushels of wheat. The manager said, "Take your contract and write eight hundred." Once again, the manager falsified the records and substantially reduced the second debtor's bill.

Through the dishonest alteration of the CEO's account (otherwise known as "cooking the books"), the manager sought to create goodwill with the debtors whose bills he reduced. These debtors, in return, would take care of the manager after he lost his job. The manager's scheme was ingenious, but it was also illegal and immoral.

Since the CEO fired the manager previously for being frivolous, we might expect the CEO to imprison the manager for fraud. However, the CEO flips the script on our expectations. Rather than punish the dishonest manager, the CEO praises him. A literal translation of Luke 16:8 is "The master praised the unrighteous manager because he acted shrewdly." The Greek adverb translated "shrewdly" (*phronimōs*) connotes the clever behavior necessary to ensure self-preservation.[5]

The manager's behavior was wrong, but it demonstrated ingenuity, and more than anything else, it demonstrated *purpose*. Rather than wait for fate, the manager intentionally, even if illegally, created a "hookup" to handle his situation.

By telling this story, is Jesus endorsing dishonesty or fraud? Absolutely not! Why then does Jesus present a fraudulent manager as an example for disciples? Through this parable, Jesus is saying, "If my followers would exemplify the same kind of purpose and shrewdness in carrying out holiness as the hustlers in the hood have in working their schemes, the kin-dom of God might show up. Don't let the hustlers in the hood surpass you in purpose, outdo you in ingenuity, outshine you in creativity. I ain't mad at a streetwise brother who has enough purpose to take care of himself. In seeking self-preservation, the manager used faulty procedures, but at least he had purpose. I can take misdirected purpose, recycle, and sanctify it."

Jesus has little tolerance for "pious people" who reverently sit on their hands waiting on God to do everything for them. People who have no passion; people who lack holy hustle; people with no "gospel get-up-and-go." When you have purpose, you are not always looking for your "pie in the sky in the sweet by and by." On the contrary, purpose pushes you to start hustling for "something sound on the ground by the pound while you are still around."

In this season of your life, strive to be a better person and create a better world on purpose. Engage in introspection and exemplify ingenuity on purpose. Get some drive, some creativity, some chutzpah on purpose. Work the system, expand your network, make some connections on purpose.

Even if your purpose is not completely pure, that's OK. Bring your purpose to the altar and let Jesus recycle and sanctify it. Imperfect purpose is better than no purpose at all.

Don't come to the Lord saying, "The Lord will make a way somehow." The Lord needs you to make a way for yourself and somebody else right now . . . on purpose. Don't stumble into a new day, a new week, a new year, and a new assignment by accident. Stride into every new season with audacity and Spirit-inspired purpose!

> *Kick a bad habit on purpose.*
> *Rebuild a torn neighborhood on purpose.*
> *Adopt a lonely child on purpose.*
>
> *Lift a discouraged person on purpose.*
> *Restore a damaged relationship on purpose.*
> *Leave a dysfunctional relationship on purpose.*
>
> *Stop eating greasy food on purpose.*
> *Exercise three times a week on purpose.*
> *Get some professional counseling on purpose.*
>
> *Update your resume on purpose.*
> *Seek some job interviews on purpose.*
> *Start your own business on purpose.*
>
> *Give more generously on purpose.*
> *Pray more fervently on purpose.*
> *Teach more courageously on purpose.*
>
> *Look evil in the eye on purpose.*
> *Tell evil that you are going higher on purpose, getting stronger*
>   *on purpose, and disrupting demonic designs on purpose.*

Don't lie down to be counted out. Rise up and be counted on—counted on as one of God's children who has the unmitigated gall to live your life . . . *on purpose!*

The Bible's *Last Word*

My Conversion to Religious Pluralism

Africa is pluralistic, and that religious pluralism has to be acknowledged and lived in a creative manner.... We need to discern the good news not only as we know it in Christianity but also as it exists in the religion of "the other."

—MERCY AMBA ODUYOYE, "THREE CARDINAL ISSUES OF MISSION IN AFRICA"

Searching for My Roots

A pilgrimage to Africa was my pathway to religious pluralism.* In 1992, I made my first trip to Mother Africa and visited the Gambia. This small African nation would play a large role in awakening me to the beauty of religious pluralism.

The trip occurred during my two-year matriculation as a Rhodes Scholar at the University of Oxford. As grateful as I was for the coveted privilege to study at Oxford, I was constantly aware while there that I was living and studying in one of the capitals of white culture. During my Oxford years, I was not the victim of overt prejudice, but in subtle and sometimes not-so-subtle

* This chapter was originally published as "The Grace of the Lord Jesus Be with All: A Minister's Conversion to Religious Pluralism," *Harvard Divinity Bulletin* 44, nos. 3/4 (2016): 57–63. Reprinted with permission of *Harvard Divinity Bulletin*.

ways, the message was conveyed that white cultural experiences were *the* measuring rod.

Surrounded so intensely by "whiteness," I felt compelled to understand more intimately my "blackness." The Gambia had figured prominently in Alex Haley's research that led to his famous book *Roots* and the subsequent television series. In an effort to reconnect with my own African roots, I chose the Gambia as my introduction to Africa, traveling there during the break between Oxford's winter and spring terms.

For more than a week in the Gambia, I immersed myself in African culture—eating the food, listening to the music, browsing through village markets, and talking with village elders. Those elders told stories, handed down through generations of oral tradition, about the faith, foibles, and feats of their Gambian forebears.

One morning during the trip, I was reading the New Testament while sitting on the porch of a sparsely furnished Gambian guesthouse near the Atlantic Ocean. The equatorial sun had warmed the early morning air. But the warm air was nothing compared to the numinous, warm presence that overshadowed me as I began hearing voices with my "third ear" that imparted wisdom to my soul. I realized that a council of invisible African ancestors had convened around me.

According to African Traditional Religions, the visible and invisible dimensions of existence are connected by Spirit—the eternal life force animating the universe with divine purpose. When honorable members of an African tribe die, they continue to live as spirits. These ancestral spirits provide moral guidance to those who are still physically alive.[1]

As the invisible ancestors surrounded me that morning in the Gambia, they irrevocably expanded the contours of my sacred universe. For several weeks before the trip, I had struggled to find an appropriate research topic for my forthcoming master's thesis at Oxford. The revelation from the ancestors instantly pierced my mental fog. Their counsel enabled me to identify my thesis topic—an unapologetic cultural reading of Christian texts through the lens of African and African American experiences. My Oxford thesis was successfully written, defended, and later expanded to a book.² In hindsight, I realized that when the ancestors speak, it is wise to listen.

This visitation introduced me to manifestations of religion that had predated Christianity by many millennia. In Africa, a continent replete with cultural and religious pluralism, my previous understandings of "exclusive salvation" through Christianity felt woefully narrow. Nevertheless, it was not lost on me that I had first met the African ancestors and experienced a powerful dimension of African Traditional Religions precisely as I was reading the Christian scriptures. Deep anchorage in the texts of my primary religious tradition (i.e., Christianity) was a bridge, not a barrier, to a greater appreciation of the diverse array of other religious traditions.

In Africa, I began to imagine religion as a kind of African music—a complex, polyphonic performance of intertwining voices giving witness to all that is sacred. Christianity, for me, was an important voice, but it was no longer the only voice. The solo had become a chorus. At age seven, I had converted to Christianity and been submerged in the waters of Christian baptism in my family's Baptist church in southwest Virginia. Sixteen years later, I traveled across the waters of the Atlantic Ocean for another conversion—a conversion to religious pluralism.

The Power of Pluralism

Since that life-altering encounter in 1992, I have been a devotee of pluralism, and my ministry and scholarship have gravitated toward interfaith settings and initiatives. In these settings, I have learned profound wisdom and witnessed beautiful practices and rituals from adherents of diverse traditions, including, but not limited to, African Traditional Religions, the Baha'i faith, Buddhism, Humanism, Islam, Judaism, and Santería. My conversation partners have ranged from orthodox religionists to unorthodox atheists, and every interfaith encounter, whether comfortable or contentious, has revealed to me important dimensions of sacred living. Eboo Patel, a noted interfaith educator and friend, provides a marvelous definition of pluralism: "A society characterized by respect for people's religious (and other) identities, positive relationships between people of different religious backgrounds, and common action for the common good."[3]

In 2009, nearly two decades after my visit to the Gambia, I participated in an interfaith gathering that further refined my abiding commitment to religious pluralism. At that time, I was the senior minister of The Riverside Church in New York City, a progressive Christian congregation known for its social activism and ecumenical approach. The Riverside Church was hosting a conference uniting Muslims, Jews, and Christians by exploring the similarities and differences in the scriptures of the Abrahamic traditions. Scholars, clerics, and interfaith advocates from Canada, the Caribbean, and across the United States convened in New York City for three days of scholarly presentations, symposia, and roundtable dialogues.

The culminating event was the Sunday morning worship service at Riverside. As the host pastor, I was invited to be the preacher. In the days leading up to the service, I grappled with how to approach this exciting and unusual preaching assignment. I was a Christian pastor and a scholar of the New Testament with profound interfaith commitments, who was preaching alongside Muslim and Jewish clergy at an interfaith conference about the scriptures of the Abrahamic traditions. How could I provide a soul-stirring, intellectually robust, and rhetorically polished witness to religious pluralism in the fleeting moments of one sermon?

Once again, the African ancestors came to my aid, speaking as clearly in the hustle and bustle of the city as they had near the picturesque Atlantic shores of the Gambia. Rather than avoid the scriptures of my tradition in service of a bland ecumenism, the ancestors encouraged me to ground my understanding of pluralism in the Christian scriptures. I had been introduced to the ancestors and, by extension, to religious pluralism, not by avoiding the Christian scriptures but by deeply engaging them.

The ancestors also reminded me of some exegetical notes I had made years earlier about a fascinating, alternative way to interpret the concluding verses of the book of Revelation, one of the most enigmatic books in the Christian scriptures. The ancestors assured me that if I wrestled long enough, the enigmas of the book of Revelation would reveal a clear, compassionate word about pluralism. Once again, the ancestors were trustworthy guides. Their guidance has usually come through gentle nudges and promptings that sharpen my perception.

They brought to my remembrance one of my graduate school mentors, Emory University biblical studies professor John Hayes. Hayes was a wise and witty interpreter of ancient texts, who encouraged students to get the "guts" of any book we read. He rightly said that we would never be able to read all that was assigned to us. Consequently, he urged us to focus on the first and last chapters of our reading assignments, and especially the last chapter, since typically, the last chapter held the book's conclusions.

The Bible's First and Last Chapters

In the spirit of John Hayes's suggestion, I revisited the first chapter of the first book in the Christian scriptures as I prepared my sermon. Genesis 1:1 declares, "In the beginning, God created the heavens and the earth."[4] The Christian scriptures open with a grand affirmation of God's creativity. God lovingly establishes divine order from the confused contents of a churning chaos.

With that in mind, I turned to the last chapter of the book of Revelation, which was written by an early Christian leader named John. As John's apocalyptic pilgrimage concludes, he receives a spectacular vision of the transformation of heaven and earth. While parts of the book of Revelation contain provocative, even disturbing, images of judgment and destruction, Revelation 22 reinforces the theme of hope that is the heartbeat of John's message. I decided to focus my sermon on some verses from this last chapter in the Christian scriptures: "Blessed are those who wash their robes so they can have access to the tree of life and can enter into the city by the gates. Outside are the dogs and the sorcerers and the sexually immoral, and the murderers, and the idolaters and everyone who loves and practices falsehood! . . . The grace of the Lord Jesus be *with all*" (Rev 22:14–15, 21; emphasis mine).

As a result of a "war in heaven," Satan—the great dragon—and other demonic forces are defeated and cast from heaven (Rev 12:7–12). After further contestation, evil is finally subdued in all realms of existence (Rev 20:7–15), and the stage is set for God to radically transform the creation. This cosmic transformation occurs when the New Jerusalem descends from heaven to earth: "Then I saw a new heaven and a new earth, for the first heaven and earth had ceased to exist, and the sea existed no more. And I saw the holy city—the new Jerusalem—descending out of heaven" (Rev 21:1–2).

In this section of Revelation, we are in the "New Jerusalem." The mention of the New Jerusalem brings to mind my childhood. Although more than forty years have passed, another voice that accompanies me—that I can still hear in my "third ear"—is the sonorous singing of Brother Herbert Wiley, that sainted deacon in my home church, First Baptist Church in Salem, Virginia. This black Baptist church was established in 1867, a mere two years after the end of the Civil War.

Rarely did a Sunday pass in my youth that I did not find myself sitting in the pew of that church. This was partly because my parents were both leaders there: my father was the pastor, and my mother is a gifted musician and religious educator. Memories of the fervent worship, the fiery religious rhetoric, and the spiritual nurture offered to me by my parents and the seasoned "mothers and fathers" of that church sustain me even to this day.

In the midweek prayer service at First Baptist Church, Deacon Wiley sang with great gusto those spirituals about the New Jerusalem:

> *I will meet you in that city of the New Jerusalem.*
> *I've been washed in the blood of the lamb.*
> *Sweeping through the gates of the New Jerusalem,*
> *Washed in the blood of the lamb.*

> *I want to be ready,*
> *I want to be ready,*

I want to be ready,
to walk in Jerusalem just like John.

Why were the spiritual elders in a small church in the foothills
of southwest Virginia singing about the New Jerusalem? They
realized that the New Jerusalem symbolized the redemption of
violence and the emergence of a new way of life where God's
unmitigated presence would be enjoyed by all. The book of Revelation declares that God will dwell among the people in the New
Jerusalem.

On that spring day in 2009, when I looked out from the ornate
pulpit of The Riverside Church at a sea of conference participants—
some in hijabs, some in yarmulkes, some in vestments—I thought
about how the image of the New Jerusalem is instructive for
interfaith cooperation. As I understand it, the New Jerusalem is
not heaven. It is *heaven on earth*. Some Christians are wistfully
waiting to be plucked into the sky during the so-called rapture.
But the book of Revelation asserts that the sky will plunge to the
earth. Thus, the New Jerusalem is a symbol of the transformation
of *this world*. In light of the need for all religions to find harmony—
and especially the Abrahamic religions—the New Jerusalem is a
relevant symbol for interfaith cooperation.[5]

Currently, Jerusalem is a site of contestation, not cooperation. Consequently, we should interpret Revelation's depiction
of the New Jerusalem not as "pie in the sky" rhetoric but rather
as an invitation for on-the-ground peaceful coexistence among
contemporary Muslims, Jews, and Christians living in and
around that ancient city. By extension, the New Jerusalem also
symbolizes an exhortation for everyone to live harmoniously on
city blocks and boulevards and rural farms and fields around
the globe.

"Let all God's people dwell together in the New Jerusalem," I
declared in the sermon. "Not the New Jerusalem in some distant,
eternal future, but the New Jerusalem in the up-close, right-now,
present." Biblical scholars Wes Howard-Brook and Anthony
Gwyther suggest that the "New Jerusalem is found wherever

human community resists the ways of empire and places God at the center of its shared life."[6]

A Closer Look at Revelation 22

The journey in Revelation 22 into the New Jerusalem, however, is neither smooth nor straightforward. There are various aspects in the last few verses of Revelation 22 that must be examined in the name of intellectual honesty and theological integrity. The pilgrimage to the end of the New Testament requires us to pass through some of the most difficult material in the book of Revelation.

Persons who want to dwell in the New Jerusalem are called to wash their robes: "Blessed are those who wash their robes so they can have access to the tree of life and enter the city by the gates" (Rev 22:14). Participation in God's *future* will be predicated upon appropriate behavior in the *present*. Earlier in the book of Revelation, the saints paradoxically whiten their robes by washing them in blood (Rev 7:14). This imagery is not the glorification of mindless martyrdom. Instead, it can be read as a metaphor for the valiant struggle and willful sacrifice necessary to resist the dehumanizing forces of empire.

The forces of empire do not die quietly. They will strike back. Some of the deadliest weapons of empire include religious and racial bigotry, gender-based chauvinism, and public policies cloaked in the respectable language of fiscal restraint that economically exploit vulnerable people while allowing corporate greed to go unchecked. Frederick Douglass, the nineteenth-century freedom fighter, declared, "Power concedes nothing without a demand." To wash our robes is to demand the dethroning of the death-dealing powers of empire in order to make room for God's *kin-dom*—the big, open house, where sacred siblings live peacefully in the presence of our heavenly father who is divine mother of us all.

The next verse, however, provides a dreadful example of *defamation* and *deformation*: "Outside are the dogs and the sorcerers and the sexually immoral, and the murderers, and the idolaters and everyone who loves and practices falsehood" (Rev 22:15). Unfortunately, this verse is filled with religiously inspired venom. The derogatory language and harsh tone are inexcusable and stand as irrefutable evidence that mean-spirited name-calling (e.g., "the dogs and the sorcerers") finds its way even into the Christian scriptures.

In my ministry, I have found it important to emphasize that critique of the Bible is not sacrilegious. Instead, it arises from a deeply held religious belief that sometimes the "Good Book" does not contain good news. So many people could be liberated from psychological and social oppression if faith leaders empowered faithful people to question sacred texts, especially when those texts "misbehave." The biblical scholar Elsa Tamez rightly suggests that faithfulness to the good news requires us to distance ourselves from the harmful elements of sacred texts.[7]

Many self-righteous Christians have used negative words like those in this verse to condemn and humiliate people who represent cultural diversity. More specifically, these parts of Christian scriptures have been used to exclude socially marginalized persons, and especially LGBTQ persons. The challenge for faith communities is to learn how to articulate passionately the central concerns of our religious traditions (e.g., love, justice, peace, alleviation of suffering, salvation, enlightenment, and fellowship with ancestral spirits) without resorting to name-calling and defamation of character.

Words like "heathen," "pagan," "unsaved," "infidel," and "hell bound" are dangerous. Such words strangle grace to death, thereby eliminating the promise of peaceful life among diverse people seeking the sacred. Preaching on Revelation in an interfaith setting, I considered it important to apologize, because the Christian scriptures are not at their best in Revelation 22:15. When we defame people, even in the supposed name of God, the best elements of our religious traditions are deformed, and we devalue the irrepressible image of God inscribed in every person. If Revelation 22:15 were the last word, we might rightly insist that the final impulses in the Christian scriptures are hatred and exclusion and not hospitality and inclusion.

Thankfully, there is still another word! The final verse in this chapter provides *rehabilitation*. The defamation that leads to deformation stands in need of rehabilitation.

The inclusive nature of God's grace resounds as Revelation 22 concludes. The best translation of this final verse is likely "The grace of the Lord Jesus be *with all*" and not as the New Revised Standard Version (NRSV) translation renders it: "The grace of the Lord Jesus be *with all the saints*." The NRSV translation "with all the saints" refers to another (and probably later) manuscript where Christian scribes altered this verse because of its original, radically inclusive, final blessing upon all. Apparently, those scribes needed to box in God's blessing, lest grace spill over on the "unsaved." Consequently, those Christian scribes changed this verse to read "all the saints," thereby restricting grace only to Christians.[8] But it is likely that the original manuscript simply extended a final benediction of grace upon all.

All Means All

The last word of the last chapter of the last book in the Christian scriptures is the most inclusive word, whether we are reading in English or Greek. In English, the last word is "all," a translation of the Greek word for "all" (*pas*). Even as the Christian Bible emphasizes the importance of Jesus, it celebrates the necessity of inclusion.

The first words in the Christian scriptures are "In the beginning, God created the heavens and the earth." The last words in the Christian scriptures are "The grace of the Lord Jesus be with all." If we want the essence of the Christian Bible and pay close attention to its opening and closing chapters, a clear message emerges: *God's ultimate plan is creative transformation that ushers in radical inclusion!* The Christian Bible begins with creativity and ends with inclusion.

In other words, there is sacred, creative energy moving through the cosmos that seeks to bring everyone and everything into harmony for the sake of goodness and peace. "All" is the last word

in the Christian scriptures. "All" is a boundary-breaking word, a defense-lowering word, a hope-instilling word.

As I have preached this message of pluralism in diverse settings, sometimes thundering the word "all" and other times whispering it, the responses have been positive and palpable. "All" relaxes anxiety-ridden shoulders. "All" causes joyful hands to clap and loving hands to embrace. "All" brings smiles to faces. The word "all" invites us to be siblings, to live peacefully together, and to learn from one another as we dwell under the expansive tent of "all."

In the word "all," there is room for the Muslim and the monk, room for Judaism and Jainism, room for the Buddhist and the Baha'i, room for the Hindu and the Humanist, room for the agnostic and the atheist, room for the skeptic and the seeker. By using the word "all," we are empowered to consider a person as our friend and, even more, our sacred sibling, if that person is hospitable to the sacred spirit of creativity moving through the cosmos to unite us.

"The grace of the Lord Jesus be with all." Pluralism celebrates polyphony. In my pilgrimage to pluralism, many voices—arising from the ancestors, the scriptures, my parents, spiritual elders, mentors, and academic texts—have taught me that when we strive to be inclusive, "all" should actually mean *all*!

Notes

Introduction

1 Emilie M. Townes, *Womanist Ethics and the Cultural Production of Evil* (New York: Palgrave Macmillan, 2006), 12.

2 Rabbi Elissa Sachs-Kohen, a progressive ally at Baltimore Hebrew Congregation in Maryland, sharpened my interpretation of the stories and themes in Genesis.

3 I use the terms "interfaith" and "interreligious" interchangeably throughout the book. Some scholars maintain that the term "interreligious" is preferable. They contend that the word "faith" in "interfaith" unjustifiably privileges Christian and Protestant approaches to religion while also excluding ethical traditions such as secular humanism. Consult Kate McCarthy, "(Inter)Religious Studies: Making a Home in the Secular Academy," in *Interreligious/Interfaith Studies: Defining a New Field*, ed. Eboo Patel, Jennifer Howe Peace, and Noah J. Silverman (Boston: Beacon, 2018), 9–11.

4 Although various forms of the quotation exist, it likely originated from this book: Oliver Wendell Holmes Sr., *The Autocrat of the Breakfast-Table* (Boston: James R. Osgood, 1873), chap. 11, http://www.gutenberg.org/files/751/751-h/751-h.htm.

5 Martin Luther King Jr., *Strength to Love* (Philadelphia: Fortress, 1963), 14.

6 Steven Johnson, *Where Good Ideas Come From: The Natural History of Innovation* (New York: Riverhead, 2010), 16.

1: "Every Time I Feel the Spirit"

1 Obery M. Hendricks Jr., *The Politics of Jesus: Rediscovering the True Revolutionary Nature of the Teachings of Jesus and How They Have Been Corrupted* (New York: Doubleday, 2006), 78.

2 Craig S. Keener, *The Historical Jesus of the Gospels* (Grand Rapids, MI: Eerdmans, 2009).

3 Amy-Jill Levine, *The Misunderstood Jew: The Church and the Scandal of the Jewish Jesus* (New York: HarperOne, 2006), 173.

4 I use the terms "African Traditional Religions" and "black churches," fully aware of the diversity of practices and beliefs conveyed by each term.

5 Adolph Hilary Agbo, *Values of Adinkra and Agama Symbols*, rev. ed. (Kumasi, Ghana: Bigshy Designs, 2006), 3.

6 Brad R. Braxton, *No Longer Slaves: Galatians and African American Experience* (Collegeville, MN: Liturgical, 2002), 96–102.

7 Delores S. Williams, *Sisters in the Wilderness: The Challenge of Womanist God-Talk* (Maryknoll, NY: Orbis, 1993), 216.

8 Jacquelyn Grant, *White Women's Christ and Black Women's Jesus: Feminist Christology and Womanist Response* (Atlanta: Scholars, 1989), 2–3.

9 Alice Walker, *In Search of Our Mothers' Gardens: Womanist Prose* (London: Harcourt Brace Jovanovich, 1983), xi.

10 Stephanie Y. Mitchem, *Introducing Womanist Theology* (Maryknoll, NY: Orbis, 2002), ix.

11 Grant, *White Women's Christ*, 220. Some scholars use "Jesus" and "Christ" interchangeably. I distinguish the terms. "Jesus" was a human prophet. "Christ" is a divine process, consummated in the resurrection, which transformed Jesus into a divine spirit.

12 Rodney S. Sadler Jr., "The Place and Role of Africa and African Imagery in the Bible," in *True to Our Native Land: An African American New Testament Commentary*, ed. Brian K. Blount et al. (Minneapolis: Fortress, 2007), 25.

13 Rodney S. Sadler Jr., "Race and the Face of Jesus: The Implications of Our Images of Christ" (unpublished lecture presented at McCormick Theological Seminary, Chicago, IL, March 15, 2010).

14 Liz Leafloor, "Reconstructing Jesus: Using Science to Flesh Out the Face of Religion," Ancient Origins, last modified December 16, 2015, https://www.ancient-origins.net/news-general/reconstructing-jesus-using-science-flesh-out-face-religion-004942.

15 Kelly Brown Douglas, *The Black Christ* (Maryknoll, NY: Orbis, 1994), 97–117.

16 Douglas, 110–13.

17 JoAnne Marie Terrell, *Power in the Blood? The Cross in the African American Experience* (Maryknoll, NY: Orbis, 1998), 7.

18 Terrell, 63.
19 Terrell, 142.
20 Christopher Rowland and Mark Corner, *Liberating Exegesis: The Challenge of Liberation Theology to Biblical Studies* (London: SPCK, 1990), 53.
21 Walter Brueggemann, *Finally Comes the Poet: Daring Speech for Proclamation* (Minneapolis: Fortress, 1989), 1.
22 Robert E. Hood, *Must God Remain Greek? Afro Cultures and God-Talk* (Minneapolis: Fortress, 1990), 151–52.
23 Joerg Rieger, *Christ and Empire: From Paul to Postcolonial Times* (Minneapolis: Fortress, 2007), 78.
24 Rieger, 96.
25 Hood, *Must God Remain Greek?*, 183–215.
26 Hood, 197.
27 Hood, 199.
28 Rosemarie Freeney Harding and Rachel Elizabeth Harding, "Hospitality, Haints, and Healing: A Southern African American Meaning of Religion," in *Deeper Shades of Purple: Womanism in Religion and Society*, ed. Stacey M. Floyd-Thomas (New York: New York University Press, 2006), 104; Barbara A. Holmes, *Race and the Cosmos: An Invitation to View the World Differently* (Harrisburg, PA: Trinity Press International, 2002), 67–91.
29 Gregg Braden, *The Isaiah Effect: Decoding the Lost Science of Prayer and Prophecy* (New York: Three Rivers, 2000), 99; Diarmuid O'Murchu, *Quantum Theology: Spiritual Implications of the New Physics*, rev. ed. (New York: Crossroads, 2004).
30 Peter J. Paris, *The Spirituality of African Peoples: The Search for a Common Moral Discourse* (Minneapolis: Fortress, 1995), 25.
31 George Cummings, "The Slave Narratives as a Source of Black Theological Discourse: The Spirit and Eschatology," in *Cut Loose Your Stammering Tongue: Black Theology in the Slave Narratives*, ed. Dwight N. Hopkins and George Cummings (Maryknoll, NY: Orbis, 1991), 46–66.
32 Cheryl A. Kirk-Duggan, "African-American Spirituals: Confronting and Exorcising Evil through Song," in *A Troubling in My Soul: Womanist Perspectives on Evil and Suffering*, ed. Emilie M. Townes (Maryknoll, NY: Orbis, 1993), 166.
33 Jürgen Moltmann, *The Spirit of Life: A Universal Affirmation* (Minneapolis: Fortress, 1992), 63.
34 James D. G. Dunn, *Christology in the Making: A New Testament Inquiry into the Origins of the Doctrine of the Incarnation*, 2nd ed. (Grand Rapids, MI: Eerdmans, 1989), 47.
35 Ched Myers, *Binding the Strong Man: A Political Reading of Mark's Story of Jesus* (Maryknoll, NY: Orbis, 1988), 123.

36 Joel Marcus, *The Way of the Lord: Christological Exegesis of the Old Testament in the Gospel of Mark* (Louisville, KY: Westminster John Knox, 1992), 12–47.

37 Brian K. Blount, *Go Preach! Mark's Kingdom Message and the Black Church Today* (Maryknoll, NY: Orbis, 1998), 55–64.

38 R. T. France, *The Gospel of Mark: A Commentary on the Greek Text* (Grand Rapids, MI: Eerdmans, 2002), 75.

39 Emerson B. Powery, "The Gospel of Mark," in Brian K. Blount et al., *True to Our Native Land*, 136.

40 Hisako Kinukawa, "The Syrophoenician Woman: Mark 7:24–30," in *Voices from the Margin: Interpreting the Bible in the Third World*, rev. ed., ed. R. S. Sugirtharajah (Maryknoll, NY: Orbis, 1995), 152.

41 Linda E. Thomas, "Anthropology, Mission, and the African Woman," in *Mission and Culture: The Louis J. Luzbetak SVD Lecture*, Catholic Theological Union (Chicago: CCGM, 2006), 4.

42 Myers, *Binding the Strong Man*, 404.

43 Rowland and Corner, *Liberating Exegesis*, 45.

44 Christopher Rowland, "Introduction: The Theology of Liberation," in *The Cambridge Companion to Liberation Theology*, ed. Christopher Rowland (Cambridge: Cambridge University Press, 1999), 7.

45 "Kin-dom" is a term coined by feminist theologians to disrupt the unjust assumption that God is "male." The term also accentuates relationality: our *relationships* with God and our *relationships* with one another. We are all *kin*folk. Ada María Isasi-Díaz, "Solidarity: Love of Neighbor in the 1980s," in *Lift Every Voice: Constructing Christian Theologies from the Underside*, ed. Susan Brooks Thistlethwaite and Mary Potter Engel (London: Harper & Row, 1990), 304n4.

46 Rieger, *Christ and Empire*, 41.

47 R. S. Sugirtharajah, *Asian Biblical Hermeneutics and Postcolonialism: Contesting the Interpretations* (Maryknoll, NY: Orbis, 1998), 119.

48 Emilie M. Townes, *In a Blaze of Glory: Womanist Spirituality as Social Witness* (Nashville: Abingdon, 1995), 47.

2: Religion, Reparations, and Racial Reconciliation

1 Ideology involves "socially produced assumptions" and socially sanctioned practices that can oppress and/or liberate groups of people. For further discussion, consult A. K. M. Adam, *What Is Postmodern Biblical Criticism?* (Minneapolis: Fortress, 1995), 45–60. The phrase "socially produced assumptions" is Adam's (48). Also, consult Louis Althusser, *Essays on Ideology* (London: Verso, 1984); and James H. Kavanagh, "Ideology," in *Critical Terms for Literary Study*, 2nd ed., ed. Frank Lentricchia and Thomas McLaughlin (Chicago: University of Chicago Press, 1995), 306–20.

2 Brad R. Braxton, *The Tyranny of Resolution: I Corinthians 7:17–24* (Atlanta: Society of Biblical Literature, 2000).

3 Sugirtharajah, *Asian Biblical Hermeneutics*, 15.

4 Mark Lewis Taylor, "Spirit and Liberation: Achieving Postcolonial Theology in the United States," in *Postcolonial Theologies: Divinity and Empire*, ed. Catherine Keller, Michael Nausner, and Mayra Rivera (St. Louis, MO: Chalice, 2004), 42.

5 Seamus Deane, "Imperialism/Nationalism," in Lentricchia and McLaughlin, *Critical Terms for Literary Study*, 354.

6 Fernando F. Segovia, *Decolonizing Biblical Studies: A View from the Margins* (Maryknoll, NY: Orbis, 2000).

7 Notable examples include Richard A. Horsley, ed., *Paul and Empire: Religion and Power in Roman Imperial Society* (Harrisburg, PA: Trinity Press International, 1997); Richard A. Horsley, ed., *Paul and Politics: Ekklesia, Israel, Imperium, Interpretation* (Harrisburg, PA: Trinity Press International, 2000); and Richard A. Horsley, ed., *Paul and the Roman Imperial Order* (Harrisburg, PA: Trinity Press International, 2004).

8 Walter Wink, *The Bible in Human Transformation: Toward a New Paradigm for Biblical Study* (Philadelphia: Fortress, 1973), 6.

9 Social scientists and cultural critics debate the meaning of the term "race." Many scholars have refuted the validity of "race" as a marker of fixed biological differences. Still, "race" as a social construction by which individuals and communities differentiate themselves remains a powerful and viable cultural force, especially in the United States. For further discussion, consult Richard Delgado and Jean Stefancic, *Critical Race Theory: An Introduction* (New York: New York University Press, 2001); and Steve Fenton, *Ethnicity* (Cambridge: Polity, 2003).

10 For another attempt to merge Pauline scholarship and dialogue about contemporary racial reconciliation, consult Braxton, *No Longer Slaves*.

11 The bicentennial commemoration occurred in Great Britain in 2007 and in the United States in 2008. While this historic legislation was signed in the British Parliament and the United States Congress in March 1807, the legislation did not become effective officially until January 1, 1808.

12 The abolition of the transatlantic *slave trade* and the abolition of transatlantic *slavery* were distinct events. Many British merchants continued in the illegal trade of enslaved Africans for years or, in some cases, decades after the parliamentary act of 1807. Also, from 1807 to 1865, the violence of chattel slavery in the United States intensified, unleashing an escalating savagery against Africans in the so-called New World. This savagery culminated in the Civil War in the United States. Thus, even after 1807, the carnage of slavery led to

even more carnage as the fledgling American nation fought internally about the fate of its enslaved.

13 For excellent historical accounts of the abolition of the slave trade and of slavery, consult Adam Hochschild, *Bury the Chains: Prophets and Rebels in the Fight to Free an Empire's Slaves* (Boston: Mariner, 2006); and Christopher Leslie Brown, *Moral Capital: Foundations of British Abolitionism* (Chapel Hill: University of North Carolina Press, 2006).

14 Consult, for example, Clarice J. Martin, "The Haustafeln (Household Codes) in African American Biblical Interpretation: 'Free Slaves' and 'Subordinate Women,'" in *Stony the Road We Trod: African American Biblical Interpretation*, ed. Cain Hope Felder (Minneapolis: Fortress, 1991), 206–31; C. Michelle Venable-Ridley, "Paul and the African American Community," in *Embracing the Spirit: Womanist Perspectives on Hope, Salvation, and Transformation*, ed. Emilie M. Townes (Maryknoll, NY: Orbis, 1997), 212–33; and Braxton, *Tyranny of Resolution*, 235–64.

15 For a cogent analysis of black people's engagement with Paul's ambiguity concerning slavery and freedom, consult Allen Dwight Callahan, "'Brother Saul': An Ambivalent Witness to Freedom," *Semeia*, nos. 83/84 (1998): 235–62.

16 The inaugural Bray Lecturer was Gerald West of the University of Natal in South Africa. He visited India and the United Kingdom in 2005. I am grateful for the generous support of USPG, SPCK, and the Anglican Communion that facilitated my travel, research, and lectures. For the history of USPG and SPCK, consult Daniel O'Connor et al., *Three Centuries of Mission: The United Society for the Propagation of the Gospel 1701–2000* (London: Continuum, 2000). In 2012 and 2016, USPG changed its name. Its current name is United Society Partners in the Gospel.

17 W. E. B. Du Bois expatriated to Ghana and provided important inspiration and counsel to Kwame Nkrumah. Both Du Bois and Nkrumah were passionate advocates of African nationalism and staunch critics of European colonialism. Consult David Birmingham, *Kwame Nkrumah: The Father of African Nationalism*, rev. ed. (Athens: Ohio University Press, 1998), 95.

18 I delivered formal lectures at Kings College, London; Ripon College, Cuddesdon; the Queen's Foundation for Ecumenical Theological Education, Birmingham; University of York; and Manchester Cathedral. I appreciate the hospitality at each of these locations and at Westminster Abbey.

19 Deadria C. Farmer-Paellmann, "Excerpt from *Black Exodus: The Ex-slave Pension Movement Reader*," in *Should America Pay? Slavery and the Raging Debate on Reparations*, ed. Raymond A. Winbush (New York: Amistad, 2003), 22.

20 For example, in political science and legal studies, Randall Robinson, *The Debt: What America Owes to Blacks* (New York: Plume, 2000); and Roy L. Brooks, *Atonement and Forgiveness: A New Model for Black Reparations* (Berkeley: University of California Press, 2004). In sociology and cultural studies, Winbush, *Should America Pay?*; and Ta-Nehisi Coates, "The Case for Reparations," *Atlantic*, June 2014, https://www .theatlantic.com/magazine/archive/2014/06/the-case-for-reparations/ 361631/. In philosophy, Janna Thompson, *Taking Responsibility for the Past: Reparation and Historical Justice* (Cambridge: Polity, 2002).

21 For a compelling exposition of the South African truth and reconciliation process in the 1990s, which involved reparations, consult Desmond Tutu, *No Future without Forgiveness* (New York: Image, 1999). For a discussion of reparations from the perspectives of pastoral theology and Hebrew Bible exegesis, consult Homer U. Ashby Jr., *Our Home Is over Jordan: A Black Pastoral Theology* (St. Louis, MO: Chalice, 2003), 134–40. For a rationale for reparations from the perspective of ethics and critical race theory, consult Jennifer Harvey, "Race and Reparations: The Material Logics of White Supremacy," in *Disrupting White Supremacy from Within: White People on What We Need to Do*, ed. Jennifer Harvey, Karin A. Case, and Robin Hawley Gorsline (Cleveland, OH: Pilgrim, 2004), 91–122.

22 Molefi Kete Asante, "The African American Warrant for Reparations: The Crime of European Enslavement of Africans and Its Consequences," in Winbush, *Should America Pay?*, 4. In an intriguing reparations case study, Virginia Theological Seminary began paying economic reparations in 2021 to the descendants of black people who were forced to work at the seminary during slavery and segregation in the United States. Will White, "Seminary Built on Slavery and Jim Crow Labor Has Begun Paying Reparations," *New York Times*, May 31, 2021, https://www.nytimes.com/2021/05/31/us/reparations -virginia-theological-seminary.html.

23 J. Louis Martyn argued that epistemology is a fundamental concern in 2 Corinthians. According to Martyn, Paul urges the Corinthians to join him in a new way of knowing God's actions. Martyn, *Theological Issues in the Letters of Paul* (Nashville: Abingdon, 1997), 89–110.

24 In 2 Corinthians 3:6, 14, Paul uses the Greek word *diathēkē*, which is normally translated as "covenant." By "covenant," Paul seems to mean something like "era." He distinguishes between the ministry of the old era and the new era. The Christ event (i.e., the life, death, resurrection, and impending return of Jesus Christ) is the dividing line between these eras. The scripture of Judaism is still an important feature within the new era. However, Paul reads that scripture in a new way—namely, through his experience with Jesus Christ.

25 Walter Brueggemann, "The Book of Exodus," in *The New Interpreter's Bible*, vol. 1 (Nashville: Abingdon, 1994), 953.

26   Phyllis Trible, *Texts of Terror: Literary-Feminist Readings of Biblical Narratives* (Philadelphia: Fortress, 1984).

27   Cain Hope Felder, "Race, Racism, and the Biblical Narratives," in Felder, *Stony the Road We Trod*, 128–29.

28   For further discussion of the "veil" in Du Bois's work, consult Stanley Brodwin, "The Veil Transcended: Form and Meaning in W. E. B. Du Bois' 'The Souls of Black Folk,'" *Journal of Black Studies* 2, no. 3 (March 1972): 303–21. Also consult Vincent L. Wimbush, "'We Will Make Our Own Future Text': An Alternate Orientation to Interpretation," in Blount et al., *True to Our Native Land*, 44–47.

29   W. E. B. Du Bois, *The Souls of Black Folk* (1903; repr., New York: Dover, 1994), 2.

30   Holmes, *Race and the Cosmos*, 76.

31   Holmes, 76.

32   Hochschild, *Bury the Chains*, 67–68.

33   For poignant analyses of the often ignored colonial violence against black women, consult Traci C. West, "Spirit-Colonizing Violations: Racism, Sexual Violence, and Black American Women," in *Remembering Conquest: Feminist/Womanist Perspectives on Religion, Colonization, and Sexual Violence*, ed. Nantawan Boonprasat Lewis and Marie M. Fortune (New York: Haworth, 1999), 19–30; and Katie G. Cannon, "Sexing Black Women: Liberation from the Prisonhouse of Anatomical Authority," in *Loving the Body: Black Religious Studies and the Erotic*, ed. Anthony B. Pinn and Dwight N. Hopkins (New York: Palgrave Macmillan, 2004), 11–30.

34   Brown, *Moral Capital*, 333–450.

35   For a detailed discussion of fundamentalism, consult James Barr, *Fundamentalism* (Philadelphia: Westminster John Knox, 1977); Karen Armstrong, *The Battle for God: A History of Fundamentalism* (New York: Ballantine Books, 2000); and Martyn Percy and Ian Jones, eds., *Fundamentalism: Church and Society* (London: SPCK, 2002).

36   Patrick Laude, "An Eternal Perfume," *Parabola: The Search for Meaning* 30, no. 4 (Winter 2005): 7.

37   For a discussion of contextual biblical interpretation on a global scale, consult Daniel Patte, ed., *Global Bible Commentary* (Nashville: Abingdon, 2004).

38   Elisabeth Schüssler Fiorenza, *Rhetoric and Ethic: The Politics of Biblical Studies* (Minneapolis: Fortress, 1999), 192–93.

3: An Experiment in Radical Religious Openness

1   The Open Church, https://theopenchurchmd.org/.

2   "Kin-dom" is a term coined by feminist theologians to disrupt the unjust assumption that God is "male."

3   Brad R. Braxton, "Extended Interview [on Marriage Equality]," Religion and Ethics Newsweekly, November 2, 2012, video, 10:06, http://www.pbs.org/wnet/religionandethics/2012/11/02/november-2-2012-brad-braxton-extended-interview/13690/.

4   Sanjena Sathian, "Where's Our Faith?," OZY, June 28, 2015, http://www.ozy.com/provocateurs/wheres-our-faith/61343.

5   Charles Kimball, *When Religion Becomes Evil* (New York: Harper-Collins, 2002).

6   Sheila Greeve Davaney, "Theology and the Turn to Cultural Analysis," in *Converging on Culture: Theologians in Dialogue with Cultural Analysis and Criticism*, ed. Delwin Brown, Sheila Greeve Davaney, and Kathryn Tanner (New York: Oxford University Press, 2001), 5.

7   The *Baltimore Sun* chronicled Douglas Church's revitalization. David L. Greene, "Here to Have Church," *Baltimore Sun*, July 10, 2000, https://www.baltimoresun.com/news/bs-xpm-2000-07-10-0007100109-story.html.

8   Amy Butler's pastorate at The Riverside Church concluded in 2019.

9   For example, Peter J. Paris et al., eds., *The History of The Riverside Church in the City of New York* (New York: New York University Press, 2004).

10 Paris et al., 46.

11 Paris et al., 47.

12 Joseph Barndt, *Understanding and Dismantling Racism: The Twenty-First Century Challenge to White America* (Minneapolis: Fortress, 2007), 143–44.

13 Kwok Pui-lan, *Postcolonial Imagination and Feminist Theology* (Louisville, KY: Westminster John Knox, 2005), 43.

14 Justo L. González, "Reading from My Bicultural Place: Acts 6:1–7," in *Reading from This Place: Social Location and Biblical Interpretation in the United States*, ed. Fernando F. Segovia and Mary Ann Tolbert (Minneapolis: Fortress, 1995), 146 (emphasis mine).

15 Joseph M. Webb, *Preaching and the Challenge of Pluralism* (St. Louis, MO: Chalice, 1998), 108.

16 Benjamin E. Mays, quoted in Lawrence Edward Carter Sr., *Walking Integrity: Benjamin Elijah Mays, Mentor to Martin Luther King, Jr.* (Macon, GA: Mercer University Press, 1998), 12.

17 Brad R. Braxton, "Interpretation for Liberation: Working with the Book" (sermon, The Open Church, Baltimore, MD, August 5, 2012).

18 Kathleen Neal Cleaver, quoted in the introduction to Harvey, Case, and Gorsline, *Disrupting White Supremacy*, 9.

19 Eboo Patel, *Acts of Faith: The Story of an American Muslim, the Struggle for the Soul of a Generation* (Boston: Beacon, 2007), xi–xix.

4: Aiding and Abetting New Life

1 Dorothy C. Bass, introduction to *Practicing Theology: Beliefs and Practices in Christian Life*, ed. Miroslav Volf and Dorothy C. Bass (Grand Rapids, MI: Eerdmans, 2002), 3.

2 Kathleen A. Cahalan and James R. Nieman, "Mapping the Field of Practical Theology," in *For Life Abundant: Practical Theology, Theological Education, and Christian Ministry*, ed. Dorothy C. Bass and Craig Dykstra (Grand Rapids, MI: Eerdmans, 2008), 79.

3 "Kin-dom" is a term coined by feminist theologians to disrupt the unjust assumption that God is "male."

4 Peter J. Gomes, *The Scandalous Gospel of Jesus: What's So Good about the Good News?* (New York: HarperOne, 2007), 196–97.

5 Samuel D. Proctor, Gardner C. Taylor, and Gary V. Simpson, *We Have This Ministry: The Heart of the Pastor's Vocation* (Valley Forge, PA: Judson, 1996), 20–21.

6 Teresa Fry Brown, "Avoiding Asphyxiation: A Womanist Perspective on Intrapersonal and Interpersonal Transformation," in Townes, *Embracing the Spirit*, 81.

7 Zora Neale Hurston, *The Sanctified Church: The Folklore Writings of Zora Neale Hurston* (Berkeley: Turtle Island Foundation, 1981), 49–50.

8 Personal conversation with Martha Simmons, ca. 2009.

9 G. Lee Ramsey Jr., *Care-full Preaching: From Sermon to Caring Community* (St. Louis, MO: Chalice, 2000), 31–58.

10 Emmanuel Y. Lartey, *Pastoral Theology in an Intercultural World* (Cleveland, OH: Pilgrim, 2006), 136.

11 bell hooks, *All about Love: New Visions* (New York: William Morrow, 2000), 93.

12 Josef Sorett and Renata Cobbs Fletcher, *Religion, Sexuality, and Black Culture Project: A Final Report* (New York: Public/Private Ventures, 2009), 28.

13 Bob Allen, "Baptist Church Postpones Vote on Including Gays in Church Directory (Updated)," Good Faith Media, December 3, 2007, https://goodfaithmedia.org/baptist-church-postpones-vote-on -including-gays-in-church-directory-updated-cms-11969/.

14 Heterosexism is "an ideology and system of power that defines what constitutes normal and deviant sexuality and distributes social rewards and penalties based on this definition." Patricia Hill Collins, *Black Sexual Politics: African Americans, Gender, and the New Racism* (New York: Routledge, 2005), 351.

15 Martha Simmons and Frank A. Thomas, eds., *Preaching with Sacred Fire: An Anthology of African American Sermons, 1750 to the Present* (New York: W. W. Norton, 2010).

16 Molefi Kete Asante [Arthur L. Smith], "Socio historical Perspectives of Black Oratory," *Quarterly Journal of Speech* 56, no. 3 (1970): 264.

17 Smith, 264.

18 James Henry Harris, *The Word Made Plain: The Power and Promise of Preaching* (Minneapolis: Fortress, 2004), 77–94.

19 Henry H. Mitchell, "African-American Preaching: The Future of a Rich Tradition," *Interpretation* 51, no. 4 (October 1997): 378.

20 Eugene H. Peterson, *The Contemplative Pastor: Returning to the Art of Spiritual Direction* (Grand Rapids, MI: Eerdmans, 1989), 32–33.

21 Obery M. Hendricks Jr., "Guerrilla Exegesis: 'Struggle' as a Scholarly Vocation—a Postmodern Approach to African-American Biblical Interpretation," *Semeia* 72 (1995): 73–90.

22 Personal conversation with Margaret Aymer, ca. 2008.

23 Ellen Ott Marshall, *Christians in the Public Square: Faith That Transforms Politics* (Nashville: Abingdon, 2008), xxi.

24 Ben Kesslen, "Anti-Semitic Assaults in U.S. More Than Doubled in 2018, ADL Reports," NBC News, April 30, 2019, https://www.nbcnews.com/news/us-news/anti-semitic-assaults-u-s-more-doubled-2018-adl-reports-n1000246; and Leila Fadel, "U.S. Hate Groups Rose Sharply in Recent Years, Watchdog Group Reports," NPR, February 20, 2019, https://www.npr.org/2019/02/20/696217158/u-s-hate-groups-rose-sharply-in-recent-years-watchdog-group-reports.

25 Victor Anderson, *Creative Exchange: A Constructive Theology of African American Religious Experience* (Minneapolis: Fortress, 2008), 3–4.

26 Iris Murdoch, *Existentialists and Mystics: Writings on Philosophy and Literature*, ed. Peter Conradi (New York: Penguin, 1997), 218.

27 Murdoch, 203.

28 Mother Teresa, *Love: The Words and Inspiration of Mother Teresa* (Boulder, CO: Blue Mountain, 2007), 87.

29 Jon Kabat-Zinn, *Wherever You Go There You Are: Mindfulness Meditation in Everyday Life* (New York: Hyperion, 1994), 12.

30 Harding and Harding, "Hospitality, Haints, and Healing," 111.

5: Baptism and Holy Communion

1 Williams, *Sisters in the Wilderness*, 205–6.

2 Consult Laurence Hull Stookey, *Baptism: Christ's Act in the Church* (Nashville: Abingdon, 1982).

3 Consult Laurence Hull Stookey, *Eucharist: Christ's Feast with the Church* (Nashville: Abingdon, 1993); and Andrea Bieler and Luise Schottroff, *The Eucharist, Bodies, Bread, and Resurrection* (Minneapolis: Fortress, 2007).

4 Stephanie Buckhanon Crowder, "Holy Communion and Epiphany Commentary," African American Lectionary, January 6, 2008, http://www.theafricanamericanlectionary.org/PopupLectionaryReading.asp?LRID=3.

5   These are the opening lyrics of the hymn "Down at the Cross" written by Elisha A. Hoffman.

6   William R. Newell wrote these hymn lyrics.

7   Lawrence S. Cunningham et al., *The Sacred Quest: An Invitation to the Study of Religion*, 2nd ed. (Englewood Cliffs, NJ: Prentice Hall, 1995), 79–80.

8   Black Lives Matter, https://blacklivesmatter.com/.

9   Daniel Funke and Tina Susman, "From Ferguson to Baton Rouge: Deaths of Black Men and Women at the Hands of Police," *Los Angeles Times*, July 12, 2016, http://www.latimes.com/nation/la-na-police -deaths-20160707-snap-htmlstory.html; Nicole Dungca et al., "A Dozen High-Profile Fatal Encounters That Have Galvanized Protests Nationwide," *Washington Post*, June 8, 2020, https://www.washingtonpost .com/investigations/a-dozen-high-profile-fatal-encounters-that-have -galvanized-protests-nationwide/2020/06/08/4fdbfc9c-a72f-11ea-b473 -04905b1af82b_story.html.

10 Christopher J. LeBron, *The Making of Black Lives Matter: A Brief History of an Idea* (New York: Oxford University Press, 2017), x.

11 Ta-Nehisi Coates, "Nonviolence as Compliance," *Atlantic*, April 27, 2015, https://www.theatlantic.com/politics/archive/2015/04/nonviolence-as -compliance/391640/.

12 Luke Broadwater and Ian Duncan, "Once Again, Baltimore's Mayor Has Fired a Police Commissioner. Will It Make a Difference?," *Baltimore Sun*, January 20, 2018, https://www.baltimoresun.com/news/ investigations/bs-md-ci-davis-fired-weekender-20180119-story .html.

13 Neil Elliott, "The Anti-imperial Message of the Cross," in Horsley, *Paul and Empire*, 168–69.

14 Gail R. O'Day, "The Gospel of John," in *The New Interpreter's Bible*, vol. 9 (Nashville: Abingdon, 1995), 834.

15 Concerning Jesus's African identity, consult Sadler Jr., "Place and Role of Africa," 23–30.

16 N. T. Wright, "Paul's Gospel and Caesar's Empire," in Horsley, *Paul and Politics*, 182.

17 Wright, 182.

18 William T. Cavanaugh and Peter Scott, introduction to *The Blackwell Companion to Political Theology*, ed. Peter Scott and William T. Cavanaugh (Malden, MA: Blackwell, 2004), 2.

19 "Kin-dom" is a term coined by feminist theologians to disrupt the unjust assumption that God is "male."

20 Thomas G. Long, *Matthew* (Louisville, KY: Westminster John Knox, 1997), 33.

21 John accentuates the radical nature of his baptismal preaching with a radical (i.e., getting to the root) metaphor in Matt 3:10: "Even now the ax is lying at the root of the tree; every tree therefore that does

not bear good fruit is cut down and thrown into the fire." The ethical commitments of our baptismal identity compel us to expose, and perhaps expunge, the roots of unjust and unproductive social systems.

22 James H. Cone, *God of the Oppressed* (San Francisco: HarperSanFrancisco, 1975), 62.

23 This is an allusion to Martin Luther King Jr.'s speech at the 1963 March on Washington. Martin Luther King Jr., "I Have a Dream," in *The Essential Writings and Speeches of Martin Luther King, Jr.*, ed. James M. Washington (San Francisco: HarperSanFrancisco, 1986), 219.

24 NPR Staff, "The Victims: 9 Were Slain at Charleston's Mother Emanuel AME Church," NPR, June 18, 2015, https://www.npr.org/sections/thetwo-way/2015/06/18/415539516/the-victims-9-were-slain-at-charlestons-emanuel-ame-church.

25 These lyrics are from the second stanza of James Weldon Johnson's "Lift Every Voice and Sing," which is referred to as the "Negro National Anthem."

26 Kelly Brown Douglas, *Stand Your Ground: Black Bodies and the Justice of God* (Maryknoll, NY: Orbis, 2015), 232.

27 Mark W. Stamm, *Let Every Soul Be Jesus' Guest: A Theology of the Open Table* (Nashville: Abingdon, 2006), 48.

28 Donna Langston, "Tired of Playing Monopoly?," in *Race, Class, and Gender: An Anthology*, 3rd ed., ed. Margaret L. Andersen and Patricia Hill Collins (New York: Wadsworth, 1998), 132.

29 Dale P. Andrews, "Preaching a Just Word in Privileged Pulpits," in *Just Preaching: Prophetic Voices for Economic Justice*, ed. André Resner Jr. (St. Louis, MO: Chalice, 2003), 169, 171.

30 Keri Day, *Unfinished Business: Black Women, the Black Church, and the Struggle to Thrive in America* (Maryknoll, NY: Orbis, 2012), 149–50.

31 These words from Assata Shakur have become a rallying cry for the Black Lives Matter movement.

6: Policy and Poetry

1 For a concise treatment of the cultural and spiritual significance of drums and drumming in African and African diasporic traditions, consult Michael Kernan, "The Talking Drums," *Smithsonian Magazine*, June 2000, https://www.smithsonianmag.com/arts-culture/the-talking-drums-29197334/. In African Traditional Religions, drums are sacred objects that convene the community and enable people to commune with African deities.

2 Anne Mackinnon, Natasha Amott, and Craig McGarvey, *Mapping Change: Using a Theory of Change to Guide Planning and Evaluation*, GrantCraft series (March 29, 2006), https://grantcraft.org/wp-content/uploads/sites/2/2018/12/theory_change.pdf.

3   Terence E. Fretheim, "Genesis," in *New Interpreter's Bible*, 1:344.

4   Fretheim, 342.

5   Fretheim, 345–46.

6   For example, consult John Hope Franklin and Alfred A. Moss Jr., *From Slavery to Freedom: A History of African Americans*, 8th ed. (New York: Alfred A. Knopf, 2000); and Molefi Kete Asante, *The History of Africa* (New York: Routledge, 2007).

7   John S. Mbiti, *Introduction to African Religion*, 2nd ed. (Oxford: Heinemann, 1991), 1–19; and Laurenti Magesa, *African Religion: The Moral Traditions of Abundant Life* (Maryknoll, NY: Orbis, 1997), 25.

8   Paris, *Spirituality of African Peoples*, 27.

9   Orlando Patterson characterizes the "social death" experienced by enslaved persons as an "institutionalized marginality" that prohibited them from enjoying the social benefits of belonging to a community. *Slavery and Social Death: A Comparative Study* (Cambridge, MA: Harvard University Press, 1982), 46.

10 Tonya Bolden, *Rock of Ages: A Tribute to the Black Church* (New York: Dell Dragonfly, 2001), 8–9.

11 James Hill Jr., "What Do People Mean by 'Theopoetics'?," Arts, Religion, and Culture, February 14, 2016, https://artsreligionculture.org/definitions.

12 The Open Church, https://theopenchurchmd.org/.

13 Howard Thurman, *Footprints of a Dream: The Story of the Church for the Fellowship of All Peoples* (New York: Harper & Brothers, 1959); Hurston, *Sanctified Church*; Cecil Williams and Janice Miriktani, *Beyond the Possible: 50 Years of Creating Radical Change at a Community Called Glide* (New York: HarperOne, 2013).

14 For examples of progressive black biblical interpretation, consult Braxton, *No Longer Slaves*; Obery M. Hendricks Jr., *The Universe Bends toward Justice: Radical Reflections on the Bible, the Church, and the Body Politic* (Maryknoll, NY: Orbis, 2011); Nyasha Junior, *An Introduction to Womanist Biblical Interpretation* (Louisville, KY: Westminster John Knox, 2015); and Mitzi J. Smith, *Womanist Sass and Talk Back: Social (In)Justice, Intersectionality, and Biblical Interpretation* (Eugene, OR: Cascade, 2018).

15 "Kin-dom" is a term coined by feminist theologians to disrupt the unjust assumption that God is "male."

16 Andrew Bradstock, "'Seeking the Welfare of the City': Public Theology as Radical Action," in *Radical Christian Voices and Practice: Essays in Honor of Christopher Rowland*, ed. Zoë Bennett and David B. Gowler (New York: Oxford University Press, 2012), 226–27.

17 John Hope Franklin, foreword to *Black Intellectuals*, by William M. Banks (New York: W. W. Norton, 1996), xi.

18 Quoted in Cornel West and Kelvin Shawn Sealey, *Restoring Hope: Conversations on the Future of Black America* (Boston: Beacon, 1997), 4.

19 Gayraud S. Wilmore, *Black Religion and Black Radicalism: An Interpretation of the Religious History of African Americans*, 3rd ed. (Maryknoll, NY: Orbis, 1998), 37.

20 Mbiti, *Introduction to African Religion*, 75–81; Monica A. Coleman, *Making a Way Out of No Way: A Womanist Theology* (Minneapolis: Fortress, 2008), 101–23.

21 Linda E. Thomas, "Womanist Theology, Epistemology, and a New Anthropological Paradigm," in Thomas, *Living Stones*, 44–45. Also consult Katie G. Cannon, "Pedagogical Praxis in African American Theology," in *The Oxford Handbook of African American Theology*, ed. Katie G. Cannon and Anthony B. Pinn (New York: Oxford University Press, 2014), 319–30.

22 Robert Darden, *Nothing but Love in God's Water*, vol. 1, *Black Sacred Music from the Civil War to the Civil Rights Movement* (University Park: Pennsylvania State University Press, 2014); Darden, *Nothing but Love in God's Water*, vol. 2, *Black Sacred Music from Sit-Ins to Resurrection City* (University Park: Pennsylvania State University Press, 2016).

23 "Lazetta Rainey Braxton," 2050 Wealth Partners, accessed March 16, 2021, https://www.2050wealthpartners.com/lazetta-rainey-braxton.

24 For discussions of the spiritual gift of speaking in tongues, consult Acts 2; 1 Cor 13–14; and John R. Levison, "Gift of Tongues," in *The New Interpreter's Dictionary of the Bible*, vol. 5, ed. Katharine Doob Sakenfeld (Nashville: Abingdon, 2009), 625–27.

25 Raquel West, "Yaa Asantewaa (Mid-1800s–1921)," Black Past, February 8, 2019, https://www.blackpast.org/global-african-history/yaa-asantewaa-mid-1800s-1921/.

26 Janelle Harris Dixon, "Why the Black National Anthem Is Lifting Every Voice to Sing," *Smithsonian Magazine*, August 2020, https://www.smithsonianmag.com/smithsonian-institution/why-black-national-anthem-lifting-every-voice-sing-180975519/.

27 Soyica Diggs Colbert, *Black Movements: Performance and Cultural Politics* (New Brunswick, NJ: Rutgers University Press, 2017), 15–16.

28 Vincent Harding, "Responsibilities of the Black Scholar to the Community," in *The State of Afro-American History: Past, Present, and Future*, ed. Darlene Clark Hine (Baton Rouge: Louisiana State University Press, 1986), 281.

7: Sanctification and Proclamation

1 Maria W. Stewart, "A Prayer for Purification (1835)," in *Conversations with God: Two Centuries of Prayers by African Americans*, ed. James Melvin Washington (New York: HarperCollins, 1994), 30.

2 Noel Schoonmaker, "Getting Your *Real* Master of Divinity" (sermon preached at Wake Forest University School of Divinity, Winston-Salem, NC, ca. 2004).

3 C. H. Spurgeon, "The Minister's Self-Watch," in *Lectures to My Students*, rev. ed. (Grand Rapids, MI: Zondervan, 1955), 7–8.

4 I am indebted to my colleague Samuel Weber, OSB, for this insight.

5 Townes, *Blaze of Glory*, 11.

6 Walter Brueggemann, *Theology of the Old Testament: Testimony, Dispute, Advocacy* (Minneapolis: Fortress, 1997), 288.

7 Kelly Brown Douglas, *Sexuality and the Black Church: A Womanist Perspective* (Maryknoll, NY: Orbis, 1999), 120.

8 Barbara A. Holmes, *Joy Unspeakable: Contemplative Practices of the Black Church* (Minneapolis: Fortress, 2004), 26.

9 For reflections on the Holy Spirit's role in preaching, consult, for example, James A. Forbes Jr., *The Holy Spirit and Preaching* (Nashville: Abingdon, 1989); Brad R. Braxton, *Preaching Paul* (Nashville: Abingdon, 2004), 69–96; and Luke A. Powery, *Spirit Speech: Lament and Celebration in Preaching* (Nashville: Abingdon, 2009).

10 Martha Simmons and Brad R. Braxton, "What Happened to Sacred Eloquence? (Celebrating the Ministry of Gardner C. Taylor)," in *Our Sufficiency Is of God: Essays on Preaching in Honor of Gardner C. Taylor*, ed. Timothy George, James Earl Massey, and Robert Smith Jr. (Macon, GA: Mercer University Press, 2010), 283.

11 Quoted in Kirk Byron Jones, *Rest in the Storm: Self-Care Strategies for Clergy and Other Caregivers* (Valley Forge, PA: Judson, 2001), 12.

12 Abraham Joshua Heschel, *The Sabbath: Its Meaning for Modern Man* (New York: Noonday, 1951), 13.

13 Quoted in Parker J. Palmer, *Leading from Within: Reflections on Spirituality and Leadership* (Washington, DC: Servant Leadership School, 1990), 9.

14 Howard Thurman, *Meditations of the Heart* (Richmond, IN: Friends United, 1953), 28.

15 Thurman, 31.

16 "Rapid Eye Movement Sleep," Wikipedia, accessed June 19, 2010, http://en.wikipedia.org/wiki/Rapid_eye_movement_sleep.

17 These lyrics are from Byron Cage's popular 2003 gospel song titled "The Presence of the Lord Is Here."

9: The Battle Cry of a New Revolution

1 Elizabeth Cady Stanton, "Seneca Falls Declaration (July 19, 1848)," Digital History, http://www.digitalhistory.uh.edu/disp_textbook.cfm?psid=1087&smtID=3.

2 Fannie Lou Hamer, "I'm Sick and Tired of Being Sick and Tired" (speech given at the Williams Institutional CME Church, Harlem, New York, December 20, 1964), https://www.crmvet.org/docs/flh64.htm.

3 Scott Bader-Saye, "Violence, Reconciliation, and the Justice of God," *Crosscurrents* 52, no. 4 (Winter 2003): 537–42.

10: A Gift for Mother Earth

1 For a concise discussion of the history and achievements of the Earth Day movement, consult https://www.earthday.org/.
2 Walter J. Burghardt, *Justice: A Global Adventure* (Maryknoll, NY: Orbis, 2004), 17.
3 Sallie McFague, *The Body of God: An Ecological Theology* (Minneapolis: Fortress, 1993), 99–100.
4 McFague, 113.
5 Consult Robert D. Bullard's classic treatment of "environmental racism," which involves discriminatory practices of directing environmental toxins toward communities of color in general and black communities in particular. Robert D. Bullard, *Dumping in Dixie: Race, Class, and Environmental Quality*, 3rd ed. (Boulder, CO: Westview, 2000).
6 Steven C. Rockefeller, "The Earth Charter: Building a Global Culture of Peace" (speech given at the Earth Charter Community Summits, Tampa, FL, September 29, 2001), https://earthcharter.org/library/the-earth-charter-building-a-global-culture-of-peace-2001/.
7 Bieler and Schottroff, *Eucharist, Bodies, Bread*, 124.

11: On Purpose

1 Kirk Byron Jones, *Holy Play: The Joyful Adventure of Unleashing Your Divine Purpose* (San Francisco: Jossey Bass, 2007), 114.
2 Janet O. Hagberg, *Real Power: Stages of Personal Power in Organizations*, 3rd ed. (Salem, WI: Sheffield, 2003), 147.
3 The source of this sermon illustration is unknown.
4 Martin Luther King Jr., "Letter from Birmingham City Jail," in Washington, *Essential Writings and Speeches*, 296.
5 Cleon L. Rogers Jr. and Cleon L. Rogers III, *The New Linguistic and Exegetical Key to the Greek New Testament* (Grand Rapids, MI: Zondervan, 1998), 150.

Epilogue: The Bible's *Last Word*

1 Mbiti, *Introduction to African Religion*; Coleman, *Making a Way*, 101–23.
2 Braxton, *No Longer Slaves*.

3   Eboo Patel, *Sacred Ground: Pluralism, Prejudice, and the Promise of America* (Boston: Beacon, 2012), 71.

4   This biblical citation and subsequent citations in this chapter are from the New English Translation (NET).

5   Each of the Abrahamic religions claims Jerusalem. For Muslims, Jerusalem is the location of the Dome of the Rock, the spot from which the prophet Muhammad ascended into heaven. For Jews, Jerusalem houses the Western Wall, the remnant of their once glorious Temple. For Christians, Jerusalem is the locale of Jesus's crucifixion and resurrection.

6   Wes Howard-Brook and Anthony Gwyther, *Unveiling Empire: Reading Revelation Then and Now* (Maryknoll, NY: Orbis, 1999), 184.

7   Elsa Tamez, "Women's Rereading of the Bible," in Sugirtharajah, *Voices from the Margin*, 52.

8   G. K. Beale, *The Book of Revelation: A Commentary on the Greek Text* (Grand Rapids, MI: Eerdmans, 1999), 1157. I typically preach from the New Revised Standard Version translation of the Bible. I departed from that practice in this sermon and instead used the New English Translation of the Bible because of the difference in the translation of Rev 22:21. This subtle difference, which is historically plausible, makes a big difference for people committed to interfaith cooperation and religious pluralism.

Bibliography

2050 Wealth Partners. "Lazetta Rainey Braxton." Accessed March 16, 2021. https://www.2050wealthpartners.com/lazetta -rainey-braxton.

Adam, A. K. M. *What Is Postmodern Biblical Criticism?* Minneapolis: Fortress, 1995.

Agbo, Adolph Hilary. *Values of Adinkra and Agama Symbols.* Rev. ed. Kumasi, Ghana: Bigshy Designs, 2006.

Allen, Bob. "Baptist Church Postpones Vote on Including Gays in Church Directory (Updated)." Good Faith Media, December 3, 2007. https://goodfaithmedia.org/baptist-church-postpones -vote-on-including-gays-in-church-directory-updated-cms -11969/.

Althusser, Louis. *Essays on Ideology.* London: Verso, 1984.

Anderson, Victor. *Creative Exchange: A Constructive Theology of African American Religious Experience.* Minneapolis: Fortress, 2008.

Andrews, Dale P. "Preaching a Just Word in Privileged Pulpits." In *Just Preaching: Prophetic Voices for Economic Justice,* edited by André Resner Jr., 169–77. St. Louis, MO: Chalice, 2003.

Armstrong, Karen. *The Battle for God: A History of Fundamentalism.* New York: Ballantine Books, 2000.

Asante, Molefi Kete [Arthur L. Smith]. "The African American Warrant for Reparations: The Crime of European Enslavement of Africans and Its Consequences." In *Should America Pay?*

Slavery and the Raging Debate on Reparations, edited by Raymond A. Winbush, 3–13. New York: Amistad, 2003.

——. *The History of Africa*. New York: Routledge, 2007.

——. "Socio-historical Perspectives of Black Oratory." *Quarterly Journal of Speech* 56, no. 3 (1970): 264–69.

Ashby, Homer U., Jr. *Our Home Is over Jordan: A Black Pastoral Theology*. St. Louis, MO: Chalice, 2003.

Bader-Saye, Scott. "Violence, Reconciliation, and the Justice of God." *Crosscurrents* 52, no. 4 (Winter 2003): 537–42.

Barndt, Joseph. *Understanding and Dismantling Racism: The Twenty-First Century Challenge to White America*. Minneapolis: Fortress, 2007.

Barr, James. *Fundamentalism*. Philadelphia: Westminster John Knox, 1977.

Bass, Dorothy C. Introduction to *Practicing Theology: Beliefs and Practices in Christian Life*, edited by Miroslav Volf and Dorothy C. Bass, 1–9. Grand Rapids, MI: Eerdmans, 2002.

Beale, G. K. *The Book of Revelation: A Commentary on the Greek Text*. Grand Rapids, MI: Eerdmans, 1999.

Bieler, Andrea, and Luise Schottroff. *The Eucharist, Bodies, Bread, and Resurrection*. Minneapolis: Fortress, 2007.

Birmingham, David. *Kwame Nkrumah: The Father of African Nationalism*. Rev. ed. Athens: Ohio University Press, 1998.

Blount, Brian K. *Go Preach! Mark's Kingdom Message and the Black Church Today*. Maryknoll, NY: Orbis, 1998.

Bolden, Tonya. *Rock of Ages: A Tribute to the Black Church*. New York: Dell Dragonfly, 2001.

Braden, Gregg. *The Isaiah Effect: Decoding the Lost Science of Prayer and Prophecy*. New York: Three Rivers, 2000.

Bradstock, Andrew. "'Seeking the Welfare of the City': Public Theology as Radical Action." In *Radical Christian Voices and Practice: Essays in Honor of Christopher Rowland*, edited by Zoë Bennett and David B. Gowler, 225–39. New York: Oxford University Press, 2012.

Braxton, Brad R. "Extended Interview [on Marriage Equality]." *Religion and Ethics Newsweekly*, November 2, 2012. Video,

10:06. http://www.pbs.org/wnet/religionandethics/2012/11/02/november-2-2012-brad-braxton-extended-interview/13690/.

———. "Interpretation for Liberation: Working with the Book." Sermon preached at The Open Church, Baltimore, MD, August 5, 2012.

———. *No Longer Slaves: Galatians and African American Experience*. Collegeville, MN: Liturgical, 2002.

———. *Preaching Paul*. Nashville: Abingdon, 2004.

———. *The Tyranny of Resolution: I Corinthians 7:17–24*. Atlanta: Society of Biblical Literature, 2000.

Broadwater, Luke, and Ian Duncan. "Once Again, Baltimore's Mayor Has Fired a Police Commissioner. Will It Make a Difference?" *Baltimore Sun*, January 20, 2018. https://www.baltimoresun.com/news/investigations/bs-md-ci-davis-fired-weekender-20180119-story.html.

Brodwin, Stanley. "The Veil Transcended: Form and Meaning in W. E. B. Du Bois' 'The Souls of Black Folk.'" *Journal of Black Studies* 2, no. 3 (March 1972): 303–21.

Brooks, Roy L. *Atonement and Forgiveness: A New Model for Black Reparations*. Berkeley: University of California Press, 2004.

Brown, Christopher Leslie. *Moral Capital: Foundations of British Abolitionism*. Chapel Hill: University of North Carolina Press, 2006.

Brown, Teresa Fry. "Avoiding Asphyxiation: A Womanist Perspective on Intrapersonal and Interpersonal Transformation." In *Embracing the Spirit: Womanist Perspectives on Hope, Salvation, and Transformation*, edited by Emilie M. Townes, 72–94. Maryknoll, NY: Orbis, 1997.

Brueggemann, Walter. *The Book of Exodus*. In *The New Interpreter's Bible*, vol. 1, 677–981. Nashville: Abingdon, 1994.

———. *Finally Comes the Poet: Daring Speech for Proclamation*. Minneapolis: Fortress, 1989.

———. *Theology of the Old Testament: Testimony, Dispute, Advocacy*. Minneapolis: Fortress, 1997.

Bullard, Robert D. *Dumping in Dixie: Race, Class, and Environmental Quality*. 3rd ed. Boulder, CO: Westview, 2000.

Burghardt, Walter J. *Justice: A Global Adventure.* Maryknoll, NY: Orbis, 2004.

Cahalan, Kathleen A., and James R. Nieman. "Mapping the Field of Practical Theology." In *For Life Abundant: Practical Theology, Theological Education, and Christian Ministry,* edited by Dorothy C. Bass and Craig Dykstra, 62–85. Grand Rapids, MI: Eerdmans, 2008.

Callahan, Allen Dwight. "'Brother Saul': An Ambivalent Witness to Freedom." *Semeia,* nos. 83/84 (1998): 235–62.

Cannon, Katie G. "Pedagogical Praxis in African American Theology." In *The Oxford Handbook of African American Theology,* edited by Katie G. Cannon and Anthony B. Pinn, 319–30. New York: Oxford University Press, 2014.

———. "Sexing Black Women: Liberation from the Prisonhouse of Anatomical Authority." In *Loving the Body: Black Religious Studies and the Erotic,* edited by Anthony B. Pinn and Dwight N. Hopkins, 11–30. New York: Palgrave Macmillan, 2004.

Carter, Lawrence Edward, Sr. *Walking Integrity: Benjamin Elijah Mays, Mentor to Martin Luther King, Jr.* Macon, GA: Mercer University Press, 1998.

Cavanaugh, William T., and Peter Scott. Introduction to *The Blackwell Companion to Political Theology,* edited by Peter Scott and William T. Cavanaugh, 1–3. Malden, MA: Blackwell, 2004.

Coates, Ta-Nehisi. "The Case for Reparations." *Atlantic,* June 2014. https://www.theatlantic.com/magazine/archive/2014/06/the-case-for-reparations/361631/.

———. "Nonviolence as Compliance." *Atlantic,* April 27, 2015. https://www.theatlantic.com/politics/archive/2015/04/nonviolence-as-compliance/391640/.

Colbert, Soyica Diggs. *Black Movements: Performance and Cultural Politics.* New Brunswick, NJ: Rutgers University Press, 2017.

Coleman, Monica A. *Making a Way Out of No Way: A Womanist Theology.* Minneapolis: Fortress, 2008.

Collins, Patricia Hill. *Black Sexual Politics: African Americans, Gender, and the New Racism.* New York: Routledge, 2005.

Cone, James H. *God of the Oppressed*. San Francisco: Harper-SanFrancisco, 1975.

Crowder, Stephanie Buckhanon. "Holy Communion and Epiphany Commentary." African American Lectionary, January 6, 2008. http://www.theafricanamericanlectionary.org/Popup LectionaryReading.asp?LRID=3.

Cummings, George. "The Slave Narratives as a Source of Black Theological Discourse: The Spirit and Eschatology." In *Cut Loose Your Stammering Tongue: Black Theology in the Slave Narratives*, edited by Dwight N. Hopkins and George Cummings, 46–66. Maryknoll, NY: Orbis, 1991.

Cunningham, Lawrence S., John Kelsay, R. Maurice Barineau, and Heather Joy McVoy. *The Sacred Quest: An Invitation to the Study of Religion*. 2nd ed. Englewood Cliffs, NJ: Prentice Hall, 1995.

Darden, Robert. *Nothing but Love in God's Water*. Vol. 1, *Black Sacred Music from the Civil War to the Civil Rights Movement*. University Park: Pennsylvania State University Press, 2014.

———. *Nothing but Love in God's Water*. Vol. 2, *Black Sacred Music from Sit-Ins to Resurrection City*. University Park: Pennsylvania State University Press, 2016.

Davaney, Sheila Greeve. "Theology and the Turn to Cultural Analysis." In *Converging on Culture: Theologians in Dialogue with Cultural Analysis and Criticism*, edited by Delwin Brown, Sheila Greeve Davaney, and Kathryn Tanner, 3–15. New York: Oxford University Press, 2001.

Day, Keri. *Unfinished Business: Black Women, the Black Church, and the Struggle to Thrive in America*. Maryknoll, NY: Orbis, 2012.

Deane, Seamus. "Imperialism/Nationalism." In *Critical Terms for Literary Study*, 2nd ed., edited by Frank Lentricchia and Thomas McLaughlin, 354–68. Chicago: University of Chicago Press, 1995.

Delgado, Richard, and Jean Stefancic. *Critical Race Theory: An Introduction*. New York: New York University Press, 2001.

Dixon, Janelle Harris. "Why the Black National Anthem Is Lifting Every Voice to Sing." *Smithsonian Magazine*, August 2020.

https://www.smithsonianmag.com/smithsonian-institution/
why-black-national-anthem-lifting-every-voice-sing
-180975519/.

Douglas, Kelly Brown. *The Black Christ*. Maryknoll, NY: Orbis,
1994.

——. *Sexuality and the Black Church: A Womanist Perspective*. Maryknoll, NY: Orbis, 1999.

——. *Stand Your Ground: Black Bodies and the Justice of God*.
Maryknoll, NY: Orbis, 2015.

Dozier, Verna J. *The Dream of God: A Call to Return*. New York:
Church Publishing, 2006.

Du Bois, W. E. B. *The Souls of Black Folk*. 1903. Reprint, New
York: Dover, 1994.

Dungca, Nicole, Jenn Abelson, Mark Berman, and John Sullivan.
"A Dozen High-Profile Fatal Encounters That Have Galvanized
Protests Nationwide." *Washington Post*, June 8, 2020. https://
www.washingtonpost.com/investigations/a-dozen-high-profile
-fatal-encounters-that-have-galvanized-protests-nationwide/
2020/06/08/4fdbfc9c-a72f-11ea-b473-04905b1af82b_story
.html.

Dunn, James D. G. *Christology in the Making: A New Testament
Inquiry into the Origins of the Doctrine of the Incarnation*.
2nd ed. Grand Rapids, MI: Eerdmans, 1989.

Elliott, Neil. "The Anti-imperial Message of the Cross." In *Paul
and Empire: Religion and Power in Roman Imperial Society*,
edited by Richard A. Horsley, 167–83. Harrisburg, PA: Trinity Press International, 1997.

Fadel, Leila. "U.S. Hate Groups Rose Sharply in Recent Years,
Watchdog Group Reports." NPR, February 20, 2019. https://
www.npr.org/2019/02/20/696217158/u-s-hate-groups-rose
-sharply-in-recent-years-watchdog-group-reports.

Farmer-Paellmann, Deadria C. "Excerpt from *Black Exodus: The
Ex-slave Pension Movement Reader*." In *Should America Pay?
Slavery and the Raging Debate on Reparations*, edited by Ray-
mond A. Winbush, 22–31. New York: Amistad, 2003.

Felder, Cain Hope. "Race, Racism, and the Biblical Narratives." In *Stony the Road We Trod: African American Biblical*

Interpretation, edited by Cain Hope Felder, 127–45. Minneapolis: Fortress, 1991.

Fenton, Steve. *Ethnicity*. Cambridge: Polity, 2003.

Fiorenza, Elisabeth Schüssler. *Rhetoric and Ethic: The Politics of Biblical Studies*. Minneapolis: Fortress, 1999.

Forbes, James A., Jr. *The Holy Spirit and Preaching*. Nashville: Abingdon, 1989.

France, R. T. *The Gospel of Mark: A Commentary on the Greek Text*. Grand Rapids, MI: Eerdmans, 2002.

Franklin, John Hope. Foreword to *Black Intellectuals*, by William M. Banks, ix–xi. New York: W. W. Norton, 1996.

Franklin, John Hope, and Alfred A. Moss Jr. *From Slavery to Freedom: A History of African Americans*. 8th ed. New York: Alfred A. Knopf, 2000.

Fretheim, Terence E. "Genesis." In *The New Interpreter's Bible*, vol. 1, 319–674. Nashville: Abingdon, 1994.

Funke, Daniel, and Tina Susman. "From Ferguson to Baton Rouge: Deaths of Black Men and Women at the Hands of Police." *Los Angeles Times*, July 12, 2016. http://www.latimes.com/nation/la-na-police-deaths-20160707-snap-htmlstory.html.

Gomes, Peter J. *The Scandalous Gospel of Jesus: What's So Good about the Good News?* New York: HarperOne, 2007.

González, Justo L. "Reading from My Bicultural Place: Acts 6:1–7." In *Reading from This Place: Social Location and Biblical Interpretation in the United States*, edited by Fernando F. Segovia and Mary Ann Tolbert, 139–47. Minneapolis: Fortress, 1995.

Grant, Jacquelyn. *White Women's Christ and Black Women's Jesus: Feminist Christology and Womanist Response*. Atlanta: Scholars, 1989.

Greene, David L. "Here to Have Church." *Baltimore Sun*, July 10, 2000. https://www.baltimoresun.com/news/bs-xpm-2000-07-10-0007100109-story.html.

Hagberg, Janet O. *Real Power: Stages of Personal Power in Organizations*. 3rd ed. Salem, WI: Sheffield, 2003.

Hamer, Fannie Lou. "I'm Sick and Tired of Being Sick and Tired." Speech given at the Williams Institutional CME Church,

Harlem, New York. December 20, 1964. https://www.crmvet.org/docs/flh64.htm.

Harding, Rosemarie Freeney, and Rachel Elizabeth Harding. "Hospitality, Haints, and Healing: A Southern African American Meaning of Religion." In *Deeper Shades of Purple: Womanism in Religion and Society*, edited by Stacey M. Floyd-Thomas, 98–114. New York: New York University Press, 2006.

Harding, Vincent. "Responsibilities of the Black Scholar to the Community." In *The State of Afro-American History: Past, Present, and Future*, edited by Darlene Clark Hine, 277–84. Baton Rouge: Louisiana State University Press, 1986.

Harris, James Henry. *The Word Made Plain: The Power and Promise of Preaching*. Minneapolis: Fortress, 2004.

Harvey, Jennifer. "Race and Reparations: The Material Logics of White Supremacy." In *Disrupting White Supremacy from Within: White People on What We Need to Do*, edited by Jennifer Harvey, Karin A. Case, and Robin Hawley Gorsline, 91–122. Cleveland, OH: Pilgrim, 2004.

Harvey, Jennifer, Karin A. Case, and Robin Hawley Gorsline, eds. Introduction to *Disrupting White Supremacy from Within: White People on What We Need to Do*, 3–31. Cleveland, OH: Pilgrim, 2004.

Hendricks, Obery M., Jr. "Guerrilla Exegesis: 'Struggle' as a Scholarly Vocation—a Postmodern Approach to African-American Biblical Interpretation." *Semeia* 72 (1995): 73–90.

———. *The Politics of Jesus: Rediscovering the True Revolutionary Nature of the Teachings of Jesus and How They Have Been Corrupted*. New York: Doubleday, 2006.

———. *The Universe Bends toward Justice: Radical Reflections on the Bible, the Church, and the Body Politic*. Maryknoll, NY: Orbis, 2011.

Heschel, Abraham Joshua. *The Sabbath: Its Meaning for Modern Man*. New York: Noonday, 1951.

Hill, James. "What Do People Mean by 'Theopoetics'?" Arts, Religion, and Culture, February 14, 2016. https://artsreligionculture.org/definitions.

Hochschild, Adam. *Bury the Chains: Prophets and Rebels in the Fight to Free an Empire's Slaves.* Boston: Mariner, 2006.

Holmes, Barbara A. *Joy Unspeakable: Contemplative Practices of the Black Church.* Minneapolis: Fortress, 2004.

———. *Race and the Cosmos: An Invitation to View the World Differently.* Harrisburg, PA: Trinity Press International, 2002.

Holmes, Oliver Wendell, Sr. *The Autocrat of the Breakfast-Table.* Boston: James R. Osgood, 1873. http://www.gutenberg.org/files/751/751-h/751-h.htm.

Hood, Robert E. *Must God Remain Greek? Afro Cultures and God-Talk.* Minneapolis: Fortress, 1990.

hooks, bell. *All about Love: New Visions.* New York: William Morrow, 2000.

Hopkins, Dwight N. *Being Human: Race, Culture, and Religion.* Minneapolis: Fortress, 2005.

———. "A Black American Perspective on Interfaith Dialogue." In *Living Stones in the Household of God: The Legacy and Future of Black Theology,* edited by Linda E. Thomas, 169–80. Minneapolis: Fortress, 2004.

Horsley, Richard A., ed. *Paul and Empire: Religion and Power in Roman Imperial Society.* Harrisburg, PA: Trinity Press International, 1997.

———. *Paul and Politics: Ekklesia, Israel, Imperium, Interpretation.* Harrisburg, PA: Trinity Press International, 2000.

———. *Paul and the Roman Imperial Order.* Harrisburg, PA: Trinity Press International, 2004.

Howard-Brook, Wes, and Anthony Gwyther. *Unveiling Empire: Reading Revelation Then and Now.* Maryknoll, NY: Orbis, 1999.

Hughes, Langston. "Draft Ideas." In *The Collected Works of Langston Hughes,* vol. 9, edited by Christopher C. De Santis, 408. Columbia: University of Missouri Press, 2002.

Hurston, Zora Neale. *The Sanctified Church: The Folklore Writings of Zora Neale Hurston.* Berkeley, CA: Turtle Island Foundation, 1981.

Isasi-Díaz, Ada María. "Solidarity: Love of Neighbor in the 1980s." In *Lift Every Voice: Constructing Christian Theologies from the Underside,* edited by Susan Brooks Thistlethwaite and Mary Potter Engel, 31–40. London: Harper & Row, 1990.

Johnson, Steven. *Where Good Ideas Come From: The Natural History of Innovation.* New York: Riverhead, 2010.

Jones, Kirk Byron. *Holy Play: The Joyful Adventure of Unleashing Your Divine Purpose.* San Francisco: Jossey Bass, 2007.

———. *Rest in the Storm: Self-Care Strategies for Clergy and Other Caregivers.* Valley Forge, PA: Judson, 2001.

Junior, Nyasha. *An Introduction to Womanist Biblical Interpretation.* Louisville, KY: Westminster John Knox, 2015.

Kabat-Zinn, Jon. *Wherever You Go There You Are: Mindfulness Meditation in Everyday Life.* New York: Hyperion, 1994.

Kavanagh, James H. "Ideology." In *Critical Terms for Literary Study,* 2nd ed., edited by Frank Lentricchia and Thomas McLaughlin, 306–20. Chicago: University of Chicago Press, 1995.

Keener, Craig S. *The Historical Jesus of the Gospels.* Grand Rapids, MI: Eerdmans, 2009.

Kernan, Michael. "The Talking Drums." *Smithsonian Magazine,* June 2000. https://www.smithsonianmag.com/arts-culture/the-talking-drums-29197334/.

Kesslen, Ben. "Anti-Semitic Assaults in U.S. More Than Doubled in 2018, ADL Reports." NBC News, April 30, 2019. https://www.nbcnews.com/news/us-news/anti-semitic-assaults-u-s-more-doubled-2018-adl-reports-n1000246.

Kimball, Charles. *When Religion Becomes Evil.* New York: HarperCollins, 2002.

King, Martin Luther, Jr. "I Have a Dream." In *The Essential Writings and Speeches of Martin Luther King, Jr.,* edited by James M. Washington, 217–20. San Francisco: HarperSanFrancisco, 1986.

———. "Letter from Birmingham City Jail." In Washington, *Essential Writings and Speeches,* 289–302.

———. *Strength to Love.* Philadelphia: Fortress, 1963.

Kinukawa, Hisako. "The Syrophoenician Woman: Mark 7:24–30." In *Voices from the Margin: Interpreting the Bible in the Third*

World, rev. ed., edited by R. S. Sugirtharajah, 138–55. Maryknoll, NY: Orbis, 1995.

Kirk-Duggan, Cheryl A. "African-American Spirituals: Confronting and Exorcising Evil through Song." In *A Troubling in My Soul: Womanist Perspectives on Evil and Suffering*, edited by Emilie M. Townes, 151–71. Maryknoll, NY: Orbis, 1993.

Langston, Donna. "Tired of Playing Monopoly?" In *Race, Class, and Gender: An Anthology*, 3rd ed., edited by Margaret L. Andersen and Patricia Hill Collins, 26–36. New York: Wadsworth, 1998.

Lartey, Emmanuel Y. *Pastoral Theology in an Intercultural World*. Cleveland, OH: Pilgrim, 2006.

Laude, Patrick. "An Eternal Perfume." *Parabola: The Search for Meaning* 30, no. 4 (Winter 2005): 6–9.

Leafloor, Liz. "Reconstructing Jesus: Using Science to Flesh Out the Face of Religion." Ancient Origins, last modified December 16, 2015. https://www.ancient-origins.net/news-general/reconstructing-jesus-using-science-flesh-out-face-religion-004942.

LeBron, Christopher J. *The Making of Black Lives Matter: A Brief History of an Idea*. New York: Oxford University Press, 2017.

Levine, Amy-Jill. *The Misunderstood Jew: The Church and the Scandal of the Jewish Jesus*. New York: HarperOne, 2006.

Levison, John R. "Gift of Tongues." In *The New Interpreter's Dictionary of the Bible*, vol. 5, edited by Katharine Doob Sakenfeld, 625–27. Nashville: Abingdon, 2009.

Long, Thomas G. *Matthew*. Louisville, KY: Westminster John Knox, 1997.

Mackinnon, Anne, Natasha Amott, and Craig McGarvey. *Mapping Change: Using a Theory of Change to Guide Planning and Evaluation*. GrantCraft series (March 29, 2006). https://learningforfunders.candid.org/content/guides/mapping-change/#highlights.

Magesa, Laurenti. *African Religion: The Moral Traditions of Abundant Life*. Maryknoll, NY: Orbis, 1997.

Marable, Manning. "Black Leadership, Faith, and the Struggle for Freedom." In *Black Faith and Public Talk: Critical Essays on James H. Cone's Black Theology and Black Power*, edited by Dwight N. Hopkins, 77–88. Maryknoll, NY: Orbis, 1999.

Marcus, Joel. *The Way of the Lord: Christological Exegesis of the Old Testament in the Gospel of Mark*. Louisville, KY: Westminster John Knox, 1992.

Marshall, Ellen Ott. *Christians in the Public Square: Faith That Transforms Politics*. Nashville: Abingdon, 2008.

Martin, Clarice J. "The Haustafeln (Household Codes) in African American Biblical Interpretation: 'Free Slaves' and 'Subordinate Women.'" In *Stony the Road We Trod: African American Biblical Interpretation*, edited by Cain Hope Felder, 206–31. Minneapolis: Fortress, 1991.

Martyn, J. Louis. *Theological Issues in the Letters of Paul*. Nashville: Abingdon, 1997.

Mbiti, John S. *Introduction to African Religion*. 2nd ed. Oxford: Heinemann, 1991.

McCarthy, Kate. "(Inter)Religious Studies: Making a Home in the Secular Academy." In *Interreligious/Interfaith Studies: Defining a New Field*, edited by Eboo Patel, Jennifer Howe Peace, and Noah J. Silverman, 2–15. Boston: Beacon, 2018.

McFague, Sallie. *The Body of God: An Ecological Theology*. Minneapolis: Fortress, 1993.

Mitchell, Henry H. "African-American Preaching: The Future of a Rich Tradition." *Interpretation* 51, no. 4 (October 1997): 371–83.

Mitchem, Stephanie Y. *Introducing Womanist Theology*. Maryknoll, NY: Orbis, 2002.

Moltmann, Jürgen. *The Spirit of Life: A Universal Affirmation*. Minneapolis: Fortress, 1992.

Mother Teresa. *Love: The Words and Inspiration of Mother Teresa*. Boulder, CO: Blue Mountain, 2007.

Murdoch, Iris. *Existentialists and Mystics: Writings on Philosophy and Literature*. Edited by Peter Conradi. New York: Penguin, 1997.

Myers, Ched. *Binding the Strong Man: A Political Reading of Mark's Story of Jesus*. Maryknoll, NY: Orbis, 1988.

NPR Staff. "The Victims: 9 Were Slain at Charleston's Mother Emanuel AME Church." NPR, June 18, 2015. https://www.npr.org/sections/thetwo-way/2015/06/18/415539516/the-victims-9-were-slain-at-charlestons-emanuel-ame-church.

O'Connor, Daniel, et al. *Three Centuries of Mission: The United Society for the Propagation of the Gospel 1701–2000*. London: Continuum, 2000.

O'Day, Gail R. "The Gospel of John." In *The New Interpreter's Bible*, vol. 9, 491–865. Nashville: Abingdon, 1995.

Oduyoye, Mercy Amba. "Three Cardinal Issues of Mission in Africa." In *Mission in the Third Millennium*, edited by Robert J. Schreiter, 40–52. Maryknoll, NY: Orbis, 2001.

O'Murchu, Diarmuid. *Quantum Theology: Spiritual Implications of the New Physics*. Rev. ed. New York: Crossroads, 2004.

Palmer, Parker J. *Leading from Within: Reflections on Spirituality and Leadership*. Washington, DC: Servant Leadership School, 1990.

Paris, Peter J. *The Spirituality of African Peoples: The Search for a Common Moral Discourse*. Minneapolis: Fortress, 1995.

Paris, Peter J., John W. Cook, James Hudnut-Beumler, and Lawrence Mamiya, eds. *The History of The Riverside Church in the City of New York*. New York: New York University Press, 2004.

Patel, Eboo. *Acts of Faith: The Story of an American Muslim, the Struggle for the Soul of a Generation*. Boston: Beacon, 2007.

———. *Sacred Ground: Pluralism, Prejudice, and the Promise of America*. Boston: Beacon, 2012.

Patte, Daniel, ed. *Global Bible Commentary*. Nashville: Abingdon, 2004.

Patterson, Orlando. *Slavery and Social Death: A Comparative Study*. Cambridge, MA: Harvard University Press, 1982.

Percy, Martyn, and Ian Jones, eds. *Fundamentalism: Church and Society*. London: SPCK, 2002.

Peterson, Eugene H. *The Contemplative Pastor: Returning to the Art of Spiritual Direction*. Grand Rapids, MI: Eerdmans, 1989.

Powery, Emerson B. "The Gospel of Mark." In *True to Our Native Land: An African American New Testament Commentary*, edited by Brian K. Blount, Cain Hope Felder, Clarice J. Martin, and Emerson B. Powery, 121–57. Minneapolis: Fortress, 2007.

Powery, Luke A. *Spirit Speech: Lament and Celebration in Preaching*. Nashville: Abingdon, 2009.

Proctor, Samuel D., Gardner C. Taylor, and Gary V. Simpson. *We Have This Ministry: The Heart of the Pastor's Vocation*. Valley Forge, PA: Judson, 1996.

Pui-lan, Kwok. *Postcolonial Imagination and Feminist Theology*. Louisville, KY: Westminster John Knox, 2005.

Ramsey, G. Lee, Jr. *Care-full Preaching: From Sermon to Caring Community*. St. Louis, MO: Chalice, 2000.

Rieger, Joerg. *Christ and Empire: From Paul to Postcolonial Times*. Minneapolis: Fortress, 2007.

Robinson, Randall. *The Debt: What America Owes to Blacks*. New York: Plume, 2000.

Rockefeller, Steven C. "The Earth Charter: Building a Global Culture of Peace." Speech given at the Earth Charter Community Summits, Tampa, FL. September 29, 2001. https://earthcharter.org/library/the-earth-charter-building-a-global-culture-of-peace-2001/.

Rogers, Cleon L., Jr., and Cleon L. Rogers III. *The New Linguistic and Exegetical Key to the Greek New Testament*. Grand Rapids, MI: Zondervan, 1998.

Rowland, Christopher. "Introduction: The Theology of Liberation." In *The Cambridge Companion to Liberation Theology*, edited by Christopher Rowland, 1–16. Cambridge: Cambridge University Press, 1999.

Rowland, Christopher, and Mark Corner. *Liberating Exegesis: The Challenge of Liberation Theology to Biblical Studies*. London: SPCK, 1990.

Sadler, Rodney S., Jr. "The Place and Role of Africa and African Imagery in the Bible." In *True to Our Native Land: An African American New Testament Commentary*, edited by Brian K. Blount, Cain Hope Felder, Clarice J. Martin, and Emerson B. Powery, 23–30. Minneapolis: Fortress, 2007.

———. "Race and the Face of Jesus: The Implications of Our Images of Christ." Unpublished lecture presented at McCormick Theological Seminary, Chicago, IL, March 15, 2010.

Sathian, Sanjena. "Where's Our Faith?" OZY, June 28, 2015. http://www.ozy.com/provocateurs/wheres-our-faith/61343.

Schoonmaker, Noel. "Getting Your *Real* Master of Divinity." Sermon preached at Wake Forest University School of Divinity, Winston-Salem, NC, ca. 2004.

Segovia, Fernando F. *Decolonizing Biblical Studies: A View from the Margins*. Maryknoll, NY: Orbis, 2000.

Simmons, Martha, and Brad R. Braxton. "What Happened to Sacred Eloquence? (Celebrating the Ministry of Gardner C. Taylor)." In *Our Sufficiency Is of God: Essays on Preaching in Honor of Gardner C. Taylor*, edited by Timothy George, James Earl Massey, and Robert Smith Jr., 272–300. Macon, GA: Mercer University Press, 2010.

Simmons, Martha, and Frank A. Thomas, eds. *Preaching with Sacred Fire: An Anthology of African American Sermons, 1750 to the Present*. New York: W. W. Norton, 2010.

Smith, Christine Marie. "A Lesbian Perspective: Moving toward a Promised Place." In *Preaching Justice: Ethnic and Cultural Perspectives*, edited by Christine Marie Smith, 134–53. Cleveland, OH: United Church, 1998.

Smith, Mitzi J. *Womanist Sass and Talk Back: Social (In)Justice, Intersectionality, and Biblical Interpretation*. Eugene, OR: Cascade, 2018.

Sorett, Josef, and Renata Cobbs Fletcher. *Religion, Sexuality, and Black Culture Project: A Final Report*. New York: Public/Private Ventures, 2009.

Spurgeon, C. H. "The Minister's Self-Watch." In *Lectures to My Students*, rev. ed. Grand Rapids, MI: Zondervan, 1955.

Stamm, Mark W. *Let Every Soul Be Jesus' Guest: A Theology of the Open Table*. Nashville: Abingdon, 2006.

Stanton, Elizabeth Cady. "Seneca Falls Declaration (July 19, 1848)." Digital History. http://www.digitalhistory.uh.edu/disp_textbook.cfm?psid=1087&smtID=3.

Stewart, Maria W. "A Prayer for Purification (1835)." In *Conversations with God: Two Centuries of Prayers by African Americans*, edited by James Melvin Washington, 30. New York: HarperCollins, 1994.

Stookey, Laurence Hull. *Baptism: Christ's Act in the Church*. Nashville: Abingdon, 1982.

———. *Eucharist: Christ's Feast with the Church*. Nashville: Abingdon, 1993.

Sugirtharajah, R. S. *Asian Biblical Hermeneutics and Postcolonialism: Contesting the Interpretations*. Maryknoll, NY: Orbis, 1998.

Tamez, Elsa. "Women's Rereading of the Bible." In *Voices from the Margin: Interpreting the Bible in the Third World*, rev. ed., edited by R. S. Sugirtharajah, 48–57. Maryknoll, NY: Orbis, 1995.

Taylor, Mark Lewis. "Spirit and Liberation: Achieving Postcolonial Theology in the United States." In *Postcolonial Theologies: Divinity and Empire*, edited by Catherine Keller, Michael Nausner, and Mayra Rivera, 39–55. St. Louis, MO: Chalice, 2004.

Terrell, JoAnne Marie. *Power in the Blood? The Cross in the African American Experience*. Maryknoll, NY: Orbis, 1998.

Thomas, Linda E. "Anthropology, Mission, and the African Woman." In *Mission and Culture: The Louis J. Luzbetak SVD Lecture*, Catholic Theological Union, 1–12. Chicago: CCGM, 2006.

———. "Womanist Theology, Epistemology, and a New Anthropological Paradigm." In *Living Stones in the Household of God: The Legacy and Future of Black Theology*, edited by Linda E. Thomas, 37–48. Minneapolis: Fortress, 2004.

Thompson, Janna. *Taking Responsibility for the Past: Reparation and Historical Justice*. Polity: Cambridge, 2002.

Thurman, Howard. *The Centering Moment*. New York: Harper & Row, 1969.

———. *Footprints of a Dream: The Story of the Church for the Fellowship of All Peoples*. New York: Harper & Brothers, 1959

———. *Meditations of the Heart*. Richmond, IN: Friends United, 1953.

Townes, Emilie M. *In a Blaze of Glory: Womanist Spirituality as Social Witness*. Nashville: Abingdon, 1995.

———. *Womanist Ethics and the Cultural Production of Evil*. New York: Palgrave Macmillan, 2006.

Trible, Phyllis. *Texts of Terror: Literary-Feminist Readings of Biblical Narratives*. Philadelphia: Fortress, 1984.

Tutu, Desmond. *No Future without Forgiveness*. New York: Image, 1999.

Venable-Ridley, C. Michelle. "Paul and the African American Community." In *Embracing the Spirit: Womanist Perspectives on Hope, Salvation, and Transformation*, edited by Emilie M. Townes, 212–33. Maryknoll, NY: Orbis, 1997.

Walker, Alice. *In Search of Our Mothers' Gardens: Womanist Prose*. London: Harcourt Brace Jovanovich, 1983.

Webb, Joseph M. *Preaching and the Challenge of Pluralism*. St. Louis, MO: Chalice, 1998.

West, Cornel, and Kelvin Shawn Sealey. *Restoring Hope: Conversations on the Future of Black America*. Boston: Beacon, 1997.

West, Raquel. "Yaa Asantewaa (Mid-1800s–1921)." Black Past, February 8, 2019. https://www.blackpast.org/global-african -history/yaa-asantewaa-mid-1800s-1921/.

West, Traci C. "Spirit-Colonizing Violations: Racism, Sexual Violence, and Black American Women." In *Remembering Conquest: Feminist/Womanist Perspectives on Religion, Colonization, and Sexual Violence*, edited by Nantawan Boonprasat Lewis and Marie M. Fortune, 19–30. New York: Haworth, 1999.

White, Will. "Seminary Built on Slavery and Jim Crow Labor Has Begun Paying Reparations." *New York Times*, May 31, 2021. https://www.nytimes.com/2021/05/31/us/reparations -virginia-theological-seminary.html.

Williams, Cecil, and Janice Miriktani. *Beyond the Possible: 50 Years of Creating Radical Change at a Community Called Glide*. New York: HarperOne, 2013.

Williams, Delores S. *Sisters in the Wilderness: The Challenge of Womanist God-Talk*. Maryknoll, NY: Orbis, 1993.

Wilmore, Gayraud S. *Black Religion and Black Radicalism: An Interpretation of the Religious History of African Americans*. 3rd ed. Maryknoll, NY: Orbis, 1998.

Wimbush, Vincent L. "'We Will Make Our Own Future Text': An Alternate Orientation to Interpretation." In *True to Our Native Land: An African American New Testament Commentary*, edited by Brian K. Blount, Cain Hope Felder, Clarice J. Martin, and Emerson B. Powery, 43–53. Minneapolis: Fortress, 2007.

Winbush, Raymond A., ed. *Should America Pay? Slavery and the Raging Debate on Reparations*. New York: Amistad, 2003.

Wink, Walter. *The Bible in Human Transformation: Toward a New Paradigm for Biblical Study*. Philadelphia: Fortress, 1973.

Wright, N. T. "Paul's Gospel and Caesar's Empire." In *Paul and Politics: Ekklesia, Israel, Imperium, Interpretation*, edited by Richard A. Horsley, 160–83. Harrisburg, PA: Trinity Press International, 2000.

Index